www.wadsworth.com

wadsworth.com is the World Wide Web site for Wadsworth and is your direct source to dozens of online resources.

At *wadsworth.com* you can find out about supplements, demonstration software, and student resources. You can also send e-mail to many of our authors and preview new publications and exciting new technologies.

wadsworth.com
Changing the way the world learns®

FROM THE WADSWORTH SERIES IN SPEECH COMMUNICATION

CASE STUDIES IN INTERPERSONAL COMMUNICATION
Processes and Problems

DAWN O. BRAITHWAITE
University of Nebraska-Lincoln

AND

JULIA T. WOOD
University of North Carolina-Chapel Hill,

EDITORS

Australia • Canada • Denmark • Japan • Mexico • New Zealand • Philippines
Puerto Rico • Singapore • South Africa • Spain • United Kingdom • United States

Executive Editor: *Deirdre Cavanaugh*
Editorial Assistant: *Dory Schaeffer*
Executive Marketing Manager: *Stacey Purviance*
Project Editor: *Cathy Linberg*
Print Buyer: *Barbara Britton*

Permissions Editor: *Robert Kauser*
Production: *Pre-Press Company, Inc.*
Cover Designer: *Stephen Rapley*
Compositor: *Pre-Press Company, Inc.*
Printer: *Thomson/West*

Printed in United States

6 7 07

For permission to use material from this text, contact us:
Web: www.thomsonrights.com
Fax: 1-800-730-2215
Phone: 1-800-730-2214

Library of Congress Cataloging-in-Publication Data

Case studies in interpersonal communication : processes / edited by Dawn O. Braithwaite, Julia T. Wood.
    p.   cm.
    Includes bibliographical references.
    ISBN-13: 978-0-534-56538-1
    ISBN-10: 0-534-56538-7
    1. Interpersonal communication Case studies. I. Braithwaite, Dawn O. II. Wood, Julia T.
    BF637.C45C367 1999
    153.6··dc21

99-16355
CIP

For more information, contact:

Wadsworth/Thomson Learning
10 Davis Drive
Belmont, CA 94002-3098
USA
www.wadsworth.com

International Headquarters
Thomson Learning
290 Harbor Drive, 2nd Floor
Stamford, CT 06902-7477
USA

UK/Europe/Middle East
Thomson Learning
Berkshire House
168-173 High Holborn
London WC1V 7AA
United Kingdom

Asia
Thomson Learning
60 Albert Street #15-01
Albert Complex
Singapore 189969

Canada
Nelson/Thomson Learning
1120 Birchmount Road
Scarborough, Ontario M1K 5G4
Canada

CONTENTS

v

PART IV
SERIOUS CHALLENGES IN RELATIONSHIPS

PART V
CHANGE AND CONTINUITY IN LONG-TERM RELATIONSHIPS

PREFACE

The two of us have taught courses in interpersonal communication for many years at community colleges, four-year colleges, and universities. Both of us love to teach interpersonal communication because we know that we are introducing students to theories, concepts, and research that apply directly to real-life relationships—both their own and those of others. We have found that traditional textbooks are insufficient resources when the goal is to teach students how to translate theory into practice. Traditional textbooks tend to discuss concepts, principles, and research findings in abstract language and they do not always accent practical application. Clearly, students should gain the conceptual knowledge that traditional textbooks present effectively. However, on its own, that kind of knowledge does not necessarily cultivate skill in applying conceptual knowledge to actual relationships. To develop that skill, students need practice in analyzing communication in relationships, recognizing and wisely assessing choices for interpretation and action, and identifying interconnections among interpersonal dynamics that continuously shape and reshape relationships.

This book grows out of our commitment to helping students develop practical skills that allow them to analyze communication in personal relationships and to make informed choices about their own interactions. In our own teaching, we have found that case studies are powerful pedagogical tools. When we use case studies in our classes, students learn to apply theory, concepts and principles to the complexity and ambiguity that are inherent in actual relationships. Working with case studies encourages active engagement, sophisticated reflection, and thoughtful application of theory and research.

Although we both use case studies in our teaching, we lacked a collection of case studies that focused on interpersonal communication and that reflected theory and research in the field of communication. The lack of theoretically grounded case studies inspired *Case Studies in Interpersonal Communication.* We first discussed the project at the 1997 International Network of Personal Relationships Conference, which was held in June at the University of Miami at Ohio. After talking with each other, we mentioned the idea of the book to others at the conference, who responded with extraordinary excitement and encouragement. We then proposed the book to Deirdre Cavanaugh, Executive Editor of Communication at Wadsworth Publishing Company, and she, too, was immediately enthusiastic and offered to support the project. Over coffee at the National Communication Conference that fall, we generated a list of key topics in interpersonal relationships, which became the chapters in the final book. We brainstormed ideas for authors of the chapters, creating our "dream list" of colleagues whose research has established them as scholars of national stature. We were delighted when our dream list became a reality. Everyone we invited to write a chapter responded with enthusiasm and with consummate skill in crafting cases that use research and theory to create rich, pedagogically useful narratives of relationship life. The result is a book that can serve as a companion to a wide range of primary textbooks that are used in introductory and advanced courses in interpersonal communication.

We open the book with a chapter that discusses the character and values of the case study method of teaching, which has a long and distinguished tradition in higher education, particularly professional education. Following that chapter are 29 cases, which are grouped into five areas that reflect prominent research and teaching interests: negotiating personal identity, developing closeness, communication processes in established relationships, serious challenges in relationships, and change and continuity in long-term relationships. One or more scholars who have conducted significant research in the area of the case study author each case. By design, these cases are compelling narratives, or stories, about people who are involved in the processes and problems of interpersonal communication. Theory and research, although clearly shaping each case, are not explicitly highlighted because that would detract from the coherence of the narrative itself. Questions following each case suggest conceptual directions for elaborating cases through in-class discussion and activities. Reflecting the complexity of relationships, the cases entail multiple interpersonal communication issues. Thus, the cases invite discussion and analysis along many lines, including but not restricted to those suggested by the questions that follow the case. For example, faculty who wish to emphasize turning points in relational life could focus discussion of any case on key junctures and their implications. Faculty interested in relational dialectics may guide students to analyze dialectical tensions in many of the cases.

Supporting this book is a web page that Scott Titsworth created. Faculty and students can access this at: http://communication.wadsworth.com. Simply locate Braithwaite/Wood in the catalogue for Speech Communication and a direct link to the page will be available to you. On the web page you will find syllabi that show how instructors around the country are incorporating the cases in this book into their classes. You will also find discussion of a range of approaches to teaching that features case studies. The web page also includes sample class activities, reaction papers and project assignments, and examination material to support the cases in this book. We invite you to become active users of the web site and contribute your own ideas for teaching and learning through case studies, ask questions of others who are teaching from case studies, and develop and post additional case studies for issues beyond those covered in this book. Our web page is meant to provide a place where people can talk productively about interpersonal communication, discuss specific case studies, and share ideas about ways to enrich the teaching–learning experience. We look forward to meeting and talking with you there!

We are grateful to many people who assisted us in the conception and development of this book. Our greatest gratitude is to the scholars who contributed cases to this book. All of them are equally committed to teaching interpersonal communication and conducting research to expand our knowledge of how relationships work. Leslie Baxter provided much useful feedback in the early stages of this project, and we thank her for her assistance and support. We also thank the extraordinary professionals at Wadsworth/ITP Publishing Company and especially Deirdre Cavanaugh, Executive Editor of Communication. Connie Buzzell was an exceptional project manager who kept us on schedule and who coordinated all members of the team for this book. We also acknowledge the key contributions of our students whom we have taught and who, in turn, have taught us about interpersonal communication. Dawn thanks her colleagues at the University of Nebraska-Lincoln for their support of her work and this project and Julia is grateful to her colleagues at the University of North Carolina at Chapel Hill, who are continuous sources of support and intellectual stimulation. And we thank our husbands, Chuck Braithwaite and Robbie Cox, who have been and continue to be our own case studies in interpersonal communication.

Dawn O. Braithwaite
Julia T. Wood

ABOUT THE EDITORS AND CONTRIBUTORS

DAWN O. BRAITHWAITE is an Associate Professor of Communication Studies and Director of Graduate Studies at the University of Nebraska-Lincoln. She is also an Affiliate Faculty member in the interdisciplinary Family Research and Policy Initiative at the university. She received her Ph.D. degree in Speech Communication from the University of Minnesota. Her research and teaching interests are centered in interpersonal and family communication, specifically communication rituals, supportive communication, communication across the life-span, and communication of persons with disabilities. She is the incoming President of the Western States Communication Association.

A native of Chicago, Professor Braithwaite lives with her husband, communication professor Charles Braithwaite, and enjoys music, entertaining, gardening, and Chicago Cubs baseball.

JULIA T. WOOD is a professor of Communication Studies at the University of North Carolina at Chapel Hill. Since completing her Ph.D. (Pennsylvania State University) at age 24, she has conducted research and written extensively about communication in personal relationships and about gender, communication, and culture. In addition to publishing over 60 articles and chapters, she has authored or co-authored 15 books and edited or co-edited 6 others. The recipient of seven awards for distinguished scholarship and seven teaching awards, Professor Wood divides her professional energies between writing and teaching.

Professor Wood lives with her partner, Robbie Cox, who is also a professor of Communication Studies at the University of North Carolina and is actively involved with the national Sierra Club. She also lives with Madhi-the-Wonder-Dog and two cats, Sadie Ladie and Ms. Wicca. When not writing and teaching, Professor Wood enjoys traveling, legal consulting, and spending time talking with students, friends, and family.

LINDA K. ACITELLI, (Ph.D., The University of Michigan), is an Associate Professor in the Department of Psychology at the University of Houston and is quite happy living without snow. Her major research interests are cognition and communication in relationships, specifically thinking and talking about relationships and the factors that determine their impact on individual and relationship well-being. In 1995, the International Network on Personal Relationships honored her with the Gerald R. Miller Award for her early career achievements.

JESS ALBERTS is an Associate Professor of Communication at Arizona State University. She received her Ph.D. degree from the University of Texas at Austin. Her research interests include the study of marital and relational communication, with special emphases on the examination of couples' discourse, conflict, flirting, and humor.

KATHERINE R. ALLEN is a Professor of Family Studies at Virginia Polytechnic Institute and State University. She is a faculty affiliate in the Center for Gerontology, a core teaching faculty member in Women's Studies, and Chair of the Academy of Teaching Excellence. She received her Ph.D. from Syracuse University. She teaches about and studies family diversity across the life course, primarily using qualitative research methods.

BETSY WACKERNAGEL BACH, is Assistant Provost for Retention and Enrollment Management and Professor of Communication Studies at the University of Montana. She received her Ph.D. from the University of Washington. She was elected as the University of Montana's Distinguished Teacher in 1991, and in 1996 she received the University's award for Administrative Excellence. Betsy is a past President of the Western States Communication Association. Her research interests lie in the area of organizational socialization.

LESLIE A. BAXTER is a Professor of Communication Studies at the University of Iowa and received her Ph.D. degree from the University of Oregon. She has published close to 80 refereed articles, chapters, and books on the topics of personal relationships and family communication.

SHERRY PERLMUTTER BOWEN, (Ph.D., University of Massachusetts, 1986), is an Associate Professor of Communication and Women's Studies at Villanova University. She has spent over ten years writing and teaching about HIV/AIDS among college students and urban African Americans. She is currently investigating the narratives of women Holocaust survivors.

CAROL J. S. BRUESS is an Assistant Professor in the Department of Communication at the University of St. Thomas, St. Paul, Minnesota. She received her Ph.D. degree from Ohio University's School of Interpersonal Communication. Her research and teaching interests are in family, interpersonal, and intercultural communication—specifically marital satisfaction and family and couple rituals.

WALTER JOHN CARL is a doctoral candidate in the Department of Communication Studies at the University of Iowa. He obtained his M. A. degree in Interpersonal and Organizational Communication at the University of North Carolina at Chapel Hill. His current research interests include the practices of community belonging, friendship groups, discourse analysis, and postmodernity. He would like to thank Nadia Marie Kubik for her inspiration on this chapter.

WILLIAM R. CUPACH (Ph. D., University of Southern California) is Professor of Communication at Illinois State University. His research pertains to the management of problematic situations such as social embarrassment, interpersonal conflict, sexual negotiation, and relationship disengagement.

SARAH E. W. DARGATZ is a Show Specialist in the Spacequest Planetarium gallery at the Children's Museum of Indianapolis. She is an undergraduate student at IUPUI, majoring in Anthropology and in Museum Studies. Her special interests are in the study of families and cultures, and archaeology.

WENDY S. DAVIES-POPELKA is the communications manager for the Mississippi Valley Girl Scout Council in Rock Island, Illinois. She received her master's degree in communication studies from the University of North Carolina at Chapel Hill in 1998. She first examined women's intrapersonal communication about their weight while writing her master's thesis.

FRAN C. DICKSON is an Associate Professor of Human Communication Studies and Director of Graduate Studies at the University of Denver. She received her Ph.D. from Bowling Green State University. Her research and teaching interests are in interpersonal and family communication, and communication and aging. Specially, she examines communication dynamics in the long-lasting later-life marriage and couples that have survived the Holocaust. Most recently, she is examining conflict in later-life couples and dating dynamics among adults over sixty years of age.

KATHRYN DINDIA is Professor and Chair of the Department of Communication at the University of Wisconsin in Milwaukee. She received her Ph.D. in Speech Communication from the University of Washington in 1981. Since then she has been teaching in the Department of Communication at UWM. Her research interests are self-disclosure, communication and relationship maintenance, and sex differences in communication. She teaches graduate and undergraduate courses on interpersonal communication and gender and communication. She received the UWM Distinguished Undergraduate Teaching Award in 1996. Kathryn is married to Jack Johnson, another professor in the Department of Communication at UWM, and has two children, John, age 8 and Katelyn, age 6, and a step-daughter, Amanda, age 17, from whom she has learned much about interpersonal communication and sex differences and similarities.

MARCIA D. DIXSON, associate professor of Communication at Indiana-Purdue University of Fort Wayne, teaches graduate and undergraduate communication courses in family, personal relationships, gender, research methods and nonverbal communication. Her research explores parent-child communication, relational communication and communication pedagogy. She is also the mother of two impressive and vexatious adolescents, Lance and Lindsay

STEVE DUCK is the Daniel and Amy Starch Distinguished Professor, Departments of Communication Studies and Psychology, University of Iowa. He has written/edited 32 books, was founding Editor of *Journal of Social and Personal Relationships,* edited two editions of the *Handbook of Personal Relationships,* and was first President of *the International Network on Personal Relationships*. He won the National Communication Association's GR Miller Book Award for his *Meaningful Relationships: Talking, Sense, and Relating* (Sage, 1994).

BELLE A. EDSON teaches at Arizona State University-West. She received her Ph.D. in Communication from the University of Denver. Her research and teaching interests are feminism and communication, rhetorical theory and criticism, and social movement theory and discourse.

BETH HARTMAN ELLIS is an Associate Professor in the Department of Communication Studies, College of Communication, Information & Media at Ball State University in Indiana. She received her Ph. D. in Organizational Communication from Michigan State University and has published in *Management Communication Quarterly, Journal of Applied Communication Research, Health Communication, Communication Research,* and *Journal of the Association for Communication Administration.* The preparation of this manuscript was funded in part by a summer research grant to Dr. Ellis from Ball State University.

LEIGH ARDEN FORD is an Assistant Professor of Communication at Western Michigan University. She received her Ph.D degree from Purdue University. Her research and teaching interests are in health communication, specifically supportive communication and the communication of health related information to disenfranchised populations.

KAREN A. FOSS is Professor and Chair of Communication and Journalism at the University of New Mexico. She received her Ph.D. in Communication from the University of Iowa in 1976. Her research and teaching interests include rhetorical theory and criticism, feminist perspectives on communication, the discourse of marginalized groups, and social movements.

KATHLEEN M. GALVIN is Associate Dean and Professor of Communication Studies at Northwestern University and a family therapist. She has co-authored seven books, including *Family Communication: Cohesion and Change* (4th ed) and developed a related 26 video distance learning package. Her research interests include stepfamily development and instructional communication.

PAGE GARBER completed her Bachelor's degree in Communication at Wheaton College in Wheaton, IL and began her graduate school work in communication at the University of Wisconsin-Milwaukee. Currently, she is enrolled in the Communication Graduate Program at Northern Illinois University and has a graduate assistantship involving research on listening and teaching assistance for a TV and film criticism course. Paige will complete her degree by December of 1999, but she will continue researching areas such as interpersonal communication, training and organizational development, and conflict resolution. Paige has worked as a teaching assistant for an interpersonal communication course at UWM and has also worked with a microenterprise development organization in the training and development department preparing training materials to be sent overseas. Future plans include a Director of Development position with Youth for Christ, a non-profit organization dedicated to helping teens.

MICHAEL L. HECHT is a professor and department head of Speech Communication and an affiliated professor in Crime, Law, and Justice at the Pennsylvania State University. He received his Ph.D. from the University of Illinois. His research interests include ethnicity and identity, inter-group relations, effective communication, communication and love, and drug prevention.

STEPHANIE HSU is a graduate student at the University of Wisconsin-Milwaukee. She is currently pursuing a Master's degree in Intercultural Communication. She received her Bachelor's at the University of Wisconsin-Eau Claire in French and Organizational Communication. A first generation Chinese-American, Stephanie keeps her intercultural ties with her relatives and other native Chinese through speaking the language. In addition to the Chinese language, Stephanie is fluent in French. Her future goals include working with U.S. businessmen and businesswomen on cultural adjustment and cross-cultural conflict prior to overseas assignments in French and Chinese speaking countries. Stephanie also hopes to further her education with a Ph.D. in Intercultural Communication.

DOUGLAS KELLEY is Assistant Professor of Communication Studies at Arizona State University West. He holds degrees in Religious Studies, Counseling, and Communication. His current research focuses on positive family functioning, intimacy, and the nature of interpersonal forgiveness.

JENNIFER A. LINDE is a faculty associate in the Department of Communication at Arizona State University. She received her M.A. in Communication from Arizona State University and her B.F.A. in Theater Education from the University of Arizona. Her scholarly interests include performance studies, rehearsal process, education through performance, and feminist criticism.

FLAVIO F. MARSIGLIA is an assistant professor of Social Work at Arizona State University. He received his Ph.D. from Case Western Reserve University. His research interests include ethnicity and identity, culturally grounded services for youth and children, substance abuse prevention, and HIV/AIDS.

STEPHANIE M. MECHMANN, B.S., is a 1999 graduate of Villanova University in Secondary Education, English. She has been extensively involved in HIV, AIDS, and sexual health education for the college-age population, with special concern as to how these issues affect women.

SANDRA METTS is a Professor in the Department of Communication at Illinois State University. She received her Ph.D. from the University of Iowa. She teaches graduate and undergraduate courses in interpersonal communication and language. Her research interests focus on the management of problematic social and relational episodes including embarrassment, relationship disengagement, deception, social support, sexual communication, and conflict.

CLARK D. OLSON is the Director of Forensics and teaches at Arizona State University in Tempe. He earned his Ph.D. in Communication from the University of Minnesota. He teaches interpersonal theory and research, and is interested in how the elderly communicate and how living environments contribute to relationships, as well as forensics pedagogy.

SANDRA PETRONIO received her BA degree from the State University of New York at Stony Brook in interdisciplinary social science with an emphasis on psychology and sociology, MA degree from the University of Michigan. She has taught at Arizona State University for 13 years and prior to that at the University of Minnesota. She is currently the Director of the Interdisciplinary Ph.D. Program at Arizona State University. Professor Petronio has published a number of scholarly articles on privacy and disclosure working to develop a theory of private disclosures. She recently received a Distinguished Award for an article with colleagues Michael Hecht, Heidi Reeder, and Teresa Mon't Ros Mandoza on disclosure of child sexual abuse.

MIKE RABBY is a doctoral student at Arizona State University. He received his Master's degree from The Pennsylvania State University. His primary research interests include interpersonal communication within a computer mediated environment as well as relationship maintenance and conflict management.

KAREN RASMUSSEN is a rhetorical critic who currently focuses on issues related to ideologies underlying the depiction of gender, class, and ethnicity. She teaches courses in rhetorical theory and criticism, argumentation, and the rhetoric of popular culture in the Communication Studies Department at California State University, Long Beach. The research for the case study included in this volume includes more than two decades' experience in support groups related to addiction and a series of in-depth interviews.

EILEEN BERLIN RAY (Ph.D., University of Washington, 1981) is an Associate Professor of Communication at Cleveland State University, where she teaches courses in health communication, organizational communication, and communication and gender. Her research focuses on supportive communication across organizational and interpersonal contexts. Ongoing research projects include studies investigating social support among disenfranchised populations. She has published articles in journals including *Communication Monographs, Health Communication,* and the *Journal of Applied Communication Research* and is the editor of *Communication and Disenfranchisement: Social Health Issues and Implications* (1996, Erlbaum), *Case Studies in Communication and Disenfranchisement: Applications to Social Health Issues* (1996, Erlbaum), *Case Studies in Health Communication* (1993, Erlbaum), and senior editor of *Communication and Health: Systems and Applications* (with L. Donohew, 1990, Erlbaum). She is currently writing *Communicating Health: Voicing Personal, Political, and Cultural Complexities* (with P. Geist and B. Sharf, for Wadsworth) and is on the editorial board of numerous journals, including *Health Communication, Journal of Applied Communication Research, and Communication Quarterly.*

JACK M. RICHMAN, Professor of Social Work, University of North Carolina at Chapel Hill, received his Ph.D. from Florida State University. He teaches Ph.D. and MSW classes in social work theory and practice. His research interests are in the areas of at-risk students, social support, and violence in childhood. Dr. Richman is a frequent contributor to the literature and is a consulting editor for *Social Work in Education*.

MARY E. ROHLFING is an Associate Professor at Boise State University. She received her Ph.D. from The University of Iowa in 1993. Her research interests include: women in rock 'n roll, friendship, and mass media depictions of feminism. She is actively involved in work to extend basic rights to gay and lesbian Americans.

LAWRENCE B. ROSENFELD, Professor of Communication Studies, University of North Carolina at Chapel Hill, received his Ph.D. from Pennsylvania State University. His research and teaching interests are in the areas of interpersonal and family communication, specifically the role of supportive relationships, marital intimacy, and how families and children manage the trauma associated with disasters. In 1995 he received the University of North Carolina's Johnston Award for Teaching Excellence. He served as Editor for the *Western Journal of Speech Communication* and *Communication Education*, and is a associate editor for journals in communication and in social work.

DEBRA-L SEQUEIRA is Professor and Chair of the Department of Communication and Journalism at Seattle Pacific University. She has published nationally and internationally in communication and language studies. Her current research focus is in culture and religion.

BRIAN H. SPITZBERG (Ph.D., University of Southern California) is Professor of Speech Communication at San Diego State University. His research interests include communication competence, interpersonal conflict, and violence and abuse in close relationships. He is currently writing *Communication Competence: Introducing the Basics* (with S. Morreale and K. Barge) for Wadsworth.

TERESA L. THOMPSON is a Professor of Communication at the University of Dayton. She received her Ph.D. degree from Temple University. Her research and teaching interests are in health communication and in communication and disability. She has published four books and numerous articles on these topics, and she edits the quarterly journal *Health Communication*.

GAIL G. WHITCHURCH is Associate Professor of Communication Studies at Indiana University-Purdue University Indianapolis (IUPUI), and counsels couples and families in private practice. She earned her Ph.D. at the University of Delaware, and did her post-doctoral work in marriage and family therapy at Butler University in Indianapolis. She is co-founder of the Family Communication Division of the National Communication Association and is a founding associate editor of *Journal of Family Communication*. Among her teaching and research interests are communication and family development theory, and applied communication research.

INTRODUCTION

LEARNING FROM CASE STUDIES

Dawn O. Braithwaite, Julia T. Wood

Imagine two scenarios. First imagine that you are in an interpersonal communication class and your teacher tells you: "Romantic partners often experience tension between the desire to be independent and the desire to feel connected." Your teacher then illustrates by saying, "For example, you may really want to be with your girlfriend or boyfriend one day and prefer not to see her or him the next day because you want some time alone."

Now imagine a second scenario. Your teacher asks you to read this story:

Cecile feels really confused about her relationship with Josh. They've been dating exclusively for six months, and for most of that time, she's felt she just couldn't get enough of him. All Cecile wanted to do was see Josh, be with him, talk to him. But that's changed in the last two weeks. Lately Cecile has felt crowded by Josh, and she's starting to resent his constant calls and demands for time. It's not that she doesn't want to see him any more. It's just that she doesn't want to spend *all* of her time with him. What she wants most right now is some time alone—her own space without Josh around. She feels she is being swallowed up in the relationship. She wants some time away from Josh to reestablish her independent identity.

Cecile wonders if her desire to spend less time with Josh means she's fallen out of love with him. Can you love someone and not want to be with him all the time? Is it inconsistent to want to be with Josh sometimes and away from him other times? Is she abnormal for feeling that she loves Josh but doesn't want to be with him all the time? Cecile wants to tell Josh what she's feeling, but she's not sure what it means or how to talk with him. She doesn't want to hurt him, but it feels dishonest not to tell him she's feeling claustrophobic.

Which scenario was more effective in giving you insight into the tension between autonomy and connection that occurs in most interpersonal relationships? In the first scenario, you were given a definition and an example of the tension between wanting independence and connection. You understood what your teacher told you and felt confident that you could recall the definition for a test.

In the second scenario, you read about Cecile's relationship with Josh. Perhaps you could identify with her confusion because you've had similar feelings at times in your own relationships. Perhaps you've wanted distance from someone you know you love and with whom you want to sustain a relationship. Perhaps you empathized with Cecile's concern that she wanted to talk to Josh but didn't know how to do so without hurting him. Did you think of ways that Cecile might discuss her feelings with Josh?

Did you understand the tension between desires for independence and connection better from the explanation in the first scenario or the story in the second one? If you're like most people, each approach offered you distinct insights. The first scenario presented you with conceptual information essential to analyzing dynamics of interaction. The second scenario provided you with a rich understanding of how this tension surfaces in a relationship. It allowed you to see how the abstract idea plays out in a real relationship with real people. The story provides a context for understanding conceptual information about tensions between desires for autonomy and connection. It also invites you to identify with Cecile's situation and think about what she might do to communicate effectively with Josh.

This book is designed for people who want to learn by exploring conceptual information in real-life situations. The cases in this book invite you to use abstract and conceptual knowledge to analyze and address concrete circumstances. This is active learning because it requires you to understand how concepts, theories, and principles apply in actual situations. By studying interpersonal dynamics in practical situations, you develop skill in applying what you learn to your own relationships. It also helps you expand your personal repertoire of communication choices so that you can adapt effectively to diverse contexts, individuals, and relationships.

This book provides you with resources for active learning about interpersonal communication. In it, you'll find case studies that are based on research and theories in the field of communication. Each case was written by individuals who have extensively studied the particular issues covered in the case. Analyzing the cases allows you to apply the abstract concepts, theories, and principles you've read about to concrete, real-life issues, problems, and processes of human relationships. Because each case is described from the perspectives of different people, you'll learn to appreciate multiple vantage points.

In this opening chapter, our goal is to explain the role of case studies in learning about interpersonal communication. We first review the tradition of case study as a method of teaching. We also identify distinct values of case study learning. In the second section of this chapter we link the case method of teaching and learning to narrative theory. Our discussion highlights the richness of a narrative approach to knowledge. The third section of this chapter describes ways you can use the case studies in this book to enhance your knowledge of interpersonal communication. Finally, we preview the organization of this book and the sequence of the case studies so that you can decide how to most effectively learn from case studies in this book.

CASE STUDIES AS PATHS TO KNOWLEDGE

There are many ways to teach and to learn. The two most conventional methods are lecture and discussion. These methods are useful in introducing concepts, principles, theories, and research. Yet these methods are not especially effective in helping us learn how to *apply* concepts, principles, theories, and research to real-life communication situations. Conventional methods of teaching and learning can be effectively supplemented by case studies, which foster rich understandings and practical skills in using knowledge.

In 1997 Robert Diamond, Assistant Vice Chancellor of Syracuse University, asserted that conventional methods of education do not prepare students to function in the real world after they leave college. According to Diamond, students must not only learn information; they must also learn how to apply it effectively. In other words, education should help students develop skills in applying knowledge in pragmatic ways. When we really know something, we can use it to improve our effectiveness in personal, social, and professional interactions.

Agreeing with Diamond is management professor Larry Hartman, who advocates teaching methods that "enable students to learn by doing," so that students leave college with experience in applying "individual communication skills, intellectual skills, and interpersonal skills" (p. 41). Knowledge consists not just of information, but also insight into how to use the knowledge effectively.

Case studies are one means of fostering skills in using knowledge effectively. Case studies are extended descriptions of particular events, situations, and people. A case tells a story, complete with the details and intricacies that characterize real life. Because cases are narratively rich, they allow us to see the complexities that mark human behavior and to appreciate the different ways that behaviors might be interpreted. Cases also encourage us to apply concepts, theories, and principles to identify options for interpretation and behavior and to generate understanding and effective courses of action.

The Case Study Tradition

The case study method of education enjoys a long and distinguished history in many fields. Perhaps the most familiar use of case studies is in religious and moral education. For centuries religious instructors of Ancient Chinese, Hebrew, and Greek used parables to teach moral principles. This tradition persists in contemporary religious teaching; parables figure prominently in Christian, Jewish, and Islamic services, and teichos (the sanskrit word for teaching) are central to Buddhist teaching.

Case studies also have an established place in secular education. Larry Hartman notes that since 1908, law schools have used case studies prominently. Cases allow law students to learn the intricacies of law as it applies in particular situations. The same is true of business schools, which rely on case studies to teach students how to assess and develop plans for improving organizational efficiency, employee morale, and so forth. Intercultural workshops and training programs rely heavily on case studies to teach diverse customs, assumptions, and expectations from different cultures. Public administration programs, such as those at Harvard and the Kennedy School of Government, feature case studies prominently.

The principles that make cases appropriate for training in law, business, and intercultural relations also render cases ideal for learning about communication. In 1990 Professor Beverly Sypher published *Case Studies in Organizational Communication*, which featured realistic cases that encouraged students to apply communication concepts to organizational processes. Eileen Berlin Ray, a professor of communication at Cleveland State University, has led the way in introducing case studies in teaching about health communication. In 1993 she edited a book of case studies in that area. Three years later, she edited a book of case studies in communication and disenfranchisement within the health-care system. The cases in Ray's books give readers complex and useful understandings of multiple and interacting issues in health contexts.

This book extends the case study method to the context of interpersonal communication. As in law, business, intercultural relations, organizational communication, and health communication, the field of interpersonal communication has a foundation in abstract concepts, principles, and definitions—essential prerequisites to effective application. As in law, business, and intercultural training programs, abstract information about interpersonal communication gains value when it is adapted and applied to particular situations, people, and relationships.

Values of the Case Study Method

Case studies are widely used educational tools because they have distinct values. Three primary values of the case study method are a focus on application, a representation of real-world complexity, and a context for practice in problem-solving and managing tensions in human communication.

Application to specific situations. A key value of case studies is that they allow students to apply concepts in actual situations. By doing so, students learn how to adapt general principles to specific circumstances in their own and others' lives. For example, courses in law school teach students that a contract is "a meeting of minds." That abstract definition, however, cannot teach students what contracts actually mean—or even when they exist—in particular cases. Is there "a meeting of minds" if one person is intoxicated when a contract is signed? What if a person feels coerced into signing a contract? What if a person doesn't understand the binding nature of a contract? Is "a meeting of minds" possible when one person doesn't understand the obligations inherent in a contract? By working with the particularities of specific cases, law students can appreciate the nuances and complexity of the abstract definition, "a meeting of minds." Working with cases helps law students realize that any abstract definition must be translated to fit the multiple details of a concrete situation.

Let's consider an example of how case studies can help us learn about communication in interpersonal relationships. Interpersonal-communication scholars define self-disclosure as "revealing information about oneself that others are unlikely to discover on their own." Knowing this abstract definition doesn't show us what self-disclosure means, or how it takes place in specific contexts.

Going beyond abstract concepts, a case study helps us analyze self-disclosure within particular settings and under specific conditions. Is it self-disclosure if a woman unintentionally reveals something about herself? Is it self-disclosure if a man who is told something personal by a friend doesn't realize the information should not be shared with anyone else? Is it self-disclosure if a person routinely reveals private information to others? Is self-disclosure equally common, and does it mean the same thing, in cultures that emphasize privacy and in those that emphasize revealing oneself to others?

A case study allows us to look at self-disclosure in particular circumstances. This encourages us to recognize that the meaning and effects of self-disclosure vary across time and contexts. We learn not only what self-disclosure is in an abstract sense but also how it operates in specific settings. As a result, we gain a more sophisticated and complex appreciation of self-disclosing communication.

Real-life complexity. Another virtue of working with case studies is highlighting the interaction among aspects of communication. Traditional methods of education introduce students to concepts individually—one at a time. This approach makes it difficult to appreciate how multiple concepts work together to shape what happens in human interaction. Because case studies present communication situations in detail, they can give us insight into multiple processes and issues that are simultaneously present and interactive.

Traditional approaches offer a definition and examples, separating self-disclosure from the contexts and circumstances that affect when, why, and how it occurs. Through a case study, we can appreciate how self-disclosing and the meaning of doing so are shaped by issues such as trust, relationship history, and self-concepts of communicators.

A good case study of self-disclosure provides insight into many dynamics involved in self-disclosing communication. We gain concrete understanding of how people decide when and to whom they will reveal private information. We might also learn how self-disclosing affects those who disclose and those who are recipients of disclosure. Does learning another person's secrets increase feelings of closeness? Does disclosure by one person encourage reciprocal disclosure by another person? We might also discover how different responses to self-disclosures—acceptance, disapproval, betraying confidence, reciprocating—affect trust, self-esteem, and willingness to invest more in the relationship.

Because case studies provide layered narratives, they invite us to recognize the complexity of interpersonal communication. They help us realize how self-disclosure is linked to previous interactions in a relationship, as well as to those that are likely to follow. Case studies can illuminate issues such as timing, context, and style of communication, and they show how these issues affect self-disclosure and responses to it.

Practice in Diagnosing and Managing Problems. A third value of studying cases is that it encourages thinking about how communication can be used to deal with your interpersonal problems and to improve your relationships outside of the classroom. When you examine a case thoughtfully, you can identify patterns of communication that lead to conflict, misunderstanding, or other problems. For example, you might ask why Cecile has waited two weeks to tell Josh that she is feeling claustrophobic. Would it have been wiser for her to talk with Josh when she first began to feel stifled? Has she been dishonest by not having said anything so far? Has this behavior pattern led her to resent Josh unfairly, because he has no way of knowing that she wants more time alone? By identifying patterns in cases, you develop the ability to detect them in your own interactions. Once you recognize patterns and their likely consequences, you are able to make more informed choices about patterns to foster or avoid in your relationships.

Conflicts and tensions are inevitable in human relationships. Case study invites you to figure out ways to address those problems and issues. You might ask how Cecile and Josh could meet her needs for independent time without jeopardizing their relationship. What could she say to assure Josh that her desire for time apart doesn't mean she doesn't love him? Thinking about how Cecile and Josh might work out their problem helps you generate practical strategies and skills for analyzing and improving communication in your own interpersonal interactions.

NARRATIVE THEORY AS A FOUNDATION FOR CASES

The case method of education begins with the assumption that knowledge can be gained from detailed accounts of people, situations, and events. This assumption is fundamental to narrative theory, which is well established in the communication discipline. One of the scholars who developed this theory is Walter Fisher, a professor at the University of Southern California. Fisher believes that humans are natural storytellers. We tell stories to make sense of our experiences and to share them with others. We listen to others' stories to understand who they are and what their lives are about. According to Fisher, we continuously learn about ourselves, others, and the world through the process of telling and hearing narratives.

What is a narrative? Most simply, it is a good story. A good story involves a series of events organized in a deliberate way that gives them coherence and meaning. We don't express events in a random fashion; we organize them to reflect the links we see among events. The organization of events shapes the meaning of a story.

In addition to an ordered presentation of events, stories also include characters and plots. We meet people and learn about their motives—why they do what they do. We learn about their backgrounds, goals, fears, and dreams, and all the information that helps us understand events and actions. We see plots develop as particular events and interactions make certain lines of future action likely and foreclose others. We see where a character's choice at one point in a story influences what can and cannot happen later.

Narratives are not just interesting stories. They are carefully constructed accounts, or explanations, of human action. They give us insight into why certain things happened and not others, and why characters did some things and not others. Narratives are not objective or true in an absolute sense. Rather they make sense from—and only from—a particular perspective. Many narratives are told from one person's point of view, so our insight into the account is shaped by that subjective point of view. Other narratives are told from more than one character's point of view and we gain insight into different, sometimes conflicting, outlooks on what is happening and what an event means. Because narratives reflect particular points of view, they teach us about individuals' perspectives on life and interaction. When we really enter into a narrative on its own terms, we gain understanding of how the narrator or character(s) sees the world.

Because narratives reflect these specific points of view, they have the power to increase our understanding of multiple perspectives and some of the reasons for them. For example, suppose you read a story about a woman who avoids conflict in her relationships. Told from her husband's point of view, the narrative portrays her as closed and unwilling to work through tough issues. His story highlights his frustration when his wife refuses to deal with conflict. It reveals that he has had conflicts in his friendships and in past romantic relationships and is comfortable confronting them.

Told from the wife's point of view, however, the story tells us that she feels profoundly scared and paralyzed when conflict threatens to arise in her marriage. Her story reveals abuse and violence that regularly erupted in her parents' marriage. We learn how helpless and scared she felt as a child watching vicious episodes between her mother and father. This insight, in turn, might make us more sympathetic to the woman and her reasons for avoiding conflict at all costs.

Which narrative is more accurate—the one reflecting the husband's or wife's point of view? It's not useful to ask whether one story is more accurate in some objective sense. What is useful is that each narrative gives us insight into how one person feels and why that person acts as she or he does. If we can discover the reasons for each person's feelings, actions, and desires, then we can better understand unsatisfying patterns of communication and suggest how they might be changed.

Case studies allow us to examine how events unfold and how relationships are affected by the choices that people make. What we learn from studying cases enlarges our understanding of a variety of people and the ways they communicate. Through what we learn, we develop our abilities to analyze communication patterns and processes in our own interactions so that we can create relationships that are healthy and productive.

LEARNING FROM CASE STUDIES

If you have not had classes that feature cases, you may wonder how to approach this book. Human Resource Management professor George Stevens suggests a three-stage process. First, read a case in its entirety to gain an overall understanding of the characters, issues, and context. Set the case aside for a while, then reread it, this time making notes to yourself—perhaps in the margins of the pages. You might use notes to identify communication concepts, principles, and issues, as well as ways of approaching the case. Then put the case aside again and leave it on the back burner of your mind. Finally, read the case a third time and refine the notes that you made on the second reading. Elaborate on conceptual issues and applications.

After you have thought about a case and made notes on your own, it's a good idea to discuss a case with others. You can learn a great deal from hearing how others view a case—how their perspectives are similar to and different from your own. What do their experiences allow them to see that you didn't see on your own? Differences in people's perceptions of cases remind us that interpretations of communication are personal and subjective. Discussing a case also allows you to refine your skills in presenting your ideas and responding to those of others. Finally, discussing a case provides an opportunity to broaden your own perspective and expand your repertoire of communication choices by learning from the unique experiences, insights, and approaches of others.

You may find it useful to let three questions guide your analysis of cases and your discussion with others. These questions direct your efforts to apply theories, principles, and concepts. First, ask what each case teaches you about interpersonal communication. Second, ask how and why various people in the case might interpret the situation differently, and how each point of view makes sense from an individual's perspective. Finally, ask how you might respond to each case if you were in that situation. We'll elaborate on how to use each of these questions when reading the cases in this book.

What Does This Case Teach About Interpersonal Communication?

This is the initial question to ask as you read a case. George Stevens, who is in the field of human resource management, asserts that case studies are extremely effective in providing opportunities to learn how theories and research findings apply to actual situations. Stevens believes that knowledge of theory and research is of little value unless students have opportunities to practice using this knowledge in life-like situations. As you read each case, ask whether it emphasizes a particular theory, concept or set of concepts, communication principle, or relational process. When you can identify the conceptual focus of the case, ask what you learn. Do you gain a better understanding of a concept such as self-disclosure? How is your understanding enlarged? What do you know now that you didn't before reading the case? What questions remain unanswered?

When thinking about what you learn from a particular case, also ask yourself how issues in this case relate to ones presented in other cases and to other topics you've discussed in your class. As we noted earlier in this chapter, in interpersonal communication, multiple issues are simultaneously present and interacting. Looking for connections among issues and concepts will lead you to recognize the complexities of interpersonal relating. For example, Case 1 focuses on decisions about keeping or changing name upon marrying. How might this topic be linked to the issues of autonomy and connection that are covered in Case 7? Can you identify connections *between* patterns of development in blended families, covered in Case 11, and efforts to balance needs for couple time with needs for family time, discussed in Case 24?

Can I Understand Alternative Perspectives on Interpersonal Communication in this Case?

This is the second question that should guide your reading of cases. This is critical because understanding different, sometimes conflicting, perspectives is one of the main skills of effective interpersonal communicators. You may not *agree* with all perspectives, and that's okay. The point is for you to understand different points of view and the reasons behind them. This gives you insight into people who think, act, and feel differently than you do. And this insight enlarges your understanding of human communication.

Understanding alternative perspectives on situations also helps you communicate more effectively, especially with people who differ from you. In our earlier example, did you identify more with the husband who was frustrated by his wife's avoidance of conflict, or with the wife who perceives conflict as frightening and dangerous? Can you stretch to understand the perspective with which you didn't originally identify? If so, then you increase your ability to recognize, respect, and deal constructively with orientations to conflict that are unlike your own. In turn, this ability makes it more likely that you can communicate effectively with people who do not share your views of what conflict means and how to deal with it.

How Might I Address the Problem in this Case?

The case studies in this book offer you opportunities to generate concrete ways to address common problems in interpersonal relationships. As you read the cases, ask how you might deal with the tensions or problems presented. What would you tell Cecile she should do about her feelings of claustrophobia in the relationship with Josh? How would you advise the husband and wife to manage their conflicts constructively?

Your ideas for approaching interpersonal communication problems should reflect what you've learned in the course this book accompanies. Thinking about how to address the issues in cases is an opportunity for you to apply the concepts you've learned and to see how they can be used to improve interpersonal communication.

Your ideas for resolving problems should respect the perspective of each person in the case. Interpersonal literally means *between people*. Thus, interpersonal communication problems occur between and among people. They involve more than one person. By extension, effective resolutions of problems cannot involve only one person. It would be unwise, for example, to suggest the wife should simply recognize that couples need to deal with their conflicts. This advice ignores her deep-seated fear of conflict, so it's likely to be ineffective in changing conflict patterns. That advice might even make her feel guilty, which could create further problems in the marriage.

For the same reason, it would not be helpful to suggest the husband should simply accept his wife's inability to confront conflict. That suggestion neglects his need to talk about problems in the marriage. It would do nothing to relieve his frustration, and it would not help the couple learn to deal constructively with conflicts. A good approach to the situation would begin with respect for both the husband's and wife's feelings and perspectives. Following that, it would be effective to make communication choices that reflect respect for both perspectives.

There is seldom only one good way to address problems in interpersonal communication. Usually there are multiple, potentially-constructive approaches to addressing problems in human relationships. An important value of discussing cases with others is that you increase your awareness of alternative ways of resolving tensions and keeping relationships healthy and enjoyable.

Extending Cases in the Classroom

There are additional ways you can work with the cases in this book to sharpen your skills in applying conceptual knowledge to real-life situations. One option is to rewrite a case, revising the choices made early so they lead to different outcomes later in the case. How might a different response to anger or disclosure affect what happens between people in a case? A second variation on this option is to enact the case and to stop at key points so that you create alternative trajectories for the story. For example, you might stop a case at a key juncture and have one or more characters make different choices about how to communicate. You can follow through by enacting what is likely to happen given the different choices. A third option is to write a continuation of a case. Working individually or with others in your class, you might compose the next chapter in the case and explore what is likely to happen, given what you know about the characters, situation, context, and choices made so far in the case.

THE ORGANIZATION OF THIS BOOK

The cases in this book reflect current theories and research about human communication processes. The cases are organized into five parts: topical areas that represent major foci of research and theory in the communication field. Within each part, the cases follow a standard format that is designed to facilitate your analysis of them.

Grouping of Case Studies

The cases in this book are organized into five major parts. The first set of case studies (Cases 1–6) focuses on how we use communication to announce, negotiate, and alter personal identity. Each case presents a situation in which identity is at stake. One, for example, explores the issue of whether to change one's name upon marrying. Another concerns how religious conversion affects individuals and their interactions. These two cases, as well as others in Part I, ask you to think seriously about how communication shapes and reflects personal identity and to consider how communication changes in response to changes in our identities over our lifetimes.

Part II of the book (Cases 7–12) presents cases involving communication during the process of developing closeness. How does communication help us define our relationships, negotiate needs for autonomy and connection, and deal with gender-related differences in interaction style? These are among the issues that focus on the evolution of friendships and romantic intimacy.

In Part III (Cases 13–18), we consider common communication processes in established and ongoing relationships. One case highlights some of the issues in balancing career and family commitments. Another case illuminates the ways in which intimates use rituals to sustain intimacy in long-term relationships.

Part IV (Cases 19–23) of the book focuses on the dark side of interpersonal relationships. The cases in this section deal with betrayals of trust, abuse between intimates, stalking, alcoholism, and incest. Each case allows you to appreciate complex communication processes that operate when relationships are troubled by major crises. These cases also invite you to think about ways to avoid serious problems in relationships you are building and how you might deal with problems and their aftermath in other relationships in your life.

In Part V (Cases 24–29) we provide cases that show how communication changes over time in long-term relationships. One case reveals how parent-child communication patterns alter when a child assumes the role of care giver for a parent. Another case illustrates some of the communication patterns that are typical in long-lasting marriages. These cases provide insight into the dynamics of enduring bonds.

The five parts in this book provide you with in-depth narratives about communication processes and problems that are common in the various relationships in our lives. Studying them will help you make sense of your own past or present interactions and anticipate ones that may be part of your future. In addition, studying these cases should enhance your understanding of others' perspectives, so that you gain an appreciation of the multiple ways people communicate and interpret what happens between them.

Format of Individual Case Studies

Each case is written by one or more scholars who have expertise in the particular topic of the case. When we conceived this book, we agreed that all authors should be established scholars who could compose cases that reflect carefully conducted research. In other words, although the cases are presented as stories, they are based on what is known from rigorous study of interpersonal communication. Although theories and research are not highlighted as they are in conventional textbooks, each case in this volume reflects theory and data from research. Thus, in reading the cases, you will learn what has been discovered by scholars who investigate human communication.

To facilitate your study, the cases are numbered sequentially, and all follow a standard format. Each opens with a list of key words that alert you to communication concepts, theories, and principles the authors have embedded in the case. Then the authors present a focused narrative—in differing formats—that sheds light on a particular topic in interpersonal communication. Typically, the narrative allows you to understand what different people in the story feel and think and how they perceive what is happening.

Following the narrative, questions guide your reflection and discussion. These questions need not limit your individual analysis or your discussion with others. In other words, the questions at the end of each chapter should stimulate your thinking, but not restrict it. You should feel free to explore issues beyond those raised in the questions the authors pose.

Each case concludes with a short list of references. These references are not meant to be comprehensive bibliographies of research in an area. Instead, they highlight primary research that underlies or relates to the case they accompany. Let these references lead you to further information about particular topics that interest you.

We hope that studying the cases in this book will prove valuable to you as you seek to learn more about human communication in your life and the lives of others.

Dawn O. Braithwaite
The University of Nebraska—Lincoln

Julia T. Wood
The University of North Carolina at Chapel Hill

REFERENCES

Cusimano, M. K. (1995). *Why do you do what you do the way you do it? Examining teaching goals and teaching methods*. [On line]. Available at gopher://csf.Colorado. EDU:70/00/ csflists/casenet/About_Case_Teaching/Cases_and_Effective_Teaching.Cusimano.

Diamond, R. (1997, 1 August). Broad curriculum reform is needed if students are to master core skills. *Chronicle of Higher Education*, p. B7.

Eisenhardt, K. M. (1989). Building theories from case study research. *Academy of Management Review, 5,* 501–508.

Fisher, W. (1984). Narration as a human communication paradigm: The case of public moral argument. *Communication Monographs, 51,* 1–22.

Fisher, W. (1987). *Human communication as narration: Toward a philosophy of reason, value, and action*. Columbia, SC: University of South Carolina Press.

Hartman, L. D. (1992). Business communication and the case method: Toward integration in accounting and MBA graduate programs. *The Bulletin, 55,* 41–45.

Ray, E. B. (Ed.). (1993). *Case studies in health communication*. Mahwah, NJ: Lawrence Erlbaum.

Ray, E. B. (Ed.). (1996). *Case studies in communication and disenfranchisement: Applications to social health issues*. Mahwah, NJ: Lawrence Erlbaum.

Stevens, C. F. (1996). *Cases and exercises in human resource management*. Chicago: Richard D. Irwin.

Sypher, B. D. (Ed.). (1990). *Case studies in organizational communication*. New York: Guilford.

PART I

NEGOTIATING PERSONAL IDENTITY IN RELATIONSHIPS

WHAT'S IN A NAME?

Negotiating Decisions about Marital Names

Karen A. Foss, Belle A. Edson, Jennifer A. Linde

KEY WORDS

■

commitment
decision making
marriage
names
relational perceptions
self-disclosure
self-identity

*M*adeline Anderson took a sip of her ice water and sighed. It still amazed her that this man who sat across the table smiling and speaking casual Spanish to the server was going to be her husband in less than six months. She gazed absentmindedly at the closed menu in front of her, certain that she could order the Frontier Special in Spanish if she truly wanted to try. Perhaps it was easier to let Martín do the ordering and save herself the embarrassment of sounding too much like a Minnesota girl trying to roll her "r's." She missed the time that she and Martín used to have when they first started dating; time for impromptu Spanish lessons and simple conversation and flirting. But Madeline also cherished the changes in their relationship that had evolved over the last two years. Martín Romero had become many things to Madeline: classmate, friend, lover, partner, Spanish teacher, and confidant; soon he would be her husband.

Another sigh escaped her lips, and this time Martín caught her eye from across the table and winked. Madeline wondered how he could read her mind. She wondered how he knew her as well as he did. It seemed to her that her parents were such strangers to one another, even after 26 years of marriage, even after living together in the same house for all this time. She marveled at the realization that she and Martín already had a way of relating that seemed to have escaped her parents' marriage entirely. Madeline knew that her ability to share her feelings with Martín and to listen and argue and work at communicating had not come from her upbringing; she wondered where she had learned it. She certainly had discovered herself in these four years of college, and she felt a twinge of sadness that graduation was just a month away and that soon she'd be saying good-bye to the routine of the University of New Mexico and the beautiful Albuquerque sunsets.

MARTÍN: Is it that serious? *(Madeline was startled out of her thoughts.)*

MADELINE: What?

MARTÍN: You stopped smiling a few minutes ago, and now you look far too preoccupied for a Friday night. Is everything okay?

MADELINE: Yup. What am I eating tonight?

MARTÍN: Cartón y plátanos. [*Cardboard and bananas.*]

MADELINE: That sounds delicious. Does it come with jalapeños?

MARTÍN: *(laughing)* Your Spanish is awful—remind me again why I'm marrying you.

MADELINE: I'm going to make a lot of money.

MARTÍN: That's right! You'll be the head of engineering for some big company within a year, and I'll get a job in a nearby school district, and then we'll have four babies and my mother will come to visit frequently.

MADELINE: Do you expect me to make a mother-in-law comment now? I'm sorry, sweetie, but I like your mother. She can come visit us anytime she wants.

N O T E S

MARTÍN: That's good—because she and Dad are coming up from Socorro next weekend.

MADELINE: Cool. Are they staying at your apartment?

MARTÍN: No, they'll stay at Aunt Yolanda's. Mom doesn't want to know that you and I are sleeping together, and this is her way of ignoring it.

MADELINE: I don't have to stay there if it bothers them.

MARTÍN: I've told you I'm not going to lie to them. Besides, I don't think it really offends them; it's just all that Catholic guilt.

MADELINE: How come *you* don't have it?

MARTÍN: I'm just a weekend Catholic.

MADELINE: I still don't understand what you mean by that.

MARTÍN: Do Lutherans go to mass on Wednesdays and Saturdays?

MADELINE: We don't have mass.

MARTÍN: *(Laughing)* You engineers are so literal. My point is that if I were full-fledged Catholic I'd be in church a lot more during the week. Sometimes I actually miss it.

MADELINE: Martín, are you really okay about getting married in my church?

MARTÍN: I'm okay with everything, mi amor—a chilly fall wedding in St. Paul, hoards of passionate Romeros doing the wedding dance to the rhythm of a polka band, my grandfather bonding with your grandfather and inviting him to come spend winters in Española, a quaint Norwegian wedding cake made by your cousins Uffda and Lefse. . . .

Madeline found herself laughing loudly at Martín's descriptions. She knew that it was his way of letting her know that he intended to make the best of this Midwest-meets-Southwest wedding. They had been planning the wedding since January, and both were tired of the stress. At times, it seemed like more hassle than it needed to be, and she and Martín had certainly had a few arguments because of it.

Madeline hated conflict. She remembered their first huge fight and how sick to her stomach she had felt. Martín seemed so comfortable with expressing emotion, probably a result of being raised by parents who encouraged their children to talk and work through problems. Martín still called his sister in San Francisco every weekend and often drove to Socorro during the week to go to his little brother's baseball games. In both relationships, she had noticed an open display of both affection and displeasure. Madeline wondered if it bothered Martín that she often side-stepped disagreements. He was pretty good at drawing her out, and she was working on being more direct about expressing conflict—but she hated to make him responsible for guessing her feelings.

For several weeks she had been avoiding talking to him about her decision to keep her family name, Anderson, when they married. She worried that Martín wouldn't understand and that he would be hurt or angry. Madeline grinned at Martín as he finished his entertaining description of their wedding, and she silently decided that tonight would be a good time to bring up the issue of names.

MADELINE: Martín, I want to talk to you about something that has been on my mind.

MARTÍN: Okay.

MADELINE: I've decided to keep my name when we get married.

MARTÍN: *(After a pause)* Okay.

MADELINE: It's not that I don't like your name—you *know* that I really love the name Romero. Its just that it's not *my* name.

MARTÍN: All right.

MADELINE: *(Pausing)* Is that all you're going to say?

MARTÍN: I'm thinking. Don't rush me. I'm just a little surprised. Do you mean you want to keep your name for professional situations?

MADELINE: Well, that, too. I don't want to change my name at all. I hope you're not hurt by this.

MARTÍN: That's not really the point, Madeline. Yeah, it hurts a little. I'm just trying to figure out why. Why don't you want to have my name?

MADELINE: Because I don't want to give up *mine*.

MARTÍN: Because it's a hassle to change your driver's license and passport and all those things?

MADELINE: Gee, Martín, I'm not *that* shallow! This has nothing to do with what's convenient. I don't want to change my name because I don't know who I would be if I wasn't Madeline Anderson.

MARTÍN: You'd be Madeline Romero.

MADELINE: Exactly. I don't know who that is.

Martín took a deep breath and tried to control the fear that was creeping into him. The idea of Madeline not changing her name bothered him more than he wanted to admit. If she didn't want his name what else didn't she want? His mind was racing with a thousand questions and a thousand reasons not to ask them. Maybe Madeline wasn't ready for this commitment; maybe he hud rushed her into getting married too soon; maybe they didn't know each other as well as he thought.

Martín's love for Madeline was very much a part of his wanting to marry and raise a family with her. He felt lucky to have grown up with parents who still laughed together and played and held hands in public. He liked the idea of marriage and the goal of building a life together. He had met Madeline in a rock-climbing class at UNM during their sophomore year, and he could still recall how funny and smart and beautiful she was to him that semester. There was no doubt in his mind that she was the one he wanted to be with for life. His family had been very supportive, and even his abuela had got past the idea that he was going to marry an anglo. Martín's stomach dropped at the thought of his abuela; how could he ever explain this to her? He knew that he needed to ask Madeline a very difficult question.

MARTÍN: Madeline, do you really want to spend your life married to me?

MADELINE: Of course I do! Martín, this isn't about *us* and our future together. I simply want to keep my name because it represents who *I am*, just as your name represents who you are.

MARTÍN: So you think being an individual is more important than being in a relationship?

MADELINE: I didn't say that! I want our marriage to be a partnership of two individuals; our relationship adds to who we are without taking anything away. I'm just trying to tell you that I've worked hard to create Madeline Anderson, and I don't want to throw all that away.

MARTÍN: By marrying me?

MADELINE: *(loudly)* That is ridiculous! I'm having a hard enough time talking about this without your questioning my commitment to you. My name is simply important to who I am—that's all. You don't even have to think about your name—you know you'll keep it. Why should it be any different for me?

MARTÍN: Don't get so angry!

MADELINE: Well, I think you're being pretty selfish.

MARTÍN: Ditto.

MADELINE: *(After a pause.)* Let's just talk about this, okay?

MARTÍN: Sweetheart, I'm trying very hard not to let this bother me, and I'm not really sure why I feel so upset—but I am. I guess there are a few issues that we need to cover.

MADELINE: *(Taking his hand.)* I'm ready to listen.

MARTÍN: I'm worried that my family will see this as your not accepting our culture. My grandmother thinks women should use the traditional Spanish *de* when they get married.

MADELINE: Madeline De-Romero?

MARTÍN: *(laughing)* No, you would be called Madeline Elaine Anderson de Romero. And don't forget to roll your r's!

MADELINE: It would take me forever to sign checks!

MARTÍN: I love my *abuelita*, and I want her to accept you.

MADELINE: *(speaking softly)* Just like I love my grandparents. Do you see how keeping Anderson is one way I can honor them? What else are you concerned about?

MARTÍN: I'm wondering what our friends will think. Won't they think it's pretty weird?

MADELINE: I'd be surprised if they do. Most of the women I know plan to keep their names when they marry.

MARTÍN: You're kidding! What is this, some kind of female conspiracy? How come guys aren't in on the conversation?

MADELINE: *(with a smile)* It's just our way of taking over the world. Keeping our names is simply the beginning. Our next move would be to stop wearing make-up and tight shoes . . . maybe stop shaving our legs.

MARTÍN: Hmmm. . . .

MADELINE: Seriously, though. Women think about it because they have to make a decision about it—and men don't. Although that raises an interesting point—you could become Martín Anderson.

MARTÍN: Radical thoughts, my love!

MADELINE: Actually, I'm serious. It is an option, just as both of us taking a completely new name is, or both of us hyphenating our names. But I like my name and my identity, so I've never thought seriously about doing any of those other things with my name. But what else are you thinking about besides female conspiracies?

MARTÍN: What about children? Whose name will they have?

MADELINE: Yours, or maybe both of ours. Or we can give the girls my name and the boys yours. Can't we figure that out when we have them? Or maybe they could choose when they got older? What do you think?

MARTÍN: Madeline, as much as I want to swallow all this and tell you I understand, I just can't. I don't think this is just your decision to make and I don't think you've considered all the angles. I'm sorry.

Martín wondered if Madeline truly wanted to know what he was thinking. He took pride in the fact that he was open and honest with her most of the time, but on this occasion he was beginning to feel that raw honesty was just going to get him into trouble. He wanted Madeline to have his name; it was that simple. Yet, he also understood her desire to stick with Anderson. He had taken a gender and communication class last semester where this very topic had come up. He remembered feeling absolutely confused by the reasons women in the class had given for wanting to keep their names. He also recalled thinking that they were pretty radical thinkers and that their experience would never be his own. Funny how life comes back to bite you sometimes!

It was complicated for Martín to sort out his feelings. He certainly didn't want Madeline or anyone else to think that he associated marriage with ownership or that she was not important as an individual, but he also saw this move as one that would destroy yet another tradition that men and women were used to sharing. Martín hated that. He thought that the loss of rituals was a danger to modern cultures, and he didn't want to participate in such a loss.

Madeline and Martín sat silently eating their meal. Each felt hurt and confused, and neither felt closer to a solution.

FOR FURTHER THOUGHT AND REFLECTION

1. What are the reasons Madeline and Martín give for their married-name preferences?

2. Considering both Madeline's and Martín's perspectives, what are the possible decisions this couple might make?

3. In what ways do married-name choices suggest different types or styles of marriage relationships? Identify the characteristics of marriage for Martín and for Madeline.

4. To what degree can cultural issues affect married-name choices?

5. In this relationship what role does self-disclosure play in defining power and control in the process of decision making?

REFERENCES

Cahn, D. D., (Ed.). (1990). *Intimates in conflict: A communication perspective.* Mahwah, NJ: Lawrence Erlbaum.

Carbaugh, D. (1996). The marital self: Styles of names used upon marriage. In D. Carbaugh, *Situating selves: The communication of social identities in American scenes* (pp. 89–112). Albany: State University of New York Press.

Duggan, D. A., Cota, A. A., & Dion, K. L. (1993). Taking the husband's name: What might it mean? *Names, 41,* 87–102.

Fitzpatrick, M. A. (1988). *Between husbands and wives: Communication in marriage.* Newbury Park, CA: Sage.

Foss, K. A., & Edson, B. A. (1989). What's in a name? Accounts of married women's name choices. *Western Journal of Speech Communication, 53*, 356–373.

Fowler, R. I., & Fuehrer, A. (1997). Women's marital names: An interpretive study of name retainers' concepts of marriage. *Feminism & Psychology, 7*, 315–320.

Gudykunst, W. B. (1989). Culture and the development of interpersonal relationships. In J. A. Anderson (Ed.), *Communication Yearbook, 12* (pp. 315–354). Newbury Park, CA: Sage.

Kline, S. L., Stafford, L., & Miklosovic, J. C. (1996). Women's surnames: Decisions, interpretations and associations with relational qualities. *Journal of Social and Personal Relationships, 13*, pp. 593–617.

Petronio, S. (1991). Communication boundary management: A theoretical model of managing disclosure of private information between marital couples. *Communication Theory, 1*, 311–335.

Scheuble, L., & Johnson, D. R. (1993). Marital name change: Plans and attitudes of college students. *Journal of Marriage and the Family, 55*, 747–754.

Stafford, L. & Kline, S. L. (1996). Women's surnames and titles: Men's and women's views. *Communication Research Reports, 13*, 214–224.

N O T E S

CASE STUDY *2*

I'M STILL ME!

Communication and Identity as a Person with a Disability

Teresa L. Thompson, Dawn O. Braithwaite

KEY WORDS

■

multiple disability
stigma
denial
deafness
identity
self-esteem

Steve Michaels pushed the control on his electronic wheelchair full throttle as he whipped down the main corridor and around the corner of the Stellar County Sheltered Workshop—nearly colliding with the smaller, more compact chair of his caseworker and mentor, Jim Thorton. "Whoa, big guy, slow down," Jim signed with his hands and said. "Rather see you late than have both of us end up in the hospital! I've already spent too much time there, you know."

Steve grinned and signed back, "It was your fault! You should already have been in your office," causing Jim to chuckle. He'd seen Steve make such great progress in his interpersonal skills over the last few years, as Steve had experienced increased opportunities for social interaction since coming to the workshop. Jim was aware that this bantering was not a behavior that Steve could have participated in when Jim first started working at the workshop. As Jim thought about this, he realized that his and Steve's experiences with disability were very different—yet they had some experiences in common as they sought to live and interact in a world where people with disabilities are often misunderstood or not accepted.

STEVE'S STORY

Like many people who are disabled from birth, Steve had spent most of his years in self-contained, special education classrooms or sheltered workshops that train clients with disabilities in work skills, obtain contracts for jobs to be completed on-site, and sometimes place clients off-premises. Since Steve spent much of his life in situations where he did not interact with many different people, he didn't experience the variety of communicative interactions and receive the subsequent feedback that other children his age experienced. His mother, Carole, had contracted rubella during the first month of her pregnancy, causing Steve to be born with cerebral palsy, a severe hearing loss, and an IQ of about 80. His limited social experiences made it harder for Steve to develop the social skills that most people acquire through ordinary interactions.

Steve's mother had a very difficult pregnancy with Steve (she had three hospitalizations), and she had feared her child would be disabled, but the extent of his disability was not immediately apparent upon Steve's birth. He was one and one-half years old before his lack of physical progress led physicians to diagnose cerebral palsy. They predicted that he would be a "vegetable" all of his life, which they predicted would last only three or four years. Because the difficulty of caring for him put a strain on the family, the physicians suggested that Steve be institutionalized. Although Steve's dad, Don, agreed, Carole refused to do so.

In fact, the doctors were very wrong about how long Steve would live. He was now 35! Their prognosis for his physical development was also inappropriately pessimistic. Although his development was severely limited, he managed to master numerous skills. Cerebral palsy can interfere with speech development, and Steve's hearing loss was not discovered until he started school at age seven. His communication problems made it difficult to assess his intelligence, so it was not until he was in high school that special educators finally judged that his IQ was probably borderline between "normal" and "impaired."

Because of his multiple handicaps, Steve's school placement was always problematic. He was originally placed in classes for physically disabled children. Because of his hearing loss, the teachers couldn't communicate with him. Steve was then moved to classes for deaf children. There, Steve no longer received the physical therapy that might have increased his physical abilities. Next, special educators raised the issue of mental retardation, and Steve was moved to classes for intellectually impaired children. These teachers did not use sign language and, although they claimed that they communicated with Steve, he understood little of what they said to him. At this point, his academic development slowed considerably. Steve was receiving no physical therapy, so his physical condition deteriorated and his body stiffened as is common with cerebral palsy. Although Steve had walked with a walker and even a little with crutches when he was younger, he now used a wheelchair exclusively.

Steve's doctors were not the only ones who thought the strain of caring for a family member with a disability would be tough to handle. Friends of Carole and Don subtly and not-so-subtly expressed their attitudes about the issue. The wife of Don's boss once sniffed to Carole, "Do you really think it's fair to your other children to keep Steve at home?" Carole was devastated by these messages. Like many parents of disabled children, she already felt guilty about her child's disability, even though she knew that it was most likely caused by the rubella and nothing she had done. But could it be the tranquilizers she had taken? Had she done something else wrong? Was it her fault? Was she now making Steve's older sisters and brother suffer? Was taking care of Steve at home fair to everyone else?

Actually, Steve was the center of the family. His cheerfulness and sweet nature attracted everyone. The family members were delighted with him. It did bring Rex, Louise, and Alyse some added responsibilities, of course. But caring for Steve never really became a burden until the fall that Carole went back to work as a realtor. At the same time Don decided to quit his job of 20-odd years and go into real estate, not a 9 to 5 job. Louise was in college by this time, and

Rex was working at a mall sporting goods store after school. That left 14-year-old Alyse to watch Steve every day after school, evenings, and on weekends. Steve required a lot more care than most kids. For example, he choked easily while eating and wasn't able to control his bladder until he was nine. Alyse never resented Steve because his cheerful nature made it difficult to be mad at him. She was, however, very angry with her parents for taking away all her free time.

A few years ago, Steve's oldest sister Louise found an essay written by a person who was deaf. The writer described the incredible feelings of loneliness when trying to communicate in a group of hearing people—feeling ignored and alone. Louise told Steve about the essay and signed, "How do you feel about being deaf?" Steve thought for a second and then replied, "Sometimes lonely, but I am happy deaf."

Having grown up with disabilities, Steve saw them as a natural part of himself. In particular, his deafness is part of his identity—just who he is. Steve grew up seeing himself as unable to do some things that other people could do and as needing help from others. Consequently, accepting help is much less difficult for Steve than it is for many people who become disabled later in life and therefore have more difficulty reconciling their desire to be independent with their need to be more dependent than they used to be.

Steve's disabilities have required that he see a lot of health-care providers. It seems, however, that only his disabilities have been treated. Other health issues were ignored. For instance, only one of his testicles dropped, but it was years before a family member helping him bathe discovered that. After one of Steve's many surgeries, a doctor removing his cast cut the back of his leg from the top of his thigh to well below his knee, leaving a thick, long scar. But the care providers acted as if it didn't matter. After all, they thought, Steve was disabled, and he would not be concerned about his appearance.

Steve stayed in high school until he turned 21, which is possible for some individuals with special needs. Then he had nothing to do—no goals or direction. By that time, his parents were divorced, an event not uncommon in families that include a child with a disability. Although he was small for an adult, Steve was too heavy for his mother to heft. He lived with his dad, who attempted to find a group home for Steve. Although a number of communities were being established for individuals with disabilities, none of them was designed for people with multiple disabilities. There were homes for intellectually impaired people and others for deaf people, but they were not wheelchair accessible. Communities for physically disabled adults required a higher level of intellectual functioning, and they did not have attendants who could use sign language. So Steve continued to live with his father. For a year, Steve stayed at home and watched television most of the time.

Finally, there was a place available for Steve at the sheltered workshop. A wheelchair-accessible bus picked him up every morning and brought him home every afternoon. The bus cost a lot more than Steve's salary at the workshop, which averaged $12 every two weeks, but going there gave new meaning and purpose to his life.

Steve began also to hear about social opportunities. A group organized by United Cerebral Palsy provided access to sporting events, plays, picnics, the zoo, and other fun activities. Even more importantly, he learned about sports for people who are physically disabled. He had tried the Special Olympics when he was younger, but found they were primarily oriented toward the intellectually impaired and didn't provide much of an athletic challenge. Now, however, he started wheelchair bowling, which he found much more interesting. Steve had always been precise in everything he did, whether it was his job at the workshop or cleaning his eyeglasses. He discovered there were sports that required this precision. Although he competed in track, soccer, and ping pong, it was bocci—Italian lawn bowling—that was *his* sport. Within a few years, he had established himself as one of the best in the nation at bocci, and was selected for the 1996 U.S. ParaOlympic team. The ParaOlympics were held at the Olympic Village in Atlanta immediately following the 1996 International Olympics. The event was the highlight of Steve's life. He won a bronze medal for the U.S. team! The only disappointment about the experience occurred during the awards ceremony. No one thought about the fact that Steve couldn't hear them announce his name. He didn't know when to wheel forward to accept his medal, and he was embarrassed and confused.

Despite his athletic success, Steve still worried about who would take care of him when he was older. His disability, coupled with his sweet nature, had always led his parents and siblings to baby him. This was particularly true of his sisters and mother. Although he was in his 30s, they did not treat Steve as an adult capable of taking care of himself and making his own decisions. This lack of independence became a key issue when Steve and Jim began working together at Stellar County Sheltered Workshop.

JIM'S STORY

Jim had been a star high-school athlete prior to suffering a spinal cord injury when he was struck by a drunk driver during his first year of college. He was in a coma for several days; his family and girlfriend thought they were going to lose him. They were relieved when he regained consciousness, and regarded the fact that he was paralyzed and paraplegic as the lesser of two evils. But that was not how Jim looked at it. At first he was sure he would walk again. Next he wished that the accident had killed him. He could not see how life could be worth living. He pushed his friends away, feeling he didn't want their pity and knowing he no longer fit into their lifestyles. In particular, he could no longer play sports with them. He soon found that their visits and concern would be temporary, and that they would quickly lose interest. Jim let only his family and girlfriend, Diane, remain close, and them only because he needed their help.

Jim's family and Diane were concerned and wanted to be helpful, but they were uncertain about how to reach out to him and help him. Jim spent a few weeks in the hospital and then was moved to a rehabilitation center. He had always been a very independent person, and he did not respond well to this new state of dependency. His loved ones constantly wanted to do things for him, yet at the rehab center, he was supposed to learn to do things for himself. Every time he tried, his mother or Diane would jump in and do it first. "I can do it myself!" he would shout in frustration. His angry response scared them, and they would just sit by meekly. Then there would come a time when he did need help, and he didn't know how to ask for it. (He had never been very good at asking for help.) So Jim would snap at them because they didn't help him. He knew he was hurting them, and that hurt him, too. He was frustrated that he didn't know how else to communicate his needs.

Diane was frustrated, too. She and Jim had been together for two years, and she loved him. Now she felt that she didn't know him! He had never snapped at her like this. She was devastated by his accident, too. This hadn't been a part of her plans for the future. She and Jim were going to get married, have kids, and have a life together. Could he even have children now? How could he help support a family? She planned to work, but she hadn't planned to have to support a husband and kids by herself. She couldn't talk to him about any of these issues, because she did not want to upset him even more. Needing someone to talk to, Diane turned to Jim's best friend, Allan. She knew that Allan cared about Jim, and she thought he might be able to help her understand Jim's behavior.

Allan tried to help Diane understand what Jim was going through, but he had never experienced anything similar himself and really didn't know what to say. He did try to comfort Diane, however. Allan, too, was feeling the tremendous loss of the friend with whom he had played sports for years, with whom he had hung out and just enjoyed life. Jim didn't want him around at all now. So Diane and Allan began spending more and more time together, sharing their losses. Diane felt sort of guilty about it, but she found it more confirming to be with Allan than to have Jim snap at her.

Once in rehab, Jim began to learn how to compensate for having only partial use of his arms. He spent months in therapy relearning many of the motor

NOTES

skills he had mastered as a child. He gradually learned new ways of doing every-day tasks, but the new skills did little to overcome his depression. However, his goal of resuming his life with Diane and their plans together kept him going. His emotional state sank when Diane told him that she and Allan had fallen in love. He was devastated. Trying to control his emotions, Jim quietly said, "I want you both to stay completely away from me." Feeling terribly guilty, she left in tears.

Now Jim saw little reason to get out of bed, let alone continue his therapy. He did continue, but only because his mother begged him to. He met some other people with disabilities at the rehab center, and he was surprised to see they did not seem to be as depressed as he was. One day, he angrily spit at two of them, "What do you two have to be so happy about?" The two quietly with-drew from the room. Shortly thereafter, a man whom Jim had seen around the center wheeled up and introduced himself as Arnold Jensen. He was a social worker, and he asked Jim if they could talk. Jim told Arnold he thought it would be a better idea to seek out Dr. Kevorkian, but he finally relented and said, "What the heck? Why not give it a try?" The two met on a daily basis for sev-eral weeks. Arnold first let Jim talk for hours about his feelings. He didn't try to tell Jim how to feel—he just listened.

After a few days, Arnold gradually began letting Jim know he was not the only person to have these feelings. Arnold shared story after story of other indi-viduals with disabilities, including himself, who had experienced similar reac-tions. But his stories didn't stop there. He continued telling Jim about the ex-periences of these individuals who came to terms with their disabilities and decided to move on with their lives. Although he didn't preach to Jim, he showed Jim other ways to see himself as a person who had a disability. Arnold said that just because a body was born one way didn't mean the body could only work in that one way. He told Jim that human beings were wonderfully flexible and resilient, and that we can adapt to whatever life brings us.

These talks helped Jim a lot and he gradually came to feel less desperate. He joined a support group of individuals who had become disabled, and he dis-covered that many of their attitudes were similar to Arnold's. Over a year's time in the group, he learned that several of the men had married after their accidents or strokes; some of them had married women who were also disabled, while oth-ers had married women without disabilities. Few of the women were married, however, which Jim later learned was typical of disabled women.

Members of the group encouraged Jim to think about his future, what he could do with his life. Jim realized how much Arnold's talks had affected him, and he began to think about ways in which he could make a similar contribu-tion. Before the accident he had been a psychology major at college. Jim decided to finish his B.A. in psychology and to then go on for graduate study in social work, much like Arnold had done.

Going back to school was a very scary proposition. Jim knew that the physical challenges would be daunting, but now he felt he could handle those with a bit of help. (He was more becoming comfortable asking for help when he needed it.) Arnold told him about programs available on campus designed to provide that help, such as retrieving library books from high shelves. Even scarier to Jim was the question of how others on campus would react to him. Would they see him as Jim, or only as a person with a disability?

It took Jim about an hour on campus to realize that his fears had not been unwarranted. Most people pretended to ignore him. Particularly upsetting was when Jim ran into people who knew him before his accident but now pretended not to see him, so that they wouldn't have to deal with the changes in him. Those who acknowledged him sometimes made him even more uncomfortable, however, with their demands for information on his disability—what had caused it, what he could and couldn't do, etc. Although he understood their curiosity, he felt like someone in a freak show. He had always been a rather private person, and he didn't respond well to being forced to disclose information to others. It helped to talk with Arnold and others in the support group about this issue, because they had all been through it before. They handled it in different ways—some through humor, some through frankness, and a few through hostility. Jim tried to look at the situation through the eyes of his fellow students, and he realized that he had been pretty naive about people with disabilities before his accident, too. He also realized that he was still naive about many types of disabilities. Just because he knew something about spinal cord injury and physical impairment didn't mean that, as a social worker, he would necessarily be very helpful to those who were visually, auditorily, intellectually, and emotionally impaired. He realized he had a lot to learn.

During the next few years of study, Jim set out to rectify his lack of experience. Through course projects, field experiences, and volunteer work, Jim learned about a variety of different disabilities and the impacts they have on the lives of others. He learned to use sign language and read braille. Jim discovered that all individuals with disabilities are socially stigmatized and that they deal with it in different ways.

Jim started dating again, but he found that the women he dated were often pressured by their parents to not become seriously attached to him. He learned that this resistance was common. He was seen as "damaged goods" by many people. But not everyone reacted to him that way. He developed new friendships and dated several women. By the time he graduated with a master's degree in social work, he had a large cheering section present. It took a while to

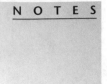

find an organization willing to hire a man with a disability, but the job at the sheltered workshop was a perfect match.

MOVING TOWARD INDEPENDENCE

Jim was assigned as Steve's case worker when Ann, Steve's former case worker, left the workshop on pregnancy leave. Jim had only been at the workshop a short time. He was struck by Steve's cheerful outlook and by the complications posed by Steve's multiple disabilities. He discovered that Steve, at age 33, lived with his mother, since his father had died a few years earlier. He asked Steve if this was what he wanted. Steve told Jim that he would like to live on his own but that they had never been able to find a place that could handle all of his disabilities. Steve said he would like more independence. He believed that his mother babied him and that she denied the fact that Steve had sexual feelings and would like relationships with women.

Jim definitely understood Steve's need for independence, and he began investigating various group homes and independent living options. He found that Steve was correct about what was out there, but he used connections he had acquired and began talking about the needs of people with multiple disabilities to those who made decisions about these buildings. It took a couple of years, but last spring Jim heard of a house that was wheelchair accessible and could be staffed 24 hours a day, primarily with care attendants who could sign. Steve's mother, Carole, was resistant; she said she was fearful for Steve's safety. Jim had to remind her diplomatically that she could not legally make these decisions for Steve. If he wanted to live on his own, she had to let him do so. Jim knew that this was a big change for Carole, who had cared for Steve all his life—a change in how she saw Steve and in how she saw herself and her role in his life.

At 35 years old, Steve began living away from home for the first time. The transition was not without obstacles. One of Steve's first housemates, Ed, beat him up before being transferred to another home. One care attendant was dismissed because of alleged sexual abuse at a past job. Other care attendants did not always carry out their responsibilities in the way contracted. Steve didn't always get meals and baths. Carole was frequently over at the house or on the phone about those issues. Although she had serious concerns, Carole could see positive changes in Steve.

The county had rules about members of the opposite sex being in residents' bedrooms, so Steve didn't have much more success with women than he had living with his mother. Even so, Steve's self-esteem and confidence increased. He was very pleased to be living on his own and making his own deci-

sions. He had felt for some time that he should be doing so, and now he was proud to be in that position. Jim could see it in his demeanor and interactions with others, and this gave Jim great satisfaction. From his own experience, he knew the importance of independence. As for Steve—well, he finally felt like an adult—at age 35!

FOR FURTHER THOUGHT AND REFLECTION

1. In what ways are disabled people stigmatized by their disabilities? How do others treat them and communicate with them?

2. What kinds of situations are particularly problematic for persons with disabilities, especially in regard to helping and maintaining privacy?

3. Some of the other cases in this book identify competing dialectical tensions that exist within relationships—independence–dependence, openness–closedness, stability–change. Which of these dialectical tensions do we see in Steve's and Jim's experiences?

4. What experiences have you had with individuals with disabilities? Does this case help you think about alternative ways of communicating with disabled people? How do you think they would like you to interact with them?

5. What impact do disability and communication patterns, as they are affected by disability, have on identity and self-esteem?

6. Do you think Steve's parents made the best decision when they elected to keep Steve at home rather than institutionalizing him?

REFERENCES

Braithwaite, D. O. (1990). From majority to minority: An analysis of cultural change from ablebodied to disabled. *International Journal of Intercultural Relations, 14,* 465–483.

Braithwaite, D. O. (1996). Persons first: Expanding communicative choices by persons with disabilities. In E. B. Ray (Ed.), *Communication and disenfranchisement: Social health issues and implications* (pp. 449–464). Mahwah, NJ: Lawrence Erlbaum.

Braithwaite, D. O., & Thompson, T. L. (1999). *Handbook of communication and people with disabilities: Research and application.* Mahwah, NJ: Lawrence Erlbaum.

Goffman, E. (1963). *Stigma: Notes on the management of spoiled identity.* Englewood Cliffs, NJ: Prentice-Hall.

Thompson, T. L., & Cusella, L. P. (1988). Help between disabled and ablebodied persons: An exploratory observational study of a feedback system. *Journal of Applied Communication Research, 16,* 51–68.

COMING OUT

Telling a Most Important Story

Clark D. Olson, Belle A. Edson

KEY WORDS

■

gay identity
coming out
relational dialectics
same-sex relationships
social support
uncertainty reduction

Twenty-one year old Doug was in a quandary. He had just received a phone call from Eric, his boyfriend of eleven months, and he learned that Eric's mother had been killed in a car accident on the West Coast. Eric was devastated. Doug and Eric had established such a close relationship that Doug was the first person Eric called. He needed help, more than a shoulder to cry on; as an only child, he needed true help. Doug knew he was going to have to be mature and help Eric through this, but he was grappling with his own predicament: just how much could he "safely" help? Although their relationship was very real, few people knew just how committed the two were to each other. Few people, that is, except for Dr. Peter Harper, Doug's mentor and sociology professor. Before he headed over to Eric's dorm, Doug wanted to call Dr. Harper.

It was Dr. Harper who had helped Doug realize he was gay. And thanks to Dr. Harper, Doug was able to tell Eric, his freshman roommate, that he was attracted to him. Doug had long known he was "different" from the other boys he grew up with. Instead of playing basketball, he chose to spend the time practicing the violin. During sports seasons, Doug would attend the symphony with his mother and grandmother, who were avid music supporters. He never dated in high school and he skipped the prom, despite much encouragement from his dad to attend. "Why would I want to go to prom? I don't even have a girlfriend." he asked his dad. Despite his six-foot frame and the fact that many people commented that he was good looking, he kept to himself, preferring to practice his violin or quietly listen to music in his room. He didn't think about creating more friendships than he already had from being in the city orchestra—the people in it were at least adults, and they didn't bother him about what he "should" be doing in high school.

Doug had met Dr. Harper his first semester in college. Despite his lack of interest in relationships up to this point, he found Dr. Harper's class on relationships fascinating. Away from home and in a new place, he felt comfortable considering new ideas. As the course progressed, Doug realized that he was more and more attracted to his roommate, Eric, and the attraction scared him. In one of his papers, Doug referenced a source that sensitive Dr. Harper picked up on. After class one day, the two of them began talking. Before long Doug told Dr. Harper about his attraction to Eric. Though he thought Dr. Harper would be open-minded, he had no idea that Dr. Harper's main research interest was gay and lesbian families. Before long, the two were sitting in Dr. Harper's office and Doug had revealed what felt like his whole life history.

Not long after that, Dr. Harper told Doug that he was gay and living with his partner of twelve years. Doug was learning far more than he ever imagined about Dr. Harper, who by this time had asked to be called Peter. Peter was at least 20 years older than Doug, nearly old enough to be his father, yet oddly Doug felt more comfortable with him than with anyone he'd ever met. So began this important relationship. Doug decided to do his final paper on gay dating, and he spent time researching in the library and on the internet. But he felt somewhat strange in the library; reading books in the HQ section, he looked carefully among the stacks to make sure no one was watching him. He even checked out several books on the Great Wall of China so that the librarian wouldn't know he was only looking at gay books. Even back in his dorm, he carefully hid the books so Eric wouldn't see them. He worked on the paper only when he was alone in his room, and he kept the door locked. Why was he so afraid? After some thought, he realized that he had never been in a position where he could be the object of discrimination. He was a young, handsome white male. And he was gay—which could make him a target for discrimination, or worse.

After reading several books on gay identity, Doug realized for the first time that he was coming to terms with himself, and who he'd really always been—a gay male living in a predominantly heterosexual world. He got an A on the paper and, after several more office conversations with Dr. Harper, was persuaded to house-sit for Peter and his partner, Charles, during winter break. Because he lived several states away, it wasn't financially possible for Doug to return home for what amounted to a long weekend, so it was convenient for him to have somewhere close to stay.

What a house Peter and Charles had! An old colonial with a Victorian living room, and an office with bookshelves to the ceiling. They also had a pretty amazing stereo, and Doug loved listening to a Brandenburg violin concerto, his favorite, on their resounding speakers. But it was in the office that Doug spent most of the break reading, without self-consciousness, their collection of gay works. Here amongst the memorabilia of a couple's life—the photos from trips, photos of family, posters and prints collected on various vacations—Doug found his greatest peace. Here he also found biographies of Oscar Wilde, Michelangelo, and Leonard Bernstein; and books by Willa Cather, Virginia Woolf, and Lillian Faderman—books about and by lesbians and gay men. Doug felt a hint of pride to be among such a distinguished group of people. Now he knew, for sure, that he was gay. But whom could he tell? His parents would be outraged; their religion didn't permit, much less condone, homosexuality. His parents always talked of how proud they would be of him at his wedding, and how they were waiting for him to start a family of his own. Isn't that why they'd wanted him to attend a private Eastern school with a fine reputation—so he could meet a nice, well-mannered girl, perhaps someone also interested in music?

Little did Doug know that Eric was taking Dr. Harper's same class in spring semester. And Eric seemed somewhat comfortable talking about Dr. Harper's research when he came home at night. Eric never actually admitted having "gay" feelings, but he seemed to know a lot more than Doug. During spring break Eric and Doug had taken a trip to Boston. To save money, they shared a small hotel room, with just one bed.

After a full day of sightseeing, Doug could hardly sleep next to Eric; he kept thinking of just how attractive Eric was. Although Eric was several inches shorter than Doug was, his muscular frame was all Doug dreamt about during the few winks of sleep he got. The next night, after a concert by the Boston Symphony, the two 19-year-olds went out for an espresso before heading back to the hotel. Before he knew it, Eric was talking about Dr. Harper's research on gay families and wondering if Doug thought it was possible for two men to actually raise a "normal" child. They debated what "normal" was by today's standards and agreed that society was changing. Before heading to bed Eric gave Doug a hug—not just any hug, but a long hug. Sometime during the night Doug remembered feeling Eric put his arm around him, just for a moment. It felt wonderful, or was it just a dream?

Doug spent the remainder of the semester thinking about Eric and practicing a difficult violin solo he was playing for the spring recital. It was rare for a freshman to be asked to play a solo, but his music teacher had convinced Doug he'd be ready. During the last week of class, Doug saw Eric's final sociology paper laying on his desk: "Two Men and a Baby: Parenting in a Gay Family." Doug started reading the paper. In it were several ideas he'd raised in their conversation in Boston. But the last paragraph stunned him. It began, "As a gay male in today's society. . . ." Doug couldn't read any further. His suspicions were true. Eric was gay too, and they'd spent an entire year living together without either of them admitting it to each other. Indeed, the college had made a fortunate choice in pairing the two of them to room together. But now just how could Doug tell Eric how he felt?

The semester ended and Doug returned home, more confused and more certain of how he felt about himself and about Eric. Twice during the summer, Doug wrote to Eric; but despite his desire to express his feelings, he just wrote about how he was spending his summer in the small town in Oregon where he'd grown up. In August, Eric wrote back. Doug couldn't believe what he read. Instead of returning to school this fall, Eric had accepted a study-abroad program lasting the entire semester. He was leaving for Europe before school began; it would be January before Doug saw Eric again. This was more than he could take. He started writing to Eric, letters that he never sent, but letters that he wished he could—letters that detailed his deep feelings for Eric.

Doug's summer ended with a barbecue hosted by his parents. One of the men his father worked with brought his daughter, soon to be a sophomore at Smith. Both men were eager for their children to meet; secretly they thought

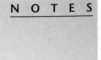

the two would make a great couple. "Great!" Doug thought, "Just what I need, a set up." Without being rude, Doug excused himself to "pack" for school. He wrote yet another unsent letter to Eric, telling him about this ridiculous situation and how he wished the two of them could be together.

Throughout the fall Doug didn't share his letters with anyone. He house-sat for Peter and Charles twice and on each visit read a few more books. On one occasion, Peter asked how he and Eric were. This was the first time Doug had ever heard their two names linked; it sounded great. Recovering from daydreaming about Eric, he confided that he'd only heard from Eric twice, but that he'd been carefully chronicling his feelings, which Peter seemed to believe was a good idea. When they returned from their latest trip, Peter and Charles invited Doug over for dinner to thank him. What a great dinner it was! Charles was a gourmet cook, and Peter fancied himself a connoisseur of fine wine. Doug would always remember this evening—not only for the fine food. He would remember this as the night he was finally able to do more than just mention his interest in Eric. In fact, he poured out his heart to the men about how much he missed Eric, about his troubles with his current roommate, his desire to get his own apartment next semester, and the horrible end-of-summer barbecue at his parents' home. Peter and Charles told him how they met in graduate school, how they told their families about their relationship, and how they had grown over the years. It was what Doug wanted, all of it—their house, their life, and Eric.

The holiday season crept by for Doug. Even the Christmas music he loved didn't seem quite so sweet that year. He missed Eric and couldn't wait to see him again. Doug returned to school, this time to his new apartment. He anticipated running into Eric on campus and was surprised when the first knock on the door of his new apartment was Eric. "Hi!" he greeted Doug with a big hug. Before Doug could ask Eric how his trip was, Eric said, "While I was away I was thinking a lot about you." Doug could hardly contain his smile. " I don't know if you know it or not, but I'm gay. And while I was away I realized that I have very deep feelings for you." Doug's heart was beating faster than he ever remembered.

Doug didn't know where to begin. He was so excited, he had so many things he wanted to blurt out at once. Instead, he said simply, " I feel exactly the same way about you." Doug retrieved the stack of letters he'd written to Eric and never sent, and they pored over them. The two of them talked all evening. Before it was over, Eric reached over and gave Doug the warmest kiss he could ever remember. It was the first time he'd been kissed by a man, and it felt wonderful. He was flooded with emotions.

The next day Doug phoned Peter to tell him what had happened. Peter was elated and invited both of them over for dinner. And that's how it began—a "double date" and a relationship that Doug had never dared hope for was happening.

But now what was Doug to do? Eric's mother was dead and neither of them had told their parents about each other, much less that they were gay. And now Eric's mother would never know. At a time like this, family was so important; but in gay relationships, acceptance by family wasn't always the norm and social support of relationships is such an important part of any healthy relationship.

During the past eleven months Doug and Eric had come to rely completely on each other. Even during the summer break, both had taken jobs near school just to be with each other. They weren't living together yet, but they might as well have been, given the amount of time they spent together. Eric was in a state of shock, he needed help. First he had to make arrangements to get home to San Diego. "He shouldn't have to face this by himself," Doug thought. He would go with Eric. But how? He couldn't afford a ticket to San Diego, and he couldn't call home to ask for one. Doug wondered how he could best help Eric. He quickly dialed Peter's number.

But Peter offered advice Doug didn't want to hear. Peter was actually suggesting he tell his parents and ask for a ticket. But what was Eric to do? Show up at his mother's funeral with a "boyfriend"? His relatives wouldn't know what to think, he would shame his mother's last memory. Doug thought a conversation with his parents could better wait for another occasion. After all, he was going home for Thanksgiving in just another week. He knew Eric would be in San Diego at least until that time. He had to see Eric.

Confused and depressed, Doug bounded over to Eric's dorm room. It was on the way that Doug thought of a solution; perhaps Eric could visit him over Thanksgiving. Eric was still in shock when Doug arrived. Before helping Eric make travel arrangements home, he suggested, "Maybe when this is all over we could spend some time together. How would you like to spend Thanksgiving with my family?" He knew Eric was not looking forward to Thanksgiving with his own family, and that would be all the more dreadful now without his mother. "That would be great," Eric said softly. Doug called the travel agent and made arrangements for Eric to fly to Oregon from San Diego. He now had one week to think about what to tell his family.

Eric left the next day, and Doug paid a visit to Peter and Charles. Doug explained how he felt pulled in two directions. On one hand, he wanted to tell his family who he really was and how Eric fit into his life. On the other hand, he wanted to spare them the embarrassment of having a gay son. Peter told him that it was natural for people to feel torn. Many of the messages received in life are ones that suggest what is normal and what is not. There is a very strong pull towards wanting to feel included as a couple, and yet gay couples are often excluded—unintentionally because they are closeted, or intentionally because they are not accepted as a couple by others, such as family. Peter further explained that all the issues couples deal with—including needing time to build a relationship and interact socially as a couple; how open a person is with their relational partner and extended family and how private they are—can be compounded for gay couples, due to society's disapproval of gays and lesbians.

With Peter's help Doug began to "practice" his coming out story for his parents. He practiced how to say he loved Eric and how he wanted his family to know him; he practiced answering questions they might ask; and he practiced how to deal with their shock and possible rejection. All of these issues were talked about and rehearsed with the help of his friends Peter and Charles. The time was right. Doug was ready for his family to know. He had already begun to tell a few close friends on campus, and he had even joined a support group sponsored by the Lesbian and Gay Academic Union at his college. Friends at the college already saw him and Eric as a couple, so now only the last piece of the puzzle needed to be completed; that was to tell his family. He wanted to tell them of the great joy the two of them experienced together, and how they couldn't contain the happiness and love they felt for each other, and how they hoped his family would share their joy. Family was an important part of Doug's life, but he didn't really know how his family would respond. After all, they were religious, as was he. It seemed as though his family would want to know about his life, and yet, this would not be what they wanted for him. Doug wondered how much to tell them. Finally he decided that he would start by telling tell them he was gay and who Eric was, and then he would let them ask any questions he hoped he could answer. Doug was almost excited to share the news with his family. This would be a Thanksgiving to remember.

FOR FURTHER THOUGHT AND REFLECTION

1. How could Doug reduce the uncertainty about how his parents will react to his coming out story?

2. How does Doug's dilemma address the integration/separation and expression/privacy poles of Baxter's dialectical theory?

3. What steps did Doug go through to begin his self-identification as a gay man? What steps could Doug continue to take to establish his identity intrapersonally and interpersonally as a gay man?

4. How did Doug's gay network of Peter and Charles help his coming out process? Why is social support for relationships important?

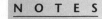
N O T E S

5. Who would it be easier to come out to: parents or friends? Why?

6. Have you ever been on the other side of this issue, wondering if someone might be gay? After reading this case, how might you act sensitively toward this person?

REFERENCES

Bauer, M. D. (Ed.). (1995). *Am I blue?: Coming out from the silence.* New York: Harper Trophy.

Baxter, L. A. (1988). A dialectical perspective on communication strategies in relationship development. In S. W. Duck (Ed.), *A handbook of personal relationships,* (pp. 257–273), New York: John Wiley.

Baxter, L. A. (1993). The social side of personal relationships: A dialectical analysis. In S. Duck (Ed.), *Social context and relationships,* (pp. 139–165). Newbury Park, CA: Sage.

Berger, C. R. (1986). Uncertain outcome values in predicted relationships: Uncertainty reduction theory then and now. *Human Communication Research, 13,* 34–38.

Berger, C. R., & Calabrese, R. J., (1975). Some explorations in initial interactions and beyond: Toward a developmental theory of interpersonal communication. *Human Communication Research, 1,* 99–112.

Due, L. A. (1995). *Joining the tribe/growing up gay and lesbian in the 1990s.* New York: Anchor.

Penelope, J., & Wolfe, S. J. (Eds.). (1989). *The original coming out stories.* San Francisco: Crossing Press.

Savin-Williams, R. C. (1997). *And then I became gay: Young men's stories.* New York: Routledge.

THE STORY OF SARA

Raising a Jewish Child Around the Christmas Tree[1]

Flavio F. Marsiglia, Michael L. Hecht

KEY WORDS

■

cultural identity
Jewish American identity
Jewish feminism
intermarriage
prejudice
stereotypes
closeting

On a sunny Fall morning Sara arrives at the office to talk. Clearly she has a lot on her mind. As a graduate student, she has been thinking about issues of identity and behavior. As a mother and wife, she has been grappling with these issues in her life. She is excited about the idea of sharing with us her own search and discovery processes as a Jewish American woman. She has been reading Michael's chapter on Jewish American identity and other short stories from "Our Voices" and wants to talk about what it means to be a Jewish American female. Sara opens the conversation by telling us that the work she is doing on our research project and recent events in her life have caused her to focus on issues of her personal identity and her family. Through her stories, she has brought her family with her. Sara's one year old son, Eli, and husband, Patrick, are very much present in the room throughout the conversation. We asked how much her female identity was determining who she is as a Jew.

SARA'S STORY

The part of myself that is now emerging is a powerful God-centered, creative, effervescent, dramatic, beautiful person. It will be very hard to tease out whether or not that is some of my Jewishness, and whether or not it has to do with being a female. I have been thinking about this a lot—my identities as Jewish and a female—since I became a mother. Motherhood has forced me to question my relationship to my religion as I try to question, integrate, and celebrate all my identities.

I think of this as a journey back into my faith. I am trying to rescue a dormant part of myself. But I don't want to blame majority society for this distance from my religion. That wasn't really the cause, although it is for some people. My childhood religion was an old religion conveyed to me in very traditional ways. While my parents did not push it on me, it was the orthodoxy of Jewish thought and practice, particularly feeling excluded as a female, that led me to move away from my faith. But at the same time, I longed for the sense of home and belonging that my community and faith offered me then and could offer my child today. So when Eli was born, I began to look for ways to raise him, to help him ground himself. This lead me to conversations with other Jewish women, many of whom were having the same experiences, and to introspection, which brought me back to my family.

Growing Up Jewish

My parents' experience with Judaism was a primary influence on my own upbringing and religious education. [Both of my parents were raised Jewish—

NOTES

actually conservative, or even orthodox Judaism—and the Jewish education was maybe shoved down their throats.] And I didn't hear my parents speaking of Judaism as a beautiful, enriching part of their lives. It seemed more to be, I think, something that they were detached from. It was part of who they were but not a part that they celebrated readily.

My parents' Jewish experience was different from my own. Because their religious and cultural upbringing was so strict, they relaxed the norms with me. Like many others of their generation, my parents did not get very involved in Jewish traditions and practices, and they never forced me to, either. In fact, I was the one who wanted to go to temple!

When I was a little girl, Anne Frank was very much an inspiration to me. I insisted on being part of a temple and going to a Hebrew school. My parents were very willing to have me not attend because they didn't want to force a Hebrew education on me. So when I asked for it, they were quite shocked, and we went to a reform temple because their feeling was, well, "Sara would have freedom to determine for herself what she does believe and what she doesn't believe." And I had the benefit of some magical teachers at the Hebrew school who taught me what God could be. I could develop my own relationship with a personal God, God could be whatever worked for me within the belief system that held there is one God and other basic Jewish tenets.

At this point in my life, religion was a refuge for me. I was very devoted to my faith, and it gave me a sense of hope. Temple was the big home and God the biblical "Father" taking care of his people as they walked through the desert. When my family went through difficult times, like during my mother's illness, my closeness to God intensified and the spiritual dimension of my Judaism was very personal.

As time went on, I decided I wanted to be a rabbi. There were very few female rabbis at the time, and I had decided to pursue that. I also wasn't pushed to pursue it. People said, "Well if that's what you want to do," but no one got excited with me. What is interesting is the maleness of God or the perception of the maleness of God. I am not even sure I think it came from my Jewish upbringing. Maybe it's one of those issues that spills over from emersion in Christian culture.

As a result, I always experienced my faith as *gendered*. But this belief intensified when I tried to find an explanation for my experience of exclusion as a female, and I didn't know where to search for explanations. The contradiction between my open and progressive religious instruction and this invisible closed door was a source of confusion and disappointment, so for a long period of time I distanced myself from my religion. Since the birth of Eli, however, I have been not only questioning and searching for my own identity as a mother but also questioning the identity of my God as well as my understanding and experiences with Judaism and with my Jewish family of origin.

Revisiting Identities Through Motherhood

After giving birth to Eli, the existentialist question "Who am I" resurfaced with the intensity of a second adolescence. The birth gave proof of God's existence in my life. There was nothing quite so profound and so miraculous as that experience. Motherhood strengthened my female identity and, through my female identity, I questioned my faith and ethnic identity formation. I am going through this process of exploring which parts of me come from my Jewishness. I am really excited about what is happening. Part of the reason is that in my prayer and meditation, since Eli has been born, I really have needed a personal connection with God. I need to have a tangible, workable relationship with God, and I need to be able to access that relationship and have my life flung from it. I started to realize the maleness of my God was not conducive to that personal relationship; I had difficulty relating to God if God is purely male.

I have also undergone a transformation more recently in looking at my own Judaism—not only my Judaism, but my own existence—and whether or not I am going to be who I am or be a reflection of what other people think I ought to be. The external versus internal struggles are a pervasive metaphor in my life these days. Up until perhaps even a year ago, if you asked me how I defined myself, the things that I would have mentioned would have included what goes on a *vita*. [However, I have developed a new sense of myself, and in the past three to six months, I have been able to gain a voice for that part of myself, which I think others might be uncomfortable with, disagree with, and perhaps even oppress me or my family.]

In the Company of Jewish Women

As part of my search I started to reconstruct or deconstruct God's identity. I talked to women, a lot of women, particularly Jewish women, about their spirituality and asking "How do you build this bridge? What works for you?" I was led to several books that have truly changed my life. One is Lynn Gottlieb's book, *She Who Dwells Within*, the subtitle of which is something like "Renewed Judaism through Feminism." The other work that has had a profound impact on me is called, *The Feminine Face of God*. Both of these books refer to *shekinah*, which is a Hebrew word for the feminine presence of God or the feminine face of God. The truth for me is that my God has masculine and feminine attributes, and that allows me to honor in a bigger way the parts of me that I may have squelched for a very, very long time because other people might find those aspects frightening or scary.

I didn't grow up in a Judaism that separated out the females. My Bat Mitzvah was given much honor and celebration. I am not quite sure of the origin of the male image that I kept conjuring up. When I pray, and when I prayed in the past, there is no picture of a person in my mind. It's more that I sense a presence of spirit or a grace. As a very little girl, the way I contended with the lack of an image was to picture the altar in a temple that had the everlasting light above it and the Torah within, and I knew that God lived within that house. So temple was a sacred place to me. I knew there was a lot of power there.

When I speak of my spiritual journey, know that I absolutely knew that God existed when I was a child. There was no intellectual question about that to me. Then I went through periods of my life where the question became intellectual. One of the things that is very Jewish in me is the questioning: Why? and how come? and I don't understand. But, ironically, the process that I have been going through has brought me back to a kind of childlike knowing the existence of God and accepting that in my life. If I were to have all the understanding I truly crave intellectually, of the least things, then my definition of God isn't big enough.

Celebrating the Jewish Woman

The cultural dimension of my Jewish identity brought other challenges, such as stereotypes of me as a female and as a Jew. My childhood sheltered me from prejudice. My definition of myself as a child was this loving acceptance of the parts of me that were dramatic and silly and all those things I said earlier. And I defined myself then very similarly to how I define myself now—as if there is some kind of core identity that I was able to embrace as a child. But through the course of my life that expressive self became, for whatever reason, very subdued. Almost caged in, so to speak, because of messages I received. And who did I receive them from? Everybody. I received a lot of overt and covert messages about how I was "supposed to behave." As I said earlier, I am a very driven person. I am very achievement oriented, so a lot of my true self got confined. In order to achieve, I had to behave in a certain fashion. It was not always clear to me who others were trying to change: the Jew? the female? Both?

It didn't serve me well to be overly dramatic, or emotional. For example, to burst into tears would have been very, very scary for people who don't know what to do with that level of emotion. So I learned, Okay, I need to control my emotions. But expressing them is a very natural thing for me. I may even cry during this interview because I feel things very deeply and they stir me to tears. That happens a lot. My father is that way, too, so I don't know if it is being female or Jewish or both.

Some of this awareness is a very recent experience that we are talking about. Since Eli has been born I think I've experienced some fear of sharing my Jewishness, and humor has always been a way to make things safe. Maybe we develop Jewish humor because we need it. But when it is from outside that humor can be very harmful. Sometimes when I hear Jewish jokes it just makes me sick to my stomach. When a woman describes herself as a Jewish-American princess, it makes people giggle. It is a silly image, conjuring up long nails, and shopping, and big earrings, and almost a caricature, which I am not. But I think people embrace the Jewish-American princess image and find it less threatening than the person I project when I say, "I am a powerful and loving Jewish female."

I know I have the prerogative of not sharing my cultural identity with others, of closeting it. Sharing is a real choice, one I struggle with because I fear prejudice. While many assume that anti-Semitism is a thing of the past, I—like most Jewish Americans—have experienced it firsthand. Because some tell me I don't look Jewish, and because of my husband's last name, many people think I am not Jewish. It's rare that I share that I am Jewish in a group, particularly out here in Arizona, just because I am very wary of the potential for prejudice. Actually one gal I really loved, brought up the topic of bosses, and she said something about rich Jews and how clueless they are. I felt the need—a very, very strong need, in a very careful way—to share my experience with her, to say that I am a Jewish person. She never treated me the same after that, and whenever the issue of spirituality came up, members of the group were afraid to go near the topic because I was present. Then I think about Eli and realize the importance of nurturing a strong sense of Jewish identity. I know that, while this identity may protect him, it also may expose him to prejudice if he chooses to express it publicly.

Negotiating a Home Identity: The Power of Symbols

Privacy issues play out powerfully as Patrick and I negotiate our home space. I want to share with you a very interesting process that Patrick and I went through when my parents gave me a mezuzah[2] for the door as a house warming gift. It is a very beautiful mezuzah because it is very southwestern, a style that is so hard to find. It has the turquoise and stone color to it, and it is really quite beautiful. Initially Patrick was fully open to having it on our door, then later he was hesitant to make a hole in the wood. But I think I was more reluctant than Patrick. I feared it would invite anti-Semitism on our home simply by virtue of being there—a symbol of our Judaism, of my Judaism.

As another wedding present we received a menorah that has the outline of a tree behind it. I really love that because I think it unifies. But a crucifix in my home would make me uncomfortable, and I actually had to discuss that with Patrick. I think Patrick is okay with it. I mean Patrick has his own crucifix and a rosary, but we don't have a family crucifix. Symbols are very, very powerful. Recently, we had a discussion about Patrick's grandmother. I love her very much, but she makes things for Christmas, ornaments and what-not, and a lot of the ornaments are very Christian: crosses and Christian prayers. I had difficulty with even having the crosses on the tree because, if we were going to decorate a tree and that was important to Patrick, then that is fine; but the more Christian it appeared to me, the more uncomfortable I was. I think that there is something to be said about the power of icons, and I remember the first time we even had a tree, I made my own star of David that needed to go on top, and the tree was my own Hanukkah bush. So there is definitely power in that. There is much overlap with the festival of light, and the presents, and the gathering of family.

Raising a Jewish Child Around the Christmas Tree

Eli is Jewish by birth, and only through baptism could he be part of his father's faith. As Eli has gotten older, I have given more thought to Eli as a Jew, and that has been profoundly comforting. The most difficult thing in making the decision about how Eli would be raised is the loyalty issue. Patrick has this profound loyalty to his family, not so much to the faith but to the parents and grandparents. My loyalty feels different because it is not to my parents but to the Jewish faith and traditions. I feel loyalty to Judaism and to passing on my Jewishness.

Around holidays, such as Passover, Patrick is very respectful, and he joins in our celebration of Seder and burns bread in different rooms. But I also had some very quiet and personal time with Eli when we sat down and I took the Haggadah and I read it to him as a story. There is a part in the Haggadah that says, if you are a parent and you don't explain this story to your child, then you are not fulfilling your responsibilities as a parent. I take that very, very seriously in terms of sharing the story with him. But I feel that I do him a disservice if I don't share with him honestly what it all means for me. I think that some bridge building is about separating out spirituality from religion, really taking what works for us, and letting the rest go.

When it comes to holidays, we improvise. Around Christmas and Hanukkah we celebrate the aspects of those two holidays that we love the most. I think we will always celebrate as an interfaith family. I will read the Passover Haggadah to Eli and I imagine him asking questions about the meaning of different symbols. Perhaps his curiosity will lead him to ask about traditions other than his own. I will try to explain these other symbols, at times with Patrick's help. I hope Eli will understand the differences and similarities. I see him one year celebrating Hanukkah, suddenly arising and taking a spin around the Christmas tree, picking up his little toy hammer and a small nail, opening the door, climbing on top of his toy bench and hanging the mezuzah.

END NOTES

1   The name Sara is fictionalized, as are all names other than in citations and those of the authors themselves. However, the characters are based on real people and these issues are theirs, as expressed by the person we have named Sara.

2   A mezuzah is a parchment containing biblical passages. It is rolled up in a small object, often rectangular in shape, and hung near or on a door. It is a sign that a Jewish family lives within and serves as a form of protection and blessing.

FOR FURTHER THOUGHT AND REFLECTION

1. What does it mean to be Jewish and American in a Christian-dominated society?

2. Which subtle stereotypes of Jewish Americans have you heard personally or seen in the media?

3. Does Sara's way of experiencing her religion distance herself from her community?

4. Have you dated a person from other racial, ethnic, or religious culture? If the answer is yes, did you face any situation similar to the one experienced by Sara. If the answer is no, why not?

5. Do you believe most women cannot fully identify with a purely male God? Do you support efforts to make translations of religious books more inclusive of women and men?

6. Are there challenges with being female and belonging to your own religion?

REFERENCES

Dershowitz, Alan M. (1997). *The vanishing American Jew*. New York: Touchstone.

Golden, D. R., Niles, T. A., & Hecht, M. L. (1998). Jewish American identity. In J. N. Martin, T. K. Nakayama, & L. A. Flores (Eds.), *Readings in cultural contexts*. Mountain View, CA: Mayfield.

Gonzalez, A., Houston, M., & Chen, V. (1997). *Our Voices: Essays in Culture, Ethnicity, and Communication* (2nd ed.). Los Angeles, CA: Roxbury.

MIRROR, MIRROR ON THE WALL

Weight, Identity, and Self-Talk in Women

Wendy S. Davies-Popelka

KEY WORDS

■

body image
identity
intrapersonal communication
race/ethnicity
self-esteem

"Hurry up, Reece, we're gonna be late for class if we don't go eat lunch now!" shouted Emma exasperatedly, as she watched her roommate check her hair and makeup in the mirror for what seemed like the hundredth time that day.

"Don't worry, Emma, we have plenty of time," said Charelle, coming down the hall and stopping in the door to Emma and Reece's dorm room. "And Reece, honey, you know you look gorgeous, so stop fussing and let's go!"

"Oh, you two, give me a break. I have to make sure my hair looks good, 'cause nothing else does today," explained Reece. She caught a glimpse of herself in the mirror: *You're fat, fat, fat*, the mirror told her.

Charelle looked at Emma with a question in her eyes. Emma nodded and then said, "Yeah, today's one of Reece's 'fat days.' She told me that before she even got out of bed this morning."

"Girlfriend, what do you weigh? All of 130?" asked Charelle.

"Fine, make fun of me all you want. You don't understand. I ate a bowl of cereal, two pieces of bread, a piece of cheese, two slices of pizza, and three chocolate chip cookies yesterday. I must have gained five pounds just since yesterday." Reece turned and glanced into the mirror on the wall above her dresser one last time, running her fingers through her straight, shoulder-length blond hair. *They don't understand what's it like to be fat*, she thought to herself. *If only I had Emma's figure; she's so thin, and she never has to watch what she eats. I'm so fat. Today I will only eat vegetables and drink water. And I have to spend 30 extra minutes at the gym. That should make up for yesterday's calories.*

Turning toward her friends, Reece grabbed her backpack off the bed and slung it over her shoulder. "Let's go then, if you two are in such a hurry to eat lunch before class."

In the Cafeteria

Reece grabbed a tray from the bin next to the front doors of the cafeteria, tossing silverware and a napkin on the tray's shiny silver surface as she slid it down the railing to the first station, the salad bar. She lifted a plate from the stack next to the salad bar and carefully selected an assortment of raw vegetables—carrots, celery, broccoli, cucumbers—ignoring the cauliflower, which she disliked with a passion. *Some ranch dressing would be really good with these veggies*, she thought to herself. *But I can't have those calories after the horrible day I had yesterday. I have to make up for all that bad food I ate. I shouldn't have eaten those cookies last night before I went to bed. I can't believe I did that. How stupid can I be?* Turning back to her friends, who were piling their plates with salad—complete with lots of dressing, she noticed—Reece said, "I'm done. I'll grab us a table."

Reece turned and walked toward the checkout line, leaving Charelle and Emma standing there looking at each other, their mouths wide open. Emma recovered first, answering Charelle's questioning look with a nod, saying, "Yeah, she's been on this weird diet kick lately. If she has a 'bad' day, like she eats something she doesn't think she should have, she tries to make up for it the next day, by just eating raw vegetables and drinking water."

"That sounds like punishment to me," replied Charelle, shuddering at the thought. "And what's up with her listing off every single thing she ate yesterday? I've never heard her do that before."

"Oh, she does that every night. She calls it her private time," explained Emma. "She told me she lies in bed at night and lists out everything she ate that day. Then she decides what she can eat the next day based on that."

"I don't understand her obsession with her weight," said Charelle. "I mean, she's not fat. She's what? A size eight?"

"Yeah, but when she was really young, she had a problem with her weight. Then she lost a whole bunch of weight in high school, but when she came to college she gained some of it back. Now she's trying to get back to where she was in high school."

At the Table

Reece leaned back in her chair and tried not to watch Emma eat the piece of carrot cake she had chosen for dessert. Even after eating most of the vegetables and drinking a glass of water, she still felt hungry. *Well, that's what you get*, she said to herself. *If you hadn't made such a pig out of yourself yesterday, you might be able to have a piece of cake. But no, you had to be a pig. That's all you are, you know. A fat pig. Ever since third grade, when those kids made fun of you. . . .* Reece's thoughts drifted back to Mrs. Wright's third-grade classroom:

Reece glanced down at her shoes as she walked to the front of the classroom. Painfully shy, she dreaded having to be in front of other children. And now Mrs. Wright had called on her to solve a math problem on the chalkboard! As she walked past Mary's desk, Reece heard Mary and Mary's best friend Lisa whispering and giggling. Then she heard Mary say under her breath, "Nice pants. Where'd you get 'em? Tents 'R Us?" Reece turned bright red and her footsteps faltered as Mary's cruel comment sank in. *I can't help it*, she thought, *that my mom makes my clothes for me. If only I weren't so fat*, she chastised herself, *I could find clothes to fit me like normal people do.* Reece continued her progression toward the front of the room, inwardly shaking at the cruelness of the two girls she so desperately wanted to be her friends. Then she heard the unmistakable whisper of Jimmy St. John coming from her left. "Boom. Boom. Boom," he chanted, ridiculing her as she walked haltingly up the seemingly endless aisle. Children around him began laughing as they heard his taunts. Reece turned an even brighter shade of scarlet and wished desperately that she could sink into the floor and disappear forever. *If only I were skinny*, she thought, *they would like me. Then I would be popular and everybody would want to be my friend.*

"Hey, girlfriend, what are you daydreaming about? Aren't you going to finish your rabbit-food lunch before it wilts?" Charelle's strident voice interrupted Reece's painful recollection and brought her back to the present with a start. She mentally shook herself, *Now there's no need to be thinking about that still. You know that you have been working hard to lose weight ever since that day in third grade. If you hadn't regained a bunch of weight when you came to college, you would still be as thin as you were in high school. No matter what it takes, you have to get back there.*

"Hey Reece, you wanna try a bite of this carrot cake? It's even better than the chocolate cake they were serving last week," offered Emma.

"No thanks, Em," Reece said. "I'll never lose those last 10 pounds if I eat cake."

"Ten pounds!" exclaimed Charelle. "Where in the world do you think you're going to lose 10 pounds?"

"I have to lose 10 pounds to get down to 120," explained Reece. "That's what I'm supposed to weigh."

"According to whom?" asked Charelle.

"I don't remember where I read it," said Reece. "One of the fashion magazines had an equation in it to figure your ideal weight. You should weigh 100 pounds if you're five feet tall and then add five pounds for every inch over five feet. Since I'm 5'4", I should weigh 120."

"What does your dad think of that equation?" Emma asked with a slight frown.

"Well, my dad says it's not right and that I shouldn't follow it," Reece said. "He has a chart from the American Medical Association that came in one of his medical journals that he gave me to look at, but it said I should weigh more than 120. And that can't be right, 'cause I'd look fat. So I'm using the equation."

"Your father the doctor said to ignore the equation you read in some fashion mag, but you think he's wrong!" exclaimed Emma questioningly.

"Well, if I want to look the way I should," said Reece defensively, "I need to lose at least 10 pounds." As she picked up a carrot stick off her plate, Reece eyed the thick slice of carrot cake on Emma's plate. *I would really like to try that carrot cake*, she thought, instantly reprimanding herself for even thinking that. *How do you think you're ever going to lose weight and be beautiful if you can't even stay away from junk food?* Even as she chastised herself, though, Reece was contemplating the carrot cake again. She reached over and pinched off a tiny piece of the cream cheese frosting, placing it on her tongue and relishing its sweetness as it dissolved in her mouth. *What an idiot!* she screamed at herself. *You are so weak. You'll never be thin. You can't resist temptation, so there's no way you're going to be able to diet. You just need to stop eating completely. Obviously you can't even come down to the cafeteria without cheating, so from now on you'll stay in your room and drink water.* She pushed her plate away from her, cringing at the harsh things she was saying to herself but unable to stop.

"You can't be full already," said Charelle. "You haven't eaten anything."

"Leave me alone," cried Reece. "I'm not hungry." She shoved her chair back from the table and stood, gathering her tray and her backpack. "I'm going to class," she said. "I have a few questions to ask Professor Lane before class starts." She turned abruptly and walked away from the table, leaving her two friends staring open-mouthed at her back, confused by her sudden burst of temper.

"What's up with that?" said Charelle. "I don't think I've ever seen her that upset. What did I say?"

"Oh nothing," said Emma. "She's like this sometimes when she's upset about her weight. She gets really quiet and withdrawn and is overly sensitive if you criticize her in any way."

"I don't understand," said Charelle. "She's not fat. I think she's beautiful just as she is."

"I know, I know. But she thinks she's fat. And nothing anyone says will change her mind."

"I just don't get why she's so hard on herself."

"I know, I don't either."

In Class Later That Afternoon

"Okay, class, quiet down. Today we're going to continue our discussion of body image by talking with Dr. Susan Holland, an expert in eating disorders." Professor Lane introduced the guest speaker to her Psychology 125 class and took a seat at the back of the room.

Dr. Holland thanked Professor Lane and the class for allowing her to visit them and share information on eating disorders.

"Did you know that dieting has reached almost epidemic proportions?" she asked the class. "Depending on what study you read, it has been estimated that as many as 60–80 percent of adolescent girls are dieting at any given time. And an obsession with being thin can lead to eating disorders."

"But doesn't that just apply to girls?" questioned one young man in the front row.

"Well, it does seem to apply especially to women, but more and more men are beginning to worry about their weight, as well. Research studies have found that women are generally more concerned and less satisfied with their physical appearance than men. Women are also more likely to weigh themselves, to describe themselves as fat, to think that that their current figure is heavier than their ideal figure, and to not see themselves as underweight even when they are," Dr. Holland continued. "I read the results from a survey done by *Psychology Today* magazine. Eighty-nine percent of all of the females responding to the survey reported that they wanted to lose weight. And I have a question for you to think about. You don't have to answer this out loud, but just think . . . how many years of your life would you give up to be your ideal weight?"

A wave of laughter and a few gasps raced through the class as the students thought about Dr. Holland's question.

I would probably give up a few years to weigh 120, thought Reece.

Emma considered the same question herself. *How can anyone give up years of their life to change their weight? Don't they know that life is precious? I can't imagine being so upset over your weight that you would actually give up years of your life!*

As the class pondered her question, Dr. Holland shared more information with them from the survey. "In response to the question I just asked you," she said, "15 percent of women and 11 percent of men said that they would sacrifice more than five years of their lives to be their ideal weight. Twenty-four percent of women and 17 percent of men said they would give up more than three years."

"I can't believe anyone would willingly give up years of their life to be a different weight," stated a young African American woman in the back of the room. "I mean, I could probably stand to lose 20 or 30 pounds if I had to, but I would never give up years of my life to do it. I mean, God gave me life, and He's the only one who can take it away. And He loves me the way I am."

"I don't know," replied a young European American woman. "I can see where people might be willing to do that. There's an awful lot of pressure put on women to lose weight. I have a lot of friends who do some pretty extreme things to try to lose weight. In fact, two of my roommates are anorexic and one of them is an exercise freak. Being thin is like an obsession with them."

"Unfortunately many women are obsessed with losing weight," said Dr. Holland. "Some people would do anything to lose weight. And their desire to lose weight may not always be linked to an actual weight problem. Who can think of things that thinness symbolizes in American culture?"

As soon as she asked the question, answers came flying from around the room.

"Beauty."

"Popularity."

"If you're thin, you have a lot of friends and people will like you."

"Thinness equals success."

"If you're thin, that means you have control over your life."

"All of those things are true," said Dr. Holland. "In our culture, thinness has come to mean many different things, and many women—especially white women—have internalized the standard of thinness and use it to judge their own attractiveness."

"I don't understand what the big deal is," said a young European American woman. "What's the big deal if we want to be slim?"

"It's a big deal," replied Dr. Holland, "when the desire to be thin begins to affect your health. And there are many health risks associated with being too thin: eating disorders can cause women to stop menstruating, cause severe damage to kidneys and other internal organs, and even lead to death.

"When women have internalized the cultural standard of thinness and use that standard to judge themselves, they often don't measure up. And if they don't measure up, if they weigh more than they think they should, they may feel less worthy, like they are less of a person. And this feeling may affect their self-esteem and their self-confidence."

"I don't really understand," said a young man in the middle of the room. "Where do women get this pressure? I mean I've never said anything to my girlfriend about her weight, but she's constantly talking about losing weight."

"It's everywhere," cried the woman sitting beside him. "You hear it from the media, from your parents, from your friends, from guys. . . ."

"Yeah, sometimes guys are the worst," said another young woman. "They are constantly making comments about really thin women, like 'She's so hot,' or 'What a body.' What are we supposed to think?"

"That's not true of all guys," exclaimed another woman in the class. "My guy friends who are African American say that they like women with a few curves. They don't want women who look like Kate Moss."

"That brings up an important issue," said Dr. Holland, raising her hand to quiet the building conversation the last few comments had inspired. "There is often a difference among racial groups. African American culture, for example, seems to be more accepting of weight than European American culture. One study done in 1993 found that even though the African American women were heavier overall as a group, twice as many African American women as European American women were satisfied with the shape of their body as it was. And a 1995 study found that European American women reported feeling significantly more pressure to be thin than did African American women."

At the end of class, Dr. Holland fielded a few final questions and then thanked the students for their lively participation. As the students filed from the room, Emma caught up with Reece and tapped her on the shoulder.

"Hey, friend," she said. "Want to go watch the women's field hockey game with me?"

"Can't," replied Reece. "I'm going to the gym to work out."

"Can't you wait and go later?" asked Emma.

"No," Reece said. "I have to put in an extra half hour today, and then I have to go to the Student Advisory Board meeting. Then I have gobs of homework to do."

"Want to meet for supper then?" Emma asked.

"No, thanks, I'm going to be too busy to eat tonight, I think," said Reece.

"Reece, come on, you have to eat. Especially after you ate hardly anything for lunch."

"No," Reece replied firmly. "If I'm going to lose weight, I have to eat less."

"Didn't you listen to what Dr. Holland was saying?" Emma asked. "Don't let the thin ideal run—or ruin—your life."

"Got to go," said Reece, ignoring her friend's question. "See you later."

Emma shook her head sadly as she watched her best friend head toward the gym. *What can I do to help her get over this obsession with her weight?* she wondered. *I'm afraid she's going to hurt herself, but she just doesn't seem to see what she's doing.*

As Reece entered the door of the gym, she mentally ran through her exercise plan for the day. *I'll stretch out and then use the Stairmaster for 30 minutes. Then I'll run two miles on the track and do another 30 minutes on the exercise bike. Maybe that'll make up for all that junk I ate yesterday. If I do 45 minutes on the exercise bike, maybe I can eat supper tonight,* she thought. Instantly, she corrected herself. *No, I can't. Those ten pounds are going to be hard to lose, and I can't let myself cheat.* As she headed for the locker room, Reece glanced in the mirrored wall by the stairs. *You're fat,* the mirror told her, *but if you work hard enough maybe someday you'll be thin.* Reece struggled in vain to ignore the hunger pangs in her stomach and tried to envision looking in the mirror and seeing her new, thin body. *Whatever it takes,* she told herself, *that's what I'll do. Whatever it takes to be thin.*

FOR FURTHER THOUGHT AND REFLECTION

1. How does Reece's intrapersonal communication about her weight affect her self-esteem? What messages does she send herself repeatedly that affect her self-esteem? Where do these messages come from?

2. How does your communication with yourself and with others affect your identity? What role does communication play in shaping your identity?

3. Not all people feel the same pressure to be thin. How much pressure do you and your friends feel to be thin? Do you hear people talking about wanting to be thin and measuring themselves against impossible standards? What might account for some people feeling an intense amount of pressure and others not feeling any pressure?

4. In this case, Reece strongly wants to lose weight and expresses her willingness to "do whatever it takes" to be thin. Do you think her desire and her behavior are unhealthy? Does her friend Emma have a responsibility to say something to Reece about her behavior? What do you think Emma should do to keep her friend from hurting herself?

5. What racial/ethnic differences in views toward weight can you see in the students' questions and comments in class? What might explain the racial/ethnic differences in views toward weight?

REFERENCES

Brumberg, J. J. (1997). *The body project: An intimate history of American girls*. New York: Random House.

Cash, T. F., & Henry, P. E. (1995). Women's body images: The results of a national survey in the U.S.A. *Sex Roles, 33*, 19–28.

Davies-Popelka, W. S. (1998). *Listening to their voices: An interpretive study of women's intrapersonal communication about weight*. Unpublished master's thesis, University of North Carolina, Chapel Hill.

Garner, D. M. (1997, January/February). The 1997 body image survey results. *Psychology Today, 30*, 30–44, 75–76, 78, 84.

Hesse-Biber, S. (1996). *Am I thin enough yet? The cult of thinness and the commercialization of identity*. New York: Oxford University Press.

Powell, A. D., & Kahn, A. S. (1995). Racial differences in women's desires to be thin. *International Journal of Eating Disorders, 9*, 329–343.

Vocate, D. R. (Ed.). (1994). *Intrapersonal communication: Different voices, different minds*. Mahwah, NJ: Lawrence Erlbaum.

Wood, J. T. (1997). *Communication theories in action: An introduction*. Belmont, CA: Wadsworth.

STRADDLING HEAVEN AND EARTH

Managing Changes Associated with Religious Conversion

Douglas L. Kelley, Debra-L Sequeira

KEY WORDS

■

identity
conversion
peer relationships
looking-glass self
turning points

NOTES

John stood in front of the mirror. He turned his body to one side and then the other, trying to get the best view possible of his lats; that is, his *latisimus dorsi* muscles. This morning, like every morning since John had joined the football team, the mirror confirmed John's own thoughts—he was a stud. Of course John would never have said this out loud to anyone, but privately he had allowed many such thoughts to run through his mind. Who would have thought two years ago, when John started playing football, that he would become the key component to the Titan defense? Having a keen nose for the ball and bulking up with weights, John had come a long way in transforming a skinny, average-looking sophomore into one of the most popular students on campus.

A year ago last fall, in the third football game of the season, John intercepted a pass during the final seconds of the game and ran it back through multiple defenders for the winning touchdown. The next day at school John found himself in the boys' bathroom at lunch, looking in the mirror to make certain that he was the same guy who had come to school the day before. His friends, somehow, seemed more friendly; seniors who had never so much as looked at him before gave him that knowing look that said, "You're in." Oh, and the girls—girls whose names he didn't even know—were suddenly finding him "soooo interesting"!

Needless to say, John liked this new persona. By the end of the season, weight training and a few good defensive plays on the field had transformed this average sophomore into a big man on campus. John's junior and senior years were a dream come true. His well-toned physique and athletic ability had provided him with all the friends he needed. Now, as he stood before the mirror he saw himself as his friends saw him, and the picture of the insecure, pimply sophomore that had once filled his mind was left behind.

John's senior year also brought some new experiences in the form of drinking with the guys on the team. Here, as well as on the football field, John expanded his popularity by being known as a risk-taker. Football and drinking allowed John to live life on the edge. And it was this edge that provided John with the "rush" that, more and more it seemed, he needed to feel good.

In the winter of his senior year, the rush John needed came in the form of a sixty-five miles per hour drive on an icy mountain road near his home. Beer and tequila subtly blurred his vision and dulled his senses. Lulled into a false sense of control, John couldn't compensate quickly enough to negotiate a forty mile per hour curve. His parents' forest green Jeep Cherokee rolled two and a half times as it careened over the embankment. A Douglas fir was the only thing that kept the car and its driver from cascading two hundred and ten feet to the bottom of the ravine. This silent sentinel was the difference between death and life.

Death was more what it felt like to John, however, when he awoke and found himself in a hospital bed, his mother by his side. Her bright eyes were a comfort to him at first, but it was a troubled smile that betrayed the truth. She told him he had been in a coma for three weeks. The doctors assured him that with physical therapy he would once again walk normally and that he should regain full mobility in his neck. However, football and the college scholarships he had counted on were out of the question.

John's first conscious week in the hospital was misery. Not only was he physically uncomfortable and begging his family to sneak him some "real food," but he had had several friends from school visit. Although their words were encouraging and uplifting, he could sense their uncertainty about how to treat him. They tried to joke as they had before, but somehow now it seemed unnatural. The look in their eyes, the distance they kept, and their short stays were like a mirror reflecting John's changed image.

Following surgery on his neck and right leg, an intense physical therapy regimen brought the Titan football star to the point where he could get out of bed. As he walked slowly around the room on his own, he paused and stood silently before a full length mirror, taking in what others' eyes had told him weeks before. His skin was pale and his face looked gaunt due to his considerable weight loss. Intravenous feeding during the coma had left his body looking somewhat ghoulish in the fluorescent light. He stared at his image in the mirror, his hopes dashed, his spirit crushed. The doctor's words, "We'll have to keep him here a couple of more weeks," echoed in his mind. His lips parted slightly. "Why me?" he whispered in anguish. "Why me?" He heard no reply.

As John pondered the effects of the physical coma, he reflected on the last two years of his life. Although they had been wild and fun in some ways, he had seldom felt any sense of true satisfaction. He was in a constant chase for more stimulation. And now look at him. A stop to the chase had been thrust upon him. John began to realize that, like the physical coma he had just come through, the last two years of his life had been lived in a coma of a different kind.

John was still standing in front of the mirror when his physical therapist, Mark, knocked on the door. "Hey, lookin' good. You've come a long way, you know."

Looking down at his two withered legs, John didn't think so. "Yeah, a long way to nowhere," he snapped sarcastically. "I've lost everything."

"Listen, you can't afford a pity party now. You've still got a lot of work to do. The doctors and I can help you learn to regain use of your legs, but the real healing is going to be between you and God."

John looked quizzically at Mark. How did he know? Each and every day, since regaining consciousness, John had cursed God for the accident. Now this man had the gall to tell him that he needed to get things right with God. "No way!" John thought to himself.

During the following few physical therapy sessions with Mark, John's recovery slowed. Mark could sense John's resistance to him, so one day in the exercise room he asked John to come to the center of the room. With the aid of his walker, John slowly worked his way out to where Mark was standing. Using mostly his upper body strength for support, John stood eye to eye with Mark.

"Give me the walker."

John couldn't believe what he was hearing. "I can't! You know that."

"Give me the walker, John."

"Look, I'm not ready for this. I'd rather work on the pneumatic machines today."

Mark slowly began to pull John's walker away from him. "John, you need to learn to put more weight on that foot. You're trying to do this with only your upper body strength."

"Hey," John almost cried out, "Don't pull this away from me. I'm serious!"

Mark put his hand firmly on John's shoulder. "John, you need to trust me— just like you need to trust Him."

John paused, then slowly let go of the walker. He stood silently, staring at his legs, which somehow were supporting his body. When he finally raised his head, Mark was looking straight at him. "A little trust can go a long way, John." John could see a mixture of strength and compassion in Mark. This man seemed so certain, so assured. John wanted that. Somehow, he felt, it was as if God was speaking directly to him.

After the session, Mark wheeled John back up to his room. "You had a good workout. I'll leave you alone to think about what happened today, and to pray."

Pray? John had not prayed since he was a small child. His strongest image of prayer was of his Vacation Bible School teacher praying out loud for Peter Skallaway's mom, whom the doctors said had only three months to live. Come to think of it, hadn't he talked with Peter's mom last year after the homecoming game? If it worked for Peter's mom, could it possibly work for him? John took a quick, irrational, look around the room to make certain no one was watching, then with eyes closed he prayed a prayer that was almost audible. He was too embarrassed to pray completely out loud, but somehow he wasn't certain that the prayer would take if he just said it quietly to himself.

The next morning John sat straight up in bed, refreshed from the first peaceful sleep he'd had since the coma. Looking around he saw Mark coming through the door.

"So John, what's up with you today? That's the first real smile I've seen from you since we started your physical therapy."

"Is it?" John felt slightly embarrassed. "You were right about me feeling sorry for myself. I've been thinking and, uh, praying."

"Great," said Mark enthusiastically. "Now that's progress. If you're up for it, I have some challenging exercises planned for today."

Later that morning, when John returned to his room, he found that he was still in good spirits. His physical therapy had gone well and he was eager to read the Bible passages that Mark had suggested. From this point on, John's attitude changed significantly and he began to look forward to his physical therapy and his talks with Mark. In fact, the change was so dramatic that family and friends remarked on how quickly his recovery was going. On one such occasion, John's mother commented on the wonders of medicine—that they could repair his neck and reconstruct his leg to such an extent that he would be able to return to an active life. John responded to her comment with enthusiasm and innocence. "The doctors are just tools in the Master's hands. It's God who really does the healing."

John's mother's face registered what could only be considered shock. The lengthy pause that followed his statement only underlined her disbelief. Clearing her throat, she artfully steered the conversation in a more comfortable and established direction. "I understand your physical therapy is progressing so well that you will be home within just a few more days."

"I can't wait to get home," John replied, squeezing him mom's hand. "But what is really great is that I've realized that I can find joy in any situation because God is watching over me."

"That's great, honey," his mom retorted, loosening his grip on her hand. "I need to go now, but I will see you tomorrow about the same time." She gave him a quick kiss on the forehead and then disappeared out the door.

John sat somewhat bewildered. He sensed his mom's discomfort as she kissed him on the head instead of lips and made a speedy departure. John's mom never left quickly from anywhere. Could it have been his mention of God? John had never spoken about God with his mom so didn't know what she believed.

The next day John's older sister, Susan, appeared late in the afternoon. "So, Goon, when are we getting you out of here?"

"Hey, Sis! The doctor says a couple of days and I'll be ready to go."

"Great! As much as I hate to admit it, I kind of miss having your obnoxious self around the house."

"Well," John retorted, "I have kind of missed seeing that special morning face and hair that you put on each day."

With this Susan laid several well aimed, but softened punches to John's mid-section. They both laughed hard.

After a long time of talking boyfriends, girlfriends, and the latest movies, Susan ventured into new territory. "So John, I see you have a Bible on your bedside. You look like you're preparing to have the priest read you your last rites." With this she gave a somewhat uncomfortable laugh, which was supposed to make this seem like a part of the normal discussion they had just been having.

"Yeah, I thought that I'd better be ready in case you all have been kidding me about my actual improvement. The other day, one of the doctors left Dr. Kevorkian's phone number on the table—just in case."

Both laughed again; however, Susan couldn't decide if John didn't pick up on her discomfort or if he simply decided not to acknowledge it. She pressed on.

"You know, Mom told me last night that you had mentioned God quite a bit yesterday when talking to her."

"Yeah! I'm living my life totally for God now. I mean think of it. If it wasn't for that one tree I would have been a goner."

"John, you know . . . um. . . . Well, it's great if that's helping you now, but when you come home . . . I mean . . . well. . . ." Susan rose to go. "I guess what I'm trying to say is, that . . . well . . . we all go through phases, and, well . . . well, when you get home everything will be able to get back to normal." With this she bent and kissed him on the head (just like his mom, he reflected), and headed out the door.

It was after church one Sunday, several weeks after arriving home from the hospital, that John called Susan into his room. "Susan," he started enthusiastically, "You've just got to hear what we talked about today in church."

Sitting side-by-side, John could feel the tension in Susan's body and see the stressed look on her face. "Are you all right, Susan?" he asked.

"John, you know I think you are the best big goon of a brother anyone could have, and I know that you've just gone through the most traumatic episode of your life, but something has happened to you. You've changed."

"I know, Sis. God has changed my life. But I'm still the same ol' guy, aren't I?"

"I don't know. That's what I'm trying to figure out. I mean, before, we used to fight and argue about trivial stuff, but there has always been this real connection. I mean, I felt like we were so similar, you know? I mean, we could talk about anything."

"Look Sis, that's exactly what I am still doing," John replied. "I'm still sharing with you the most important things in my life. It just happens that God is a big part of that now."

"I know," said Susan reservedly, "but it's just that it's not the same. It's like you talk about different things and use different words than you used to. I mean, I guess I'm glad for you and all, but somehow it's just different between you and me now."

"But it doesn't have to be that way," John quickly retorted. "I'm still sharing with you. It seems to me you're the one who's changed. I'm still telling you what's important to me, it's you who won't share about your life."

"Okay, okay, it's just that. . . ."

"What?"

"It's just that I'm not so sure that you really approve of me and my friends anymore."

"What do you mean?" John asked in disbelief.

"Well," Susan began hesitantly, "I mean, you don't really think drinking is cool anymore and, well, I know what you think about Jennifer and Amy. I can see it all over your face whenever they are here."

"Oh come on, Sis, they're okay. And I don't really care whether you drink or not. I just want you and your friends to experience God's grace in the way that I have."

"See, that's what I mean!" Susan suddenly exploded. "What is this 'God's grace' crap? It's like you're talking in secret code. It's like . . . well, it's like you think you're better than us!"

"Hold on, Sis. That's unfair. It's just that I want you to experience the joy I've found. I mean, I am happier and more at peace than I have ever been before."

"Oh, great! So God brings you more happiness than you're own family ever has."

John hesitated, "Well, I wouldn't say it just like that."

"Look John. . . ." Susan stood, then paused longer than what seemed comfortable. "I've got to go. By the way, Tyler called and wants you to call him back." This said, Susan turned down the hall.

As the door shut behind her, John sat looking straight into a full-length mirror that hung on the back of his door. Had he really changed? He knew that his encounter with God was real and that he wasn't the same person spiritually that he had been before. But did this mean he was different in other ways, too? He truly just wanted to share with his family and friends what he had found. Why was this such a big deal? As he stared hard at the mirror he thought to himself that he was really not so different after all. Susan would get over it. Call Tyler—it was time to see the old gang.

The call to Tyler lifted his spirits. They laughed together and he found out some friends were getting together that very night, and he, John, would be the guest of honor.

As John walked up to the steps of Tyler's apartment, he paused and took a deep breath. While he had spoken by phone to some of his friends since being home, he had not seen most of them. John stood silently, listening to the laughter inside the apartment and the deep bass from some song whose title he could not remember, when he almost jumped out of his skin. He was so intent on his own thoughts that he hadn't heard Tyler come up behind him. John's heart almost leaped out of his chest when Tyler's hand had touched his shoulder.

"Tyler, what are you doing out here?" John blurted out in an almost accusatory tone.

"Had to get some ice," Tyler responded, shoving John toward the door. "What are *you* doing out here? Go on in."

As John entered the room, eyes lit up and myriad voices said how great he looked and how they had meant to call. The sensation of voices, warm air, moving bodies, slaps on the back, and the blur of faces was almost numbing.

"What'll you have?" someone shouted.

"Huh?" John was looking to put a face with the voice.

"What'll you have?" It was Tyler standing at the bar. People began chanting "Chug King, Chug King, Chug King." Somehow he had forgotten. John had been the beer chugging champion at various parties, and was affectionately called "Chug King" by his adoring fans. John looked at the chanting, hopeful faces.

"Uh, well . . . I um. . . ." John wasn't quite sure what to think. He hadn't been a Christian for very long and wasn't quite sure what he believed about drinking.

Suddenly an open can of beer came flying from behind the bar. John caught the can mid-flight as Tyler proposed a toast in his honor. "Friends, we've gathered here tonight to bring one of our own home. John's life has taken a few unexpected turns lately, but he's back with us tonight." Tyler hopped the bar, put his arm around John, and raised his beer high. "Here's to John!" With this, beer cans clanked all around the room and John took his first sip of beer in ten weeks.

The next two hours of conversation went as well as expected—mostly shallow and surfacy, no risks. But finally, the moment he had been dreading came.

"Hey everybody, it's chugging time! Clear a path to let the Chug Meister and any challengers come to the front." A cheer from the crowd went up; John and two reluctant challengers were pushed forward.

"Hey, you know, they don't let you chug much in the hospital so I'm kind of out of practice. Maybe these two. . . ."

"Not to worry," Tyler interrupted, "we know this is your first time out of the chutes since before the accident." With this Tyler tossed a can of beer to each of the three contestants. "Ready, steady, you're. . . ."

"Wait, wait, I . . . well, I. . . ." interrupted John.

"What is it, Ol' Chug King?" Tyler said with an air of mock subservience. "What is your bidding?"

"Well, I just am not exactly ready that's all."

"So what are you going to need to be ready, John?" Tyler asked impatiently.

"Well, it's just that. . . ." John began.

"Just that John's found religion, that's all," came a voice from the crowd.

John wheeled around quickly, only to see Susan's friend Amy smiling at him. "Amy, what are you doing here?" John asked desperately.

"Renee invited me," replied Amy with a little too much sugar in her voice.

Then John wheeled back to the sound of Tyler's voice. "Is this true old Chug King? Has the Chug King found religion?"

The silence in the room was deafening to John. He could hear nothing but his own heart pounding erratically in his chest; all eyes were fixed on him. John had no idea how much time had passed when he finally spoke, but not a person had moved.

"No, I haven't really found religion . . ." John started.

"Good!" Tyler interjected.

"It's more like God has grabbed a hold of my life."

Tyler feigned to faint on the floor, and the rest of the crowd turned and began to mill around again amidst a cacophony of moans and hushed discussion. John hung out for a while longer, chatting with a few friends who seemed to listen politely and then, when no one seemed to really notice, he quietly slipped out the door.

John drove home slowly and then quietly slipped into his parents' house, and into his room. With the latch of the door Susan rolled over in bed; the clock read 10:30—too early for John to be home. She rose, went into the hall, and tapped softly on his door.

"I'm not here," John called.

"Hey, it's your Sis, you big goon. Open the door."

A moment later the lock clicked and Susan opened the door. "So how was the party?"

"Fine."

"Fine, and you're home at 10:30? Come on, level with me."

"Your friend Amy was there," John said.

"Oh, really?" Susan said hesitantly.

"When I was trying to avoid a chugging contest she told the whole group, 'John's found religion.'"

"Oooooh, I'm sorry. What happened?" Susan asked, putting her arm around her bigger younger brother.

"Well, after Tyler fell on the floor, that pretty much ended things and I just slipped out. Is it really so bad to follow God? Am I really so different?"

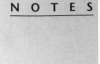

"John, we all still love you. It's just been a bit of a surprise, you know? I mean, it's just quite a change from who you were before."

"I know. But I really want things to get back to normal and yet, every time I see the way you or Mom looks at me, it's a reminder that I'm different somehow. But when I'm just sitting here with you talking," at this point both John and Susan looked at their reflection together in the mirror on the back of the door, "it's like nothing has ever changed."

Susan took a long look at the two of them in the mirror. "Maybe you're right. Maybe we've been a little rough on you. It's just that you've sorta forced us to look at ourselves and we haven't liked it. Okay, I haven't liked it, and I'm not ready to change."

"I'm not asking you to change, Sis. I'm just hoping you can accept me as I am now. I really didn't mean to put a guilt trip on everyone."

"But John," she pleaded, "can you accept me for who I am now? Will you judge me every time I go out with my friends?"

John felt a twinge in his stomach—his first recognition that following God wasn't going to mean that life would now be easy. His next words seemed to lift the weight of uncertainty from Susan. "Sis, I love you and, even though we're not always going to agree on everything, you've got to know that I'm always here for you no matter what."

John's words and the look on his face were all she needed. Her brother was finally home.

FOR FURTHER THOUGHT AND REFLECTION

1. What was it about John's behavior that made Susan so uncomfortable?

2. Have you ever had a situation where you still felt like "you" on the inside, but others began treating you differently? How did this affect your self-image?

3. Imagine six months from now. How will Susan and John interact together? What factors might affect the future of this relationship? Imagine a year from now. Do you think John will be "back to normal" with his other family members and friends?

4. Put yourself in Susan's position. How would you interact with your friends when John is around? Put yourself in John's position. Are there ways you can communicate the changes in your life without causing your family or friends discomfort? If so, how? Can discomfort ever be positive in a relationship?

5. Have you ever taken a position or held a belief that put you at odds with the majority of your peers? If so, how did you handle it? How did they react?

6. What were the turning points in John's relationships with his family? His friends? What types of turning points could occur that would strengthen or weaken his current relationships?

REFERENCES

Baxter, L.A., & Bullis, C. (1986). Turning points in developing romantic relationships. *Human Communication Research, 12,* (4), 469–493.

Baxter, L. A., & Montgomery, B. M. (1996). *Relating: Dialogues and dialectics.* New York: Guilford.

Berger, C.R., & Bradac, J.J. (1982). *Language and social knowledge: Uncertainty in interpersonal relations.* London: Edward Arnold.

Berger, C.R. & Calabrese, R.J. (1975). Some exploration in initial interaction and beyond: Toward a developmental theory of interpersonal communication. *Human Communication Research, 1,* 99–112.

Duck. S. (1994). *Meaningful relationships: Talking, sense, and relating.* Thousand Oaks, CA: Sage.

Mead, G.H. (1934). *Mind, self, and society.* Chicago, IL: University of Chicago.

Sherif, M., & Hovland, C.I. (1961). *Social judgment.* New Haven, CT: Yale University Press.

Sherif, M., Sherif, C., & Nebergall, R. (1965). *Attitude and attitude change: The social judgment involvement approach.* Philadelphia: Saunders.

PART II

COMING TOGETHER: DEVELOPING CLOSENESS WITH OTHERS

I NEED SOME SPACE

Friends Through Good Times and Bad Times

Kathryn Dindia, Stephanie Hsu, Page Garber

KEYWORDS

■

relational dialectics
openness/closedness
autonomy/connection
novelty/predictability

Turning left down the street, Ashley saw for the first time the immense dorm she would be living in for the upcoming school year. Butterflies began to flutter in her stomach. As her father pulled the van into the lot, Ashley took a deep breath to prepare herself for what was to come. Then, Ashley and her parents got out of the car and began unloading her belongings. Grabbing the first couple of boxes, Ashley headed to the dorm to find her room.

Down the hallway, Ashley spotted her roommate and best friend of four years, Jennifer. Ashley smiled when she saw Jennifer and ran to give her a big hug. It was a relief to see a familiar face, when there were so many strangers around her. As best friends, Ashley and Jennifer were excited to have the opportunity to attend the same college and share the same dorm room. They were looking forward to learning new things and growing closer.

After Ashley's last box was brought to her room, she knew it was time to say good-bye to her family. Teary-eyed, she gave her parents one last hug. Ashley's father wiped a tear from his cheek and said, "I want you to know how proud we are of you."

When Ashley's family left, Jennifer came back into the room. "Are you all right, Ash?" she asked.

Ashley replied. "I'm okay. I just think it's going to take some time to adjust to living away from home and my family."

"I know exactly what you mean. Giving up the comforts and security of home will be tough, but the excitement of being independent and exploring life on our own will be a great experience. You know that if you ever feel that you want to talk about something, I am always here for you."

"I know," Ashley replied. "And you know that you can always come to me for advice or anything else, too, Jen."

For four months, Ashley and Jennifer were inseparable. They made the same friends, joined the same clubs, ate dinner together almost every night, and went out to the same places. But by the fifth month, Ashley felt as if she was suffocating in her friendship with Jennifer and needed some space. Granted it was nice to start college with the security of a built-in friend. It made the transition from living at home to being at college less frightening. But now Ashley was ready to venture out on her own, make some other friends. On the weekends, she began to associate with new acquaintances outside of her previous social circle. However, every time Ashley was invited to go somewhere with her new friends, Jennifer would tag along without asking. The situation grew to be such a problem that Ashley started to sneak out of her dorm room to be alone with her friends.

There were several times when Ashley planned to tell Jennifer what she was feeling. She thought: *I need time to myself, and I want time with my new friends without having Jennifer constantly around. But I'm afraid that saying something to Jen would hurt her feelings and our friendship.*

Over the weeks that followed, Jennifer noticed that Ashley was not in the room as often, and she wondered if something was wrong. She thought, *I really need to find out what is going on with Ashley. We don't really do much together anymore, which is really weird.*

One day, Ashley came back to the room from class in a bad mood. She noticed a large pile of Jennifer's laundry on the floor. Just as Ashley walked out of the room, Jennifer walked in. "Jen, what's your junk doing all over the floor? I can't even walk through the room without seeing all of your crap lying on the floor!"

Jennifer apologized. "Look, I am sorry that everything is everywhere. I was just trying to organize some of my stuff. Besides, I didn't think you would be back for another hour because I thought you were going to be in the chemistry lab."

"Whatever!" Ashley snapped.

Jennifer ignored Ashley's comment and looked directly at her. "Ashley, we really need to talk about some things."

"Like what?" Ashley said harshly.

"Like the fact that over the last month or so you have been incredibly moody, we barely ever do anything together, and you're never in the room anymore! I feel like our friendship is going downhill, and I really want to know what is going on. Ashley, we've been best friends for a long time! You know you can tell me what's on your mind."

Ashley moved toward the couch and sat down. "You're right, Jen. There has been something bothering me, and I should have told you right away. But I was scared that you would be mad at me."

"Ash, tell me what it is! I really care about our friendship and want to work things out."

"Jen, I really care about you, too. But I guess the big problem is that I feel I don't have any freedom in our friendship. Every time I tell you I am going somewhere with friends, you never ask if you can come along. You just invite yourself. Don't get me wrong. I really do like spending time with you, but I also like to hang out with other people I have become friends with."

Jennifer was surprised. "Wow. I guess I didn't know I was doing that. I thought it was a given that we always do things together. I'm sorry that I got on your nerves that much, but it's not fair that you are so angry with me. You could have at least come talk to me instead of getting so defensive about the situation."

"Yeah, I guess you're right, but it wasn't that easy to talk to you about it."

"What do you mean?" asked Jennifer.

"Well, it's hard to say what I want without hurting your feelings, making you angry, and straining our friendship."

"The fact that you have been avoiding me for the past several weeks has hurt me more than if you had told me up front." After a moment of silence, Jennifer said, "Ash, let's promise that if we ever have a problem with one another, no matter what it is, we will tell each other right away?"

"Deal!" Ashley replied.

Jennifer and Ashley smiled at each other and hugged.

Before the start of the second school year, Ashley and Jennifer agreed it was best to room with other people. They felt that more time apart would ease some of the strains in their friendship. For one thing, Ashley had a new boyfriend, Steve, and Jennifer wasn't too fond of him. Jennifer thought Steve was trouble and had told Ashley so. Ashley moved to an apartment complex with two friends from her French class, and Jennifer moved into an apartment building two blocks away. Ashley balanced her time around Steve and her friends, and Jennifer began meeting new people. Although Ashley and Jennifer did not see each other as often, they made it a point to stay in touch by a phone call or a weekly get-together at a café. As the weeks passed, Jennifer and Ashley's friendship grew stronger and they enjoyed the time they spent together.

One night, as Jennifer was walking to the library, she passed the cafeteria and noticed Ashley's boyfriend Steve, kissing another girl. Jennifer got a closer look to make sure it was really him, and to her dismay, it was! She was so upset and enraged at that point, she wanted to confront Steve. At the same time, she felt that she should tell Ashley first. But she ended up at the library sitting at a table for two hours, staring at her books and trying to figure out what she was going to do. Jennifer was torn. Should she tell Ashley everything she witnessed, or should she pretend that nothing had happened? That night, Jennifer could not sleep. She decided that, as a best friend, she needed to tell Ashley. But she tossed and turned, trying to come up with the best way to do so.

The next day, Jennifer called Ashley. "Ashley, we need to talk about something."

"It sounds serious. What is it?"

Jennifer hesitated. "Well, I, I can't tell you over the phone. It's something I need to tell you in person. I'll be at your place in a few minutes."

Ashley was waiting outside for Jennifer when she arrived at the apartment. Once inside, Jennifer said, "I've been agonizing over what I am about to tell you, and it's very serious."

"You're really scaring me, Jen!" Ashley nervously replied.

"I want you to know that as my best friend, Ash, I care about you and only want what is best for you. I think you better sit down."

"I don't want to sit down. Just tell me!" Ashley demanded.

Jennifer took a deep breath. "Okay, here it goes. . . . A few nights ago, I was walking to the library and I saw Steve. He was with another girl, and they were kissing."

Immediately denying the accusation, Ashley yelled, "How could you say that about him? There's no way he would ever do that to me." Ashley caught her breath and said more calmly, "You probably saw someone who looked like Steve."

"No! I've never been more clear about what I saw; it was Steve with another girl. I am so sorry, Ashley. I didn't mean to hurt you, but I wanted you to know before you got further into the relationship and ended up getting hurt even more."

Running to her room and slamming the door, Ashley began to cry uncontrollably. Jennifer wanted to do something to help, anything that would make Ashley feel better. She hated seeing her in this state. After waiting five minutes, Jennifer softly knocked on Ashley's door. "Ashley, I am going to leave you alone. I know you need some time alone to think about things. When you're ready to talk, call me! Don't forget that I am here for you."

"Thank you, Jennifer." Ashley softly replied.

Later that evening, Jennifer received a call from Ashley. They decided to meet at a coffee shop, and Ashley told Jennifer what happened after she had left her apartment. "I called Steve and asked him to come over. I confronted him face-to-face about that other girl. At first, he denied it, but then I told him what you saw and he admitted it. I couldn't believe that he lied to me! I told him that I had to break up with him because I could never trust him again. I can't believe that I was in love with that jerk! Jen, I should have taken your advice when you warned me he was trouble. I guess I wanted to believe that he was a good person."

Jennifer smiled. "I know you did, Ash. For a long time, I tried to accept the fact that you were in a relationship with Steve, even though I didn't like him. As long as you were happy, I was happy."

"Jennifer, I want you to know how much our friendship means to me. You really saved me from making one of the biggest mistakes in my life. I don't know what I'd do without you. Thank you."

Jennifer smiled. "I know I don't say this too often, but you've always been a big part of my life, too, Ash. You've supported me through a lot of things and even put up with my annoying habits!" Ashley and Jennifer began to laugh. "I know I can always count on you if I need someone to talk to. I am so thankful for the friendship we have had for the past six years."

* * *

The summer had ended, and Ashley and Jennifer's third year of college had begun. Ashley had decided to study in France for six months of the school year. Jennifer wanted to go along, but opted to stay in the States because going abroad would have delayed her graduation, and she wanted to graduate the same time as Ashley. The semester before Ashley left, Jennifer and Ashley had decided to try to live together again, but this time in an apartment. Three months went by without problems. Ashley still spent time with her other friends, and Jennifer started dating a new man.

Ashley was always curious about the guy Jennifer was dating. She constantly asked her who he was, but Jennifer would always reply, "Oh, just a guy."

Ashley found it very awkward that Jennifer would never mention his name or bring him to the apartment to introduce her. After four weeks, Ashley nonchalantly asked Jennifer about the mystery man. "So, when am I ever going to meet this boyfriend of yours?"

"One day." Jennifer quickly answered.

Several days later, Ashley stopped by the grocery store after class to pick up some items she needed to fix dinner. As she walked past a checkout counter, she saw Jennifer holding hands with the mystery guy. When he turned around, Ashley could not believe who she was seeing. It was Steve! Ashley immediately realized why Jennifer had been so secretive about her relationship. Ashley was so stunned that she dropped a glass bottle she was carrying. Several people turned around to see what happened, including Jennifer and Steve. Jennifer looked up just in time to see Ashley run out of the store. She tried to run after her, but Ashley was too fast. She knew that Ashley had seen her with Steve. Jennifer had been nervous for so long about telling Ashley, because she was not sure how Ashley would take the news. As Ashley ran back to the apartment, she thought to herself, "How could Jennifer do this to me? I thought she was my best friend!" Ashley unlocked the door, went to her room, buried her head under her pillow, and cried.

Jennifer had known she would have to tell Ashley sooner or later, but this was not the way she'd anticipated doing it. Jennifer arrived at the apartment and knocked on Ashley's door. "Ashley, open up."

"Go away!" Ashley demanded.

"Please Ashley! I'm sorry!"

"Don't talk to me ever again!" Ashley screamed.

Jennifer backed away from the door. She thought to herself, *There goes the greatest friendship I have ever had. I know there is probably no way Ash is ever going to forgive me for what I have done to her. But I thought that, maybe because we are friends and she cared about me, she would try to be happy for me!*

One week passed, and not one word, not even eye contact was exchanged between Ashley and Jennifer. Tension grew whenever they were in the same room. Another two weeks went by, and nothing changed. Finally, one afternoon during lunch, Jennifer tried to open the line of communication. "Ashley, I know how upset you are with me about seeing Steve. And I know I am a hypocrite for saying how bad Steve was for you. I can't explain how we even got together! All I can do is hope that you can forgive me. We can't go on ignoring each other for the rest of our lives. Maybe we'd feel a little better if we talked about it. Ashley, I would do anything possible to try to salvage our relationship! It means more to me than staying in a relationship with a guy."

Ashley turned to Jennifer. "Jen, you know you really hurt me. How could you ever go out with a guy I dated, whom you saw cheating on me?"

"I really am sorry for all the pain I caused you Ash. I swear, I didn't get together with Steve to intentionally hurt you."

"You know, Jen, it's going to take a long time for me to build up trust in you."

"I know it will." Jennifer sadly said.

The first semester ended and winter break approached. Jennifer and Ashley spent much of their time talking about the situation with Steve and where their friendship stood. Even though they sorted out some of their problems, they knew that their friendship would not be the same. Trust between Ashley and Jennifer was still fragile. The new year began and it was time for Ashley to leave for France. She and Jennifer decided that they would take the time they would be apart and think about how they could turn their friendship around. Jennifer went to the airport with Ashley and her family to send Ashley off. Ashley hugged her parents, but only waved good-bye to Jennifer and told her to take care of herself.

When Ashley arrived in France, she felt a sense of relief; relief from the pressures of home and friends. So much had happened between her and Jennifer, it was a wonderful feeling for her to get away from it all. At the same time, she knew that she would miss Jennifer and her family.

It was two months since Ashley had left, and Jennifer had not heard from her. Jennifer had no idea how Ashley was or what she was doing. Jennifer made the effort to keep in contact through letters. No responses came from Ashley, and that made Jennifer feel lonely. No one was here to talk with. Jennifer thought that maybe Ashley was still angry with her and the relationship with Steve.

Three weeks later, Jennifer finally received a letter from Ashley. She was so excited. In the letter, Ashley apologized for not writing sooner. She had been so busy with schoolwork and exploring all of Europe. She also wrote that she had forgiven Jennifer for the situation with Steve and that she missed her a lot. A large smile drew across Jennifer's face. For the remaining two months of Ashley's trip, she and Jennifer corresponded several times.

The night before Ashley was to come home, Jennifer could hardly sleep a wink. She was excited to see Ashley, but also nervous because she wasn't sure how Ashley would react when they saw each other. Even though they had corresponded, it was not the same as seeing each other in person.

The day finally came when Jennifer and Ashley's parents went to pick up Ashley. As Ashley walked out of the terminal, her family ran to her and embraced. Jennifer stood and watched. Ashley then approached Jennifer. "Hi Jen. It's good to see you again!"

"Hi Ashley. How was your flight?" Both of them acted awkward; both were unsure about the status of their friendship. Gradually, they began to talk about what had happened to them since they had last written to each other.

The summer began and Ashley continued to tell Jennifer stories about her time abroad. Ashley also told her that she had met someone in her program. His name was Jerome and she was planning to go back to France to visit him. Jennifer was happy to hear about it. Nothing made Jennifer more happy than seeing Ashley happy. Jennifer told Ashley that she had begun to see someone new and that she wanted to introduce him to Ashley. "Ash, I am sorry about the way things were before you left for France. I know that in the first letter you sent to me you said that you forgave me, but I still feel terrible."

"Jen, after thinking about things in France, I learned to forgive and forget. I learned not to take things, especially our close friendship, for granted. I want us to be best friends again."

Jennifer smiled, "I would really like that too."

Ashley's and Jennifer's final year at college approached. They decided to live together again. They promised each other to make their last year their most memorable and positive experience. Neither knew what was going to happen after graduation. They had some ideas, but they were not ones that would allow them to be near each other. Ashley wanted to move to France to be with her boyfriend, and Jennifer wanted to move to California and teach.

The entire year went without any major problems, and before they knew it, graduation day was here. Jennifer and Ashley could not believe how fast their four years in college had gone. They were both excited to start their new lives, but at the same time they were sad about leaving each other. Jennifer received a teaching job in Arizona, and Ashley was leaving for France at the end of the summer to live with Jerome.

After the graduation ceremony, Jennifer and Ashley congratulated one another and hugged. "Ash, when are we going to see each other again?"

"I don't know, but it definitely is going to be strange without you." Both Ashley and Jennifer began to well up with tears.

"I promise to write and call often," Ashley declared.

"Me, too," Jennifer said. "Let's promise that we will always be friends, no matter what, Ash!"

"Friends forever. Jen, that is something I will treasure for the rest of my life!"

FOR FURTHER THOUGHT AND REFLECTION

1. According to Baxter (1988) there are at least three dialectical tensions inherent in all relationships: autonomy/connection, novelty/predictability, and openness/closedness. Identify the dialectical tensions apparent in Jennifer and Ashley's relationship. Can you find specific examples of each of the dialectical tensions in the relationship? Which dialectical tension is most predominant in Jennifer and Ashley's relationship?

2. Relationship partners, knowingly or unknowingly, use strategies to deal with the dialectical tensions in their relationship. What are the strategies researchers have identified for managing dialectical tensions (Baxter, 1988, Baxter-Montgomery, 1998; Wood, 1995, 1997). Which of these strategies did Jennifer and Ashley use to manage the dialectical tensions in their relationship? Which dialectical tensions did these strategies address? What was the principle dialectical strategy used to manage the openness/closedness dialectic in their relationship?

3. Dialectical tensions are often experienced in varying degrees of intensity and at different times by each partner in a relationship. Find specific examples of Jennifer and Ashley experiencing the tensions to different degrees or at different times in their relationship. How did their different experiences of the dialectical tensions lead to conflict in their relationship?

4. How relationship partners respond to dialectical tensions influences relationship development. How did Jennifer and Ashley's relationship develop (decline) and change as a result of their responses to the dialectical tensions? What dialectical tension did you feel was most important for Ashley and Jennifer to be able to maintain their relationship? What strategies were most effective in maintaining Jennifer and Ashley's relationship?

5. Dialectical tensions are interrelated in personal relationships. How does the autonomy/connection tension affect the openness/closedness tension, and vice versa, in Jennifer and Ashley's relationship? How does the novelty/predictability tension affect the openness/closedness tension, and vice versa, in Jennifer and Ashley's relationship?

REFERENCES

Baxter, L. A. (1988). A dialectical perspective on communication strategies in relationship development. In S. W. Duck (Ed.), *Handbook of personal relationships* (pp. 257–273). London: John Wiley & Sons.

Baxter, L. A. & Montgomery, B. M. (1998). Rethinking communication in personal relationships from a dialectical perspective. In S. W. Duck (Ed.), *Handbook of personal relationships* (2nd ed., pp. 305–351). London: John Wiley & Sons.

Montgomery, B. M., & Baxter, L. A. (1998). *Dialectical approaches to studying relationships*. Mahwah: Lawrence Erlbaum.

Rawlins, W. K. (1992). *Friendship matters: Communication, dialectics, and the life course.* New York: Aldine de Gruyter.

Wood, J. T. (1997). *Communication theories in action*. Belmont, CA: Wadsworth.

Wood, J. T. (1999). *Interpersonal communication: Everyday encounters*. Belmont, CA: Wadsworth.

WHAT TO TELL

Deciding When, How, and What to Self-Disclose

Lawrence B. Rosenfeld and Jack M. Richman

KEY WORDS

■

self-disclosure
relational intimacy
benefits and risks of self-disclosure
disability communication

T he summer went by too quickly. All the plans for the trip to college had to fall into place *now*.

"Katy-Leigh, hurry up and get your bags down here so we can pack the car!" Katherine's mother shouts, even though the house is small enough that shouting isn't necessary.

Katherine's father comes into her room and helps move her bags out to the hallway. He stops by the door, turns, and tells Katherine, "I remember when I went off to college . . . the first day . . . getting ready. I was excited and scared, happy and downhearted. . . . Yes, I was a bit bewildered! So, I was wondering how you were feeling."

Katherine looks at her father, confused, thinking, *I thought Mom would be talking to me about this? What's Dad up to?* "Well, yeah," she tells him, "I'm feeling pretty okay about all this."

"Okay, let's get these bags into the car," Katherine's Dad tells her. "I guess we can talk later, if you want."

Three hours and a hundred and forty miles later, they arrive at Western State University. As Katherine looks at the long set of stairs leading up the hill to her dormitory, all she can think about is getting her stuff into her room, meeting her roommate, and getting started on her first year of college. She grabs the smallest, lightest bag and hustles up to her dorm room so she can get to see her roommate before her parents embarrass her!

"Hi, my name's Katherine."

"Great to meet you. I'm Kim. I guess we're going to be spending the year together."

"Yeah, I see you've got your stuff in the closets already. I guess you want that side of the room." Katherine thinks, *Maybe I wanted that side of the room*, but says, "No problem, I'll take this side. I need to warn you: my parents will be up here in a minute, and there's no telling what they'll ask you. Just nod a lot. My folks are really great . . . most of the time."

"No problem! My mom just left—and if you had been here she would have grilled you about anything and everything. She has to be sure her daughter isn't living with a lunatic!"

Katherine's parents enter loaded down with boxes and suitcases, and the process begins—of moving in, meeting Kim, and making jokes that cover the tension everyone feels. Within a few hours everything is put away, the beds are made, and Katherine and her parents, with Kim, go out for dinner.

Later, Katherine and Kim collapse on their beds and wonder what's next. The answer appears in the doorway in the shape of the Resident Advisor, "Sarah-the-RA" (which seems to be her full name), telling them about the dorm meeting scheduled for 8:00 P.M. Living in a co-ed dorm means meeting the other women and men.

"Kim?" Katherine asks without posing a question. "Do you realize that we have a rare opportunity here? I mean, in an hour we'll be meeting lots of people, but right now they don't know us. We can be whoever and whatever we want to be! I'm not sure whether I want to be 'Katherine' or 'Kathy,' or even 'Katy-Leigh,' my parents' nickname for me."

"I can be 'Kim' or 'Kimberly,' or even 'Kimmy,' but I never liked that nickname. My brother uses that when he wants to be really obnoxious."

"I'm not sure what kind of impression I should make. Should I be 'sophisticated Katherine'? Or should I be 'easy-to-get-to-know Kathy'?"

"I think we're going to be whoever we are, whatever we call ourselves. But I agree with you, we're probably all feeling a little insecure and flustered. When we get back here, you can let me know how I came across, and I'll let you know. But we have to be honest with each other!"

The meeting is in the lounge on the first floor, between the elevators and the Coke machines. A hundred people scatter on the chairs and floor, and lean against the walls. Sarah-the-RA calls the meeting to order, and what follows is a lengthy speech about rules and regulations, quiet hours, and planned social events. Ears perk up at the mention of social events. Then Sarah-the-RA offers soft drinks and cookies to encourage the residents to hang around.

"Kathy?" a voice calls out to her. "Kathy? It's me, Russ. I was a year ahead of you in high school—remember? We went out once. I've been here a year, but I still like living in the dorms."

"Oh, yeah, Russ . . . sure . . . high school. You were friends with those kids on the basketball team." Katherine thinks, *I really liked you . . . and wanted to get to know you better . . . I don't know why you never called me again after we went out.*

After a moment of awkward silence, Katherine asks, "How do you like Western? I'm registering for classes tomorrow. Any suggestions?"

They talk about Western, classes, the weather, majors, "do-ya-know-so-and-so" questions, and other topics that are safe and usual. They agree to meet the next day for lunch after registration. Kim walks up, nudges Katherine, and clears her throat loudly.

"Russ, this is Kim. She's my roommate. Kim, this is Russ . . . he's a sophomore here . . and he went to my high school."

"Hi, Russ! Sorry to interrupt, but I just wanted to tell Katherine . . . or is it Kathy? . . . or is it Katy-Leigh—have you decided? Well, I just wanted to tell you that I'm meeting some friends from Smith Hall. There's a guy there I know from high school. See ya!" Without waiting for a response, Kim is gone.

"What's up with Kim? Doesn't she know your name?" Russ asks.

"Oh, it's nothing. She was just kidding."

Later that night, lying on her bed, Katherine stares at the ceiling and goes over the day in her head. *I never did get to have that conversation Dad wanted. . . . I can't believe I'm in college, in a dorm room, away from home! . . . What would I be doing at 10:00 P.M. at home on a Sunday night—probably not much less than this! . . . Am I boring? What is this place really, really like? I think Kim is already having a better social life than I am. . . . I wish she asked me to go with her! Why did she mention that "name thing" to Russ? How embarrassing!*

Katherine's thoughts come to an abrupt halt when she hears a key in the door. Kim comes in and says, "How was your night? Russ is cute!"

"Oh, we just talked for a few minutes. I'm meeting him tomorrow after registration. A lunch thing."

"Do you like him?"

Katherine hesitates. *I'd like to tell Kim that Russ and I went out once, and about my feelings for him, whatever they are. I want to talk to Kim and sort out my feelings—about Russ, being away for the first time, college. But . . . I'm not ready. I mean, should I trust her? What if I say something really stupid? What if she thinks I'm an immature jerk?* She says, "He's OK. What did you do?"

"It was weird! I went over to meet Mike, and the first thing I notice is he's cut all his hair off! I'm not sure I like that! I really liked him in high school, but I don't know if I want to jump into a relationship—not with all these other guys around! You see . . . I was in a relationship for two years, and while it was good in a lot of ways, it felt a little like prison . . . a nice prison, but a prison anyway. You know what I mean?"

"I've had some boyfriends, but nothing as serious as two years. What was it like?"

Katherine and Kim talk about high school and the pros and cons of dating someone for a long time, and Katherine wonders, *Maybe I can tell her how I felt being left at the meeting, and about her mentioning the Katherine-Kathy-Katy-Leigh thing to Russ. After all, she's told me so much about herself.* "When I was talking to Russ, and you left . . . and I came up here by myself. It was . . . well . . . a little scary. I mean, it dawned on me, I really am alone here."

"How terrible! I didn't mean to leave you! I know how that feels. You know? I've felt the same way. I grew up in a single-parent family, and had a lot of responsibility, and I used to think that I was alone, having to figure out everything for myself. I'm sorry."

Katherine thinks, *I'm lucky! Kim really seems to understand me . . . and she's a great listener!* "It's OK, I'm probably a little hyper today. First day. Our relationship isn't going to be a 'prison,' even if we're roomies for four years!"

Lunch the next day comes at the perfect moment: Katherine is closed out of several classes, registers for a class in Botany that meets a science requirement but isn't something she's particularly interested in taking, and finds herself with a schedule that requires being on campus from 8:00 A.M. until 5:00 P.M. five days a week. Frustrated, she meets Russ and plunks her books on the table. Russ tells her, "You look terrible!"

"Thanks. You would too if you had to work so hard to get the awful schedule I'm stuck with! I couldn't get Dr. Rawlings for English, like you told me to, so I had to sign up for Dr. Spencer. I hear she requires a lot of reading!"

"Well, welcome to college! Only the learning disabled *really* have trouble keeping up!"

Katherine is surprised: *He said "learning disabled" like it was a horrible disease, and he doesn't know that I "have it"! I wonder what he would think if he knew I was ADD? A lot of reading is a real challenge for me. I have to stick with it for a long time. I've worked so hard to overcome my disability . . . why does it have to be a problem?*

The rest of the conversation follows the first-lunch rules: Say nothing too deep, ask nothing too personal, and keep yourself looking good. And it ends with plans to meet again on the weekend. But later that day, Katherine recognizes old feelings: *How can I tell Russ about my ADD? I never even heard of attention deficit disorder, much less "ADD," which is what everyone calls it, until I found out I had it. And why should I have to explain myself to him in the first place? What will he think about me? He seems to think that anyone with a learning disability is less than a real student? I like him, but can I have a relationship with him?*

Katherine needs some advice. She calls her mother and tells her about the problems with registration and with Russ. "What can I do?" she asks her mother.

"Look, Katy-Leigh, one reason we selected Western was because they're supposed to have a great Learning Disabilities Center. Remember, when we met Dr. O'Neill, he said to come by any time. So why not call him? I'm sure you're not alone in having to tell people about your ADD."

"I know I'm not alone, but I sure feel alone."

Following her mother's advice, Katherine calls the Learning Disabilities Center and makes an appointment for the next day with Dr. O'Neill.

"What's up, Katherine? I'm glad to see you chose Western. What can I do for you?"

"Well, for starters, you can give me a magic pill that'll get rid of my ADD!"

"You sound frustrated. How is your ADD a problem? Classes don't begin until next week."

Katherine recounts her conversation with Russ, and about needing some advice. "How can I tell him about my ADD, which I have to if I want any kind of relationship with him that's more than superficial? I'm afraid he'll not want any relationship at all if I tell him."

"OK, you're feeling conflict over being honest with him and with risking the potential for a close relationship."

"That's it! So what do I do?"

"First, you need to decide if being open with Russ is what you want to do. There are no hard-and-fast rules about when and what to tell someone about yourself. Don't panic; you're in control here. Now, is this about Russ thinking bad things about you, or is it about your own fears about college and how well you'll do?"

"It's not the ADD. I know my problem with organizing, about having to concentrate when I listen in class, about not getting distracted, about following through on assignments. I've learned ways to sustain my concentration and mental effort when I'm doing my school work. I know all that. I've been taught how to use structure in my life, use time-outs when I get really frustrated, and to keep a sense of humor about the whole thing."

"So what's the problem?"

"The problem is how do I tell Russ, and my roommate, Kim, and anybody else at Western—without feeling exposed, unprotected, and maybe unworthy of being here."

"OK, I get the point. You need some guidelines. Well, every relationship is different, and it's not safe to make generalizations, but that's never stopped me before! Really, here are some things to think about. First of all, you need to think about how important Russ or Kim or anyone else is to you. Is the person you want to tell a big risk or a small risk? I mean, how much can you trust the person to treat what you say confidentially and with respect? Holding back with people you don't feel comfortable with may not be a bad idea! Second, you have to think about whether what you want to say about yourself is an appropriate topic to talk about. Your ADD may be something important to tell your teachers, but not just any student in one of your classes. See what I mean?"

"I see. But it seems relevant to tell Russ because he obviously has negative feelings about people with a learning disability. And if we're going to have any friendship at all—of any kind—this has got to get cleared up. I guess I just decided it's worth the risk!"

"Seems like it! Also, think about *when* you're going to tell Russ. You need a space that's comfortable and that allows for privacy. You don't want Russ to feel as if he *has* to be polite and say the 'right thing.' And here's a last consideration. You need to think about the possible outcomes and be prepared for whatever might be said. Why don't we do a few role plays. I'll play you and you can be Russ, then you can be yourself and I'll play Russ. This way you're sure to be clear and understandable if you decide to be open with him."

Katherine and Dr. O'Neill practice what Katherine might say to Russ, and she leaves his office feeling more confident in her ability to interact with Russ successfully and deal with whatever his response might be. Walking up the

NOTES

stairs to her dorm room, she thinks: *If Kim asks me where I've been, I'll tell her about meeting Dr. O'Neill and see how she reacts. I think it's worth the risk with Kim. We're going to be living together, and she seems to be understanding.*

As if on cue, Kim asks her, "So what's going on?"

"I'm just getting back from the Learning Disabilities Center."

"Getting a tutoring job?"

"Not really—I may be one of those who needs tutoring!"

"I don't understand."

"I saw Dr. O'Neill, the Center's Director. I wanted to talk to him about how to tell people about my learning disability."

"Great, so tell me."

"I have ADD—that's Attention Deficit Disorder. And Russ made some insensitive put-down of people with learning disabilities. So Dr. O'Neill and I decided how best to deal with all this. Am I clear? I can hear myself sounding scattered—shifting topics. Welcome to my ADD! This is what happens when I get nervous."

"OK, so you have ADD. What's the problem? You must be doing something right if you got into Western?"

"The problem is I need to work harder than most people just keeping myself on task, on organizing my work. And sometimes I think I don't belong here . . . and I'm afraid the other students are going to judge me. That's why I feel so alone sometimes!"

"I don't know much about ADD, but if it helps, it looks to me like you're pretty task oriented and you seem organized. Is there anything I can do?"

"No, just listening to me helps. It feels good just to have someone know and be supportive. It would be great if you could learn to sleep with the light on while I'm taking the extra time I need to study. Just kidding!"

"So what's the issue with Russ? He doesn't seem like a jerk, except maybe for his remark about learning disabilities."

"That's the point. I don't know."

"Well, if you talk to him, you can clarify how you feel and how he feels. I'm sure he'll tell you if you tell him! And then you'll get it off your chest. You know, he may even think you're brave to tell him. I think you're brave! It takes guts to be up front with someone. . . . Anyway, it'll give him a chance to understand how his remark hurt you and to apologize, or let you know he's not worth having a relationship with."

"That makes sense. But if he says more insensitive stuff, I'll probably be so frustrated and angry that I'll want to hit him!"

"Yeah, being rejected, even if it's by a jerk, still hurts. But, it's either tell him, or plan on nothing more than nodding hello when you pass him on campus."

"I'm meeting him this weekend. I'll take the risk."

That Saturday night, sitting across from each other at a local pizza parlor, Katherine looks Russ in the eyes and says, "You said something when we were having lunch a few days ago, and I need to talk to you about it."

FOR FURTHER THOUGHT AND REFLECTION

1. When Katherine and her parents are getting ready to leave for college, Katherine chooses not to respond to her father's self-disclosing statements. She also chooses several times not to disclose to Kim, her roommate, or to Russ. What are the drawbacks to disclosing that might have motivated her to remain private?

2. During her first few days at Western State University, Katherine makes decisions about disclosing to her mother, Kim, Russ, and Dr. O'Neill. What are the possible benefits for Katherine of self-disclosing? Why did it seem easier for her to self disclose to her mother, Kim, and Dr. O'Neill than to Russ?

3. Dr. O'Neill's four guidelines for considering when to self-disclose were provided in the context of whether Katherine should disclose to Russ. How do the guidelines apply to Katherine and Kim's relationship?

4. How do Kim and Katherine use self-disclosure to create impressions with each other and with others on campus?

5. Self-disclosing communication can vary in intensity, in the degree to which it is personal. How does self-disclosure reflect the way in which Katherine and Kim's relationship develops, and how does it help them create a more trusting and intimate relationship?

REFERENCES

Cline, R. J. W. (1989). The politics of intimacy: Costs and benefits determining disclosure intimacy in male-female dyads. *Journal of Social and Personal Relationships, 6,* 5–20.

Derlega, V. J., Metts, S., Petronio, S., & Margulis, S. T. (1993). *Self-disclosure.* Newbury Park, CA: Sage.

Foubert, J. D., & Sholley, B. K. (1996). Effects of gender, gender role, and individualized trust on self-disclosure. *Journal of Social Behavior and Personality, 11*(5), 277–288.

Laurenceau, J. P., Barrett, L. F., & Pietromonaco, P. R. (1998). Intimacy as an interpersonal process: The importance of self-disclosure, partner disclosure, and perceived

NOTES

partner responsiveness in interpersonal exchanges. *Journal of Personality and Social Psychology, 74,* 1238–1251.

Petronio, S., Martin, J., & Littlefield, R. (1984). Prerequisite conditions for self-disclosing: A gender issue. *Communication Monographs, 51,* 268–273.

Rosenfeld, L. B. (in press). Overview of the ways privacy, secrecy, and disclosure are balanced in today's society. In S. Petronio (Ed.), *Balancing the secrets of private disclosures.* Mahwah, NJ: Lawrence Erlbaum.

Rosenfeld, L. B. (1979). Self-disclosure avoidance: Why I am afraid to tell you who I am. *Communication Monographs, 46,* 63–74.

Rosenfeld, L. B., & Kendrick, W. L. (1987). Choosing to be open: Subjective reasons for self-disclosing. *Western Journal of Speech Communication, 48,* 326–343.

Toukmanian, S. G., & Brouwers, M. C. (1998). Cultural aspects of self-disclosure and psychotherapy. In S. S. Kazarian & D. R. Evans (Eds.), *Cultural clinical psychology: Theory, research, and practice* (pp. 106–124). New York: Oxford University Press.

Wintrob, H. L. (1987). Self-disclosure as a marketable commodity. *Journal of Social Behavior and Personality, 2,* 77–88.

HE SAYS/SHE SAYS

Misunderstandings Between Men and Women

Julia T. Wood

KEY WORDS

■

gendered communication patterns
speech communities
instrumental communication

Ginger walks out of her last class of the day to find Luke waiting for her, as he usually does on Tuesdays and Thursdays. She greets him with a hug and they fall into a matched pace that soon will lead them to the library.

"Becky got an offer from DuPont," Ginger says, knowing Luke will be interested because Becky is a mutual friend of theirs.

"Yeah? That's great." Luke says as he watches a roller blader whiz by. "We'll have to take her out to celebrate."

"Well, she hasn't accepted yet."

"What's she waiting for? A red carpet?"

"Chicago is pretty far away, you know, so it's a big decision," Ginger explains. She thinks how hard it would be for her to move away from Luke and all her friends and family. She adds, "And Ben doesn't want her to leave because they might not be able to manage a long-distance relationship. He's encouraging her to turn down the offer."

"That's selfish. They can visit and use email to stay in touch. Lots of people have long-distance relationships."

"Maybe, but it's not the same as being together. Besides, I think she's worried that taking the job might end the relationship with Ben."

"Let's focus on the job offer, not the relationship," Luke suggests. "That's the issue for her right now."

"But the two are connected. How can Becky decide about the job without making a decision about Ben?" Ginger thinks about all the relationships Becky has had and how short-lived each was. "In the three years we've known Becky, she's never stayed with anyone for long. Whenever a relationship starts to get serious, she bolts. The question is whether she's going to do that again with Ben."

"So you think she won't take the job?" he asks, glancing at a construction site they are passing.

"What I really think is that this offer may be an easy way to end the relationship." Ginger tries to make eye contact with Luke, but his eyes remain focused on the construction. "I think she has a pattern of bailing out of relationships because her parents divorced when she was 12. Maybe she doesn't trust a relationship to last."

"Maybe a job is more trustworthy," Luke says. "Besides, this is the time for her to launch her career. She can settle down later if she wants, but opportunities like DuPont don't come along every day."

"Neither do relationships," Ginger says sharply.

"Well, I think she should take the job."

Ginger is irritated by Luke's advice. It's not his business to say what Becky should do. Ginger wonders how she would feel if her parents had divorced. Would she be wary of committing to a relationship? Sharing her thoughts with

Luke, Ginger asks, "Do you think people whose parents divorced are less able to form commitments?"

"Beats me," Luke replies, only half listening to Ginger. He gets frustrated when she starts a conversation on one topic and then wanders onto another and another. He finds it hard to follow her thinking, and there's never any closure on a topic.

"Becky told me once that she felt her whole world blew up when her parents divorced." Ginger looks at Luke and asks, "If your parents had divorced, do you think you would shy away from relationships? Do you think we wouldn't be together?"

"I don't know," he replies, watching a crane lower building materials. How is he supposed to answer a hypothetical question? His parents didn't divorce, so he has no idea how he'd feel if they had. And what does any of this have to do with Becky and the offer from DuPont, he wonders. Why can't Ginger ever stick with just one topic?

"It just seems like it would affect a young child in a pretty major way," Ginger says. "I was so vulnerable at 12. Can you remember what you were like when you were 12?"

"Yeah, I guess," he mumbles, working hard to figure out where this conversation is going. "I was into baseball big time. That was my life."

"But what about your family? How would it have affected you if your parents had split up when you were 12?"

"Ginger, I've told you, I don't have any idea. They didn't split up, so how can I tell you how I would have felt if they had? Can you get back to the point?"

"This is the point. The point is about Becky's feelings about relationships," Ginger snaps.

"You started by telling me Becky had an offer from DuPont, and now we're talking about hypothetical family dynamics. Can we focus on whether she should take the job offer?"

"It's not my place to say what she should or shouldn't do, and it's not your place either. I'm more interested in her issues with relationships," Ginger says crossly. "Why can't you ever let a conversation evolve naturally?"

"There's a difference between a conversation that evolves and one that rambles all over," he growls. "I'd just like you, for once, to stay on topic."

"I am on topic! Lots of things are linked together. Do you think what Becky does about DuPont's offer is irrelevant to Ben or her parents' divorce?"

"It's a job offer. She takes it, or she doesn't," Luke replies. "Whether or not her parents divorced and whether or not she is serious about Ben, she has to decide about the offer. Even if the divorce did upset her, she's 21 years old. She should get beyond that and get on with her life."

N O T E S

Ginger lets out an exasperated sigh. She is so tired of trying to have a real talk with Luke and having him try to force the conversation into some narrow cubby hole or flood her with advice she hasn't asked for and doesn't want.

"Let's just drop it," she says.

"Fine with me," Luke replies. He is happy to drop this conversation—one more in a long line of conversations where he and Ginger wind up irritated with each other. He loves her but feels frustrated when she wanders all over in their conversations. If she would just stick to the point. . . .

Michelle drops by Luke's room that afternoon and says, "Hey, guy, what's happening?"

He smiles, glad to see Michelle. They first met during freshman orientation and become fast friends. In the four years since, Michelle and he have seen each other through academic anxieties, minor medical problems, and many, many relationships. He finds it so easy to talk with her about whatever is on his mind. He doesn't have to put up a false front and avoid showing he is upset or feels vulnerable, as he sometimes does with his guy friends. Michelle always takes him as he is and empathizes with his feelings.

"Nothing much, really; just kind of aggravated with Ginger," he replies, clearing his clothes off a chair so Michelle can sit.

"Trouble in Paradise?" When Luke doesn't smile, Michelle asks, "So is there a problem between you two?"

"No, not really—just a problem that keeps coming up when we talk. She starts a conversation about one thing, and the next thing I know we're all over creation. She's unable to stick to a topic. The minute I try to respond to one thing she's said, she's bouncing off somewhere else." Luke describes what happened today to Michelle and then says, "I mean why bring up the job offer if she wants to talk about how divorce affects children?"

Michelle laughs, "Oh, that's easy. She wasn't just trying to talk with you about the job offer or divorce."

Luke's face reflects his perplexity. "Huh? She brought up those topics. What do you mean she didn't want to talk about them."

"Well she did and she didn't," Michelle explains. "She was talking about them because they were on her mind, but mainly she just wanted to be in touch with you and share herself with you. It could have been other topics. It could have been plans for graduation day or anything."

"That's crazy."

"No, it's just not how *you* think and talk."

"But it's incoherent," Luke insists. "You can't have a conversation about one thing, like a job offer, if you're jumping to relationships and divorce and everything else."

"But, Luke, in Ginger's mind, what Becky decides to do about the offer *is* related to her relationship with Ben and Becky's parents' divorce. She probably feels that Becky would be less likely to take the job and to stay near Ben if her folks hadn't divorced. If you understand that, then you understand why Ginger would bring up those other things."

"Is that why she got angry when I offered advice?"

"She probably was more interested in having you tune into what she was thinking and feeling than in getting any advice. You don't always have to fix things, you know."

"But the only reason I give her advice is because I care about her," he protests.

"Maybe you two should talk about what you want in conversations," Michelle suggests. "It sounds to me as if you are really talking past each other."

That evening Ginger is hanging out with her roommate, Cassandra. She describes the earlier conversation with Luke and expresses her frustration that he never seems willing to talk in a free-flowing kind of way.

"I know what you mean," Cassandra says, nodding vigorously as their eyes connect. "The same thing happens with me and Aaron. I'll start talking about something and that will lead naturally to something else, and then he's all over my case for rambling. But it's not rambling to me to deal with a lot of issues that are so related."

"Exactly," Ginger says, "and no matter what I bring up, Luke's first response is to give advice. That drives me crazy—like I need his advice or something. Mr. Answer Man."

"It used to drive me crazy too," Cassandra agrees. "But in my Gender and Communication course I learned why this happens. It's not just you and Luke and me and Aaron. It's a problem a lot of women and men have when they talk."

"Oh, I've heard about that stuff. Didn't John Gray write a book about how different men and women are?"

"You mean *Men Are from Mars, Women Are from Venus?*" Ginger nods and Cassandra laughs. "On the first day of the class, our teacher said that John Gray was from Mars but women and men are from the same planet."

"But you just said that women and men have trouble understanding each other."

"They do, but not because they are from different planets or are different species, as John Gray says. It's that you and I and Luke and Aaron belong to the same planet, so we're are alike in most ways," Cassandra explains, looking at Ginger to be sure she's following. "But in the early years of life when we are learning how to interact with others, boys and girls tend to play with members of their own sex. As a result, a lot of boys and girls learn some different ways of interacting."

"Such as?" Ginger prompts.

"Our teacher told us that women usually learn to weave issues and people together in conversations, but men generally learn to compartmentalize topics and people. To them it feels logical to deal with one topic at a time, but to us it feels logical to mix everything together."

"So it's a basic gender difference?"

"Well, not entirely. Gender isn't the only thing that affects how we communicate," Cassandra qualifies. "We read some research that shows there are differences between how, say, Black and White and Asian people communicate, so ethnic communities also affect how we interact. You can't say 'All women do this, and all men do that,' but you can say there are some general patterns."

Cassandra thinks back to her class. The teacher used the term "speech communities" to describe the different ways women and men generally communicate. Her teacher explained that researchers who observed young boys and girls playing had discovered that the boys and girls played in different ways. The boys tended to play games such as football and war, which are structured by rules (for example, what counts as a touchdown; what counts as victory in battle), whereas girls tended to play games such as house and school, in which there are no clear-cut rules. The girls had to talk with each other to connect their worlds and work out how to play their games. As a result, girls were more likely to learn that talk builds relationships and is a way to link people together. In their games, the boys used communication mainly to define events (calling out a foul) and to plan strategy (the huddle). The researchers concluded that men learn to use communication to achieve specific things, whereas women learn to use communication to create relationships. Thinking back over what she has learned in her class, Cassandra tries to translate it for Ginger.

"I think it's like this: You were talking to Luke about Becky's job offer more to connect to him than to report on the job offer, right?"

Ginger shrugs. "Sure, why else would we talk?"

"Exactly," Cassandra says, "but Luke probably saw the conversation as about the job offer, so he addressed that. He didn't understand the topic was mainly a way for you and him to relate."

"Weird." Ginger shakes her head. "Why would you talk to someone if you weren't trying to relate to them?"

"If you were a guy, you might talk to resolve an issue or accomplish something like telling news or solving a problem or giving directions or offering advice."

"But I didn't ask him for advice. I was just trying to talk with him about Becky and the connections between the job offer and her relationship with Ben and her parents' divorce. Why does he feel compelled to give advice instead of just listening or talking with me?"

"He was trying to help, trying to support you and Becky by figuring out what she should do."

"But why won't he connect with me first and then offer advice, if he feels he has to do that?" Ginger asks. "I mean, isn't that the point of talking, anyway?"

"To you, it is, but it may not be to Luke because he may not perceive the point of conversation the same way that you do," Cassandra reiterates. "And he may find your way of talking just as confusing as you find his. He probably thinks it's really weird that you don't stick to just one topic. And he probably thinks it's really strange that you didn't want his advice. He was trying to help, after all."

"It's so interesting how people misunderstand each other," Ginger muses. "I remember once I wanted to show my mother how special I thought she was, so I gave her a gift certificate for a day at a spa. She thought I was saying she needed to have a facial and stuff."

"I know what you mean! My mother and I have had some really strange breakdowns, too," Cassandra empathizes, looking at Ginger and laughing. "The worst was my freshman year when I was waiting for her to call—to tell me she missed me and see how I was doing—but she was trying not to infringe on my independence, so she didn't call."

Ginger laughs, "Mothers!"

"And boyfriends," Cassandra adds, smiling at Ginger.

"Maybe I should take the course you're taking. What you've said is the first thing that's helped me understand why Luke and I sometimes get so irritated with each other."

After class the next Thursday, Ginger finds Luke waiting in the usual spot. She walks over to him and hugs him hello. "Becky turned DuPont down," Ginger announces.

"Wow, that's news," he replies as they start walking.

"She decided not to leave the relationship with Ben. We had a long talk about how she always does that, and she said she didn't want to continue that pattern."

"So does she think its because her parents divorced?"

Ginger stops and looks at him. "What's going on? You don't sound like yourself."

"Well, I'm beginning to understand a bit better why you put all these things together in a conversation, and I'm trying to follow the connections you make instead of always telling you what ought to happen or to stay on topic."

"That's so strange, because I talked with Cassandra the other night and she helped me understand why you like to tackle one topic at a time and that when you give me advice you are trying to help—not saying you think you have all the answers or that I can't solve my own problems."

"So Becky really turned DuPont down, did she?" Ginger nods. "Is she interviewing with other companies now?"

"Right now she wants to focus on the relationship with Ben and see where it might go," Ginger replies.

"But this is prime time for interviewing. She shouldn't delay that or she might not get a job at all."

"So your advice is that she should be interviewing?" Ginger asks with a mischievous smile.

He grins and says, "Even when you start to understand gendered patterns of communication, it's hard to break out of them, isn't it?"

FOR FURTHER THOUGHT AND REFLECTION

1. Reread the conversations between Ginger and Luke, Ginger and Cassandra, and Luke and Michelle. Can you identify gendered patterns in the three conversations?

2. Why do you think Luke talked with a woman friend instead of a man friend? Whom do you talk with when you are upset or frustrated, and why?

3. In what ways does understanding the sources of gendered conversational patterns help men and women to avoid misunderstandings and frustrations in their interactions?

4. In this case, Cassandra noted that gender is not the only aspect of identity that affects communication. Drawing on your experience and observation, point out ways in which communication is influenced by race, economic class, and other aspects of social identity.

REFERENCES

Inman, C. C. (1996). Friendships among men: Closeness in the doing. In J. T. Wood (Ed.), *Gendered relationships* (pp. 95–110). Mountain View, CA: Mayfield.

Johnson, F. L. (1996). Friendships among women: Closeness in dialogue. In J. T. Wood (Ed.), *Gendered relationships* (pp. 79–94). Mountain View, CA: Mayfield.

Maltz, D., & Borker, R. (1982). A cultural approach to male-female miscommunication. In J. J. Gumpertz (Ed.), *Language and social identity* (pp. 196–216). Cambridge, UK: Cambridge University Press.

Tannen, D. (1990). *You just don't understand: Women and men in conversation*. New York: William Morrow.

Wood, J. T., & Inman, C. C. (1992). In a different mode: Masculine styles of communicating closeness. *Journal of Applied Communication Research, 21,* 279–295.

Wood, J. T. (1998). *But I thought you meant . . . : Misunderstandings in human communication*. Mountain View, CA: Mayfield.

LET HER EAT CAKE

Recognizing and Coordinating Rules for Communicating[1]

Betsy Wackernagel Bach

KEY WORDS

■

communication rules
implicit rules
explicit rules
rule-following
rule-breaking
organizational socialization

Ruth was excited. She could hardly contain herself. She had just waved good-bye to her father and was running up the stairs of her dormitory. She didn't wait to watch him turn the corner so that she could wave one last time. It's not that Ruth didn't love her father. She did. And she knew that she would miss her father and her mom and two sisters—eventually. But not now. There was too much to do. She had the campus to explore, roommates to meet, and sorority rush to attend. Decisions had to be made about how to arrange the furniture and which posters to put up on the bare walls of the dorm room. She savored the moment of being on her own for the very first time, and she breathed a sigh of relief. "I can finally have a life!"

Background

Ruth had grown up in Deere, a small ranching community of 6,000, about 500 miles from Northern Rockies University, the place she was now glad to call home. She knew almost everyone in Deere, because the community was close-knit. All 40 people in her high school graduating class had been born and raised in Deere. She knew a great deal about all of her classmates, their families, and even their extended families. Although Ruth had been popular and well liked all through high school, she was thrilled about being among the more than 15,000 students on the Northern campus. She was anxious to have some anonymity, as well as the opportunity to make new friends.

Ruth meets Kay

Ruth arrived on campus early because she signed up for sorority rush, a two-week event during which women wishing to join sororities can learn more about sorority life. During rush, women visit sorority houses, talk with sorority members, and (if they seem compatible with other members), are extended invitations to join a sorority. During a freshman orientation session she had attended in July, Ruth had received a "Greek Life" brochure and an invitation to participate in "rush." The brochure listed many benefits of being in a sorority, one of which was the opportunity to make friends. Ruth thought that making friends on a large campus might be difficult, and she figured that going through rush would be an excellent way to meet people.

Two days after her arrival at Northern Rockies, Ruth began the flurry of rush activities. She was assigned to a group of 20 other women, and during the first three days of rush, she visited 19 sorority houses, where she was treated to goodies and introductions. Ruth began to make friends from her group of 20, and she started to spend time with Kay, who was also from a small town. Ruth and Kay found that they had a lot in common, particularly the fact that they were excited about getting away from small town life.

Over the next two weeks, Ruth and Kay attended sorority parties and learned that they got invited back to the same two sororities: Sigma and Delta. Ruth was glad that the members of Sigma and Delta seemed to like both her and Kay because they had decided that they would like to join the same sorority. As the last day of rush approached, Ruth and Kay decided that they would join Sigma, whose members seemed very friendly, genuine, and fun to be around. Sigma members had taken an interest in both women and had spent a lot of time with them at parties—talking, laughing, and offering advice and encouragement. Ruth and Kay found the Sigma sorority house very elegant—much more elegant than their own homes. There was a grand piano, brand new plush carpeting, and a beautiful stained glass window of the Sigma crest hanging in the dining room (which had lace tablecloths)! Ruth and Kay hoped they would be invited to join Sigma and nervously awaited the delivery of "bids"—invitations to become a member of a particular sorority.

On Friday the bids arrived. Ruth and Kay had decided to open their bids together so that they could celebrate or commiserate, depending upon the outcome. Each held her breath as they tore open the envelopes and read aloud similar greetings. Much to their relief, both Ruth and Kay received invitations to join Sigma. The invitations read, "You are cordially invited to join Sigma. We welcome you with open arms to our friendship circle! Should you decide to join us, kindly notify us of your acceptance by 3:00 P.M. on Friday. At 4:00 P.M. on Friday, we request your presence at our sorority house." Ruth and Kay screamed and hugged. They were ecstatic, not only because they had been invited to join Sigma, but because they would be together.

Learning and Breaking Rules

Ruth and Kay arrived at the Sigma house just a few minutes before 4 o'clock on Friday and were asked to wait outside the front door. They met 22 other women who had also been asked to join the sorority. Promptly at 4:00 P.M. a sorority member opened the front door and invited the new members inside. They were directed to sit on the floor of the living room. The woman introduced herself as Sharon, their "pledge trainer." Sharon continued by saying, "From now until the end of January, you will be known as 'pledges' of Sigma and members-in-training. Every Monday night after dinner here, you will be instructed in the rules and regulations of Sigma and participate in 'pledge training.' You will learn about who we are and about our purpose. You will, over the next four months, be required to spend time with each active member, one of whom will be your 'big sister.' You will also spend a great deal of time with your fellow pledges. All of this is a way to help you understand us, so that you can become members who contribute to and value what we do. I have been put in charge of helping you to become a valued member of Sigma. We are proud of this sorority and want you to be, too."

After explaining the history of Sigma, Sharon handed out small pins in the shape of a crescent to the 24 pledges. "These pins are 'pledge pins.' They signify to others that you have decided to join Sigma. They should be worn while you are in public, but especially every Monday night for formal dinner which, by the way, begins promptly at 6 o'clock." Finally, Sharon closed the meeting by handing out the music and words to the sorority song. "I strongly advise you to learn it by Monday," she instructed with a wry smile. "I'd hate to have you regret it."

Ruth and Kay spent much of the weekend with the other pledges learning the song. Much to their relief, they knew the words and the tune by Monday afternoon. Ruth hummed the tune while getting ready for her first formal dinner at the Sigma house. She choose a nice pair of slacks and a top, much like what she saw Sigma members wear during rush. She ran outside to meet Kay so that they could walk to the "house" together. Kay was dressed in a similar manner. They sang the sorority song softly as they made their way to the house, where they arrived promptly at 5:59 P.M.

When they arrived at the house, they found that they were the only ones outside. They cautiously opened the front door and observed everyone inside talking and laughing. They became very dismayed. "Damn, they're going to hate us!" Kay whispered to Ruth. "We're the only ones who were late and the only ones in pants. Everyone else has on a dress. Boy, do I feel like a jerk!" Ruth retorted, "Well, we're not psychic. How were we supposed to know that we had to arrive ten minutes early to socialize and wear a dress? Nobody *said* anything! Maybe if we sing our hearts out, they'll let us stay in."

Although no one looked at them in a disapproving manner, Ruth and Kay decided to listen and observe during dinner, and they tried to keep a low profile. They were intimidated by the formality of what they had observed. The dining room was set with lace tablecloths and china, and there were men dressed in white shirts, black ties, and short white jackets standing by the kitchen door ready to serve dinner. Ruth and Kay learned that these were the "houseboys," and that they were hired to serve dinner and do the dishes on Monday nights. The housemother, introduced to the pledges as "Mrs. P," stood by the door and hushed all the women before she walked over and turned on a light behind the stain-glassed Sigma crest that Kay and Ruth had admired during rush. She then lead the women into the dining room.

Ruth began to follow the housemother when she felt a gentle hand on her shoulder pulling her back. "Don't get ahead of Mrs. P. or our officers," the voice commanded. The order was quickly followed by a stage whisper. "It's Nancy. We talked quite a bit during rush. I'm your big sister. It's my job to help you understand what's expected around here, despite what Sharon tells you. Sit with me during dinner and I will help you out." Ruth breathed a sigh of relief. As she stood next to Nancy, she noticed that Mrs. P. and all the Sigma officers moved to a head table and that everyone else filed in behind them, scattering to other tables of eight. As Ruth pulled out her chair to sit down, Nancy again placed her hand on Ruth's shoulder. "Not yet. First we sing grace." Ruth noticed that everyone pulled out the chair to her left prior to sitting down, rather than pulling out their own chairs. "Whew," Ruth thought to herself. "I'm glad that Kay and I decided to observe. At least I didn't blow *that* one."

Dinner went smoothly and Ruth began to relax. Nancy kept her posted on what would be happening by saying, "Look, Ruth, I know that you weren't born in a barn. But, since Monday dinners are quite formal, let me remind you of a few things. Remember always to use the utensil on the outside first and work toward your plate. Also, we pass everything to the head of the table and let that person serve herself before we take anything. And," Nancy added, "when you serve yourself, pass everything to the left." Ruth was most grateful for the refresher course on etiquette. By dessert, she was actually enjoying herself. "I'm going to get along here just fine," she thought. "Nancy sure is helpful and I think I can ask her almost anything. I'm glad that she's my big sister. I wonder, though, why she made that comment about how she can help me out 'despite what Sharon says'?" Her thoughts were interrupted as a houseboy brought her an absolutely divine looking piece of chocolate cake covered with rich, creamy, chocolate frosting. Although she was not hungry and did not want dessert, she allowed him to put a piece of cake at her place. At that moment Ruth looked over at Kay, who appeared dismayed. Kay was hanging her head and her cheeks were flushed. She had been assigned Sharon, the pledge trainer, as her big sister; and Sharon appeared to be "lecturing" Kay about something. Ruth noticed that Kay had refused a helping of chocolate cake. "It would be tough being allergic to chocolate like Kay," Ruth reminded herself. "Geez, I wonder why Sharon is talking so sternly to Kay. Certainly Kay's refusal of cake is nothing to be lectured about."

Ruth's thoughts were interrupted as Nancy laughed and gently chided her, "If you're not going to eat your dessert, pass it down to Joan, as she would love to have seconds." Ruth complied, happy to keep her waistline intact.

After dinner, the housemother rang a bell for the houseboys to come and clear the dessert plates. Sigma members engaged in lively chatter until the houseboys had completed their task. As the last plate was removed, the Sigma president rose and announced, "We will now close dinner with a sorority song that the pledges were instructed to learn. After that, all pledges will meet with Sharon in the T.V. room while the rest of us attend Chapter." Nancy leaned over to Ruth and offered her some encouragement. "Now's your first chance to show that you want to belong. Go for it!" Ruth sang in as animated a fashion as she could. While she sang, she noticed that (despite her *faux pas* of arriving late and wearing pants) several sorority members were looking at her while smiling and nodding approval.

At the pledge meeting after dinner, Sharon approached them in a very stern manner. "Despite the fact that you have been invited to join Sigma, realize that you are not yet permanent, active members. You have to prove to us that you are worthy of active membership. From what I saw tonight, not many of you want a place in our sorority. Frankly, your singing was abysmal. You'd better learn quickly how things work around here if you want to be initiated! It's my job to teach you the rules, and I don't want you to make me look bad. Here is a list of house rules of conduct. Make sure that you know them by next Monday. By the way, Ruth and Kay, you will be fined $5.00 for wearing pants to Chapter dinner. You can pay next week. Also, make sure that you all get together with your Big Sisters at least twice this week. Meeting adjourned. I'll see you next week."

Ruth and Kay quietly left the house, and Ruth could sense that Kay was upset. Once they were out of earshot of the other pledges, Kay sobbed, "I hate Sigma. I just had the most horrible dinner of my life! I can't believe that Sharon is my big sister. What a wretch! She rode my butt throughout dinner and treated me like I was stupid. All she did was criticize me in front of all the others. I've never been criticized in front of other people before. In my family, if someone bugged us we would talk it out privately with them, not in front of an audience! We also never ate formally at my house. We don't even own a lace tablecloth. We're just not like that. What difference does it make which way you pass a damn dish? Who cares which fork you use as long as you chew with your mouth closed? I can't stand this! And, to be fined five bucks for wearing pants! How the hell were we supposed to know? What stupid idiot decided that?" Ruth tried to console Kay, but with no success. Ruth was worried that Kay might decide to leave Sigma, so she decided to talk with Nancy the following day.

When Ruth poured out Kay's problem to Nancy, she found her big sister supportive, yet firm. "I feel very bad for Kay," Nancy proclaimed. "Unfortunately she is stuck with Sharon, as we don't change big sisters after they have been assigned. I guess that we shouldn't have given Sharon the task of being both a big sister and a pledge trainer. Perhaps it's too much for her. However, in Sharon's defense, I must say that learning proper etiquette is something we take very seriously. It is very important later on in life." Nancy continued, "That aside, I am very angry that you both got fined, although it is something that I would expect Sharon to do. Over the summer, Sharon turned into a by-the-book person. She was much more relaxed before we elected her as our pledge trainer. It almost seems like a little bit of power has gone to her head! In July she took it upon herself to rewrite the house rules of conduct, and she is determined to stick by them as we haven't closely adhered to house rules in the past. Although the house rules need to be enforced, there should be some room for flexibility. It's unclear to me whether or not we should fine pledges, particularly for a first-time violation. Let me talk with the President and see what can be done. If past practice is followed, people do not pay the first time they are fined." Nancy concluded, "I understand that it's difficult to learn new ways, but that's what pledge training is all about. Some things you will be taught directly, such as our house rules. Other things you just pick up by observing what is going on or by being corrected, like at dinner last night."

"Dinner last night . . . ," mused Ruth. "Oh, you mean when you reminded me to pass the mashed potatoes to the left?"

"Well, sort of," replied Nancy. "Remember when I told you to give your chocolate cake to Joan? You may not have realized it, but it is very important around here to take dessert even when you don't want it. During formal dinner, we are only allowed one helping of dessert—it's Mrs. P's hard and fast rule. Some people would like to have more than one dessert. So, even if you don't want a dessert, you should take it and save it for anyone else at the table who wants seconds."

Nancy continued. "As long as we're talking about dinner last night and how to behave during formal meals, I should tell you that Joan mentioned that you did not talk with her at all. You simply handed your cake to her at my request. It is a pledge's responsibility during formal dinners to initiate conversation with every active member seated within comfortable talking distance. So, you should be sure to talk with any active members sitting on either side of you or directly across from you at the table. You're considered arrogant if you don't talk to everyone seated near you."

Ruth was relieved. She left the house feeling much better and was anxious to tell Kay what she had learned. Perhaps making new friends outside of Deere was not going to be as easy as she thought. "Dinner at Sigma is certainly unlike anything I've ever experienced—geez, all the formality," she mused. "Oh, well, I guess that's why I joined. I'll get used to it, I'm sure."

Ruth talked with Kay and explained everything she had learned from Nancy. They acknowledged that Sharon was rigid (non to mention a bit power hungry) and that she probably had Kay's best interest at heart when she corrected her. However, they decided that when the time was right, Kay would explain her feelings about the public reprimand to Sharon. "Hopefully Sharon will ease up a bit as time goes on and I will be able to talk with her," Kay said wishfully.

After thoroughly discussing Kay's relationship with Sharon and what could be done to improve it, Ruth laughed out loud. "I just have to tell you this," she giggled. "You won't believe it. When I was talking to Nancy she told me that everyone always takes dessert during formal dinner whether or not they want it. They then give it to people at the table who want seconds, because Mrs. P won't allow anyone to get seconds from the kitchen! I'll make sure that I sit next to you every time we have chocolate, so you can give me your dessert. Do we have a deal?"

"No," said Kay giggling, "I noticed that Sharon wolfed down not one but two pieces of cake at dinner. I'd better make sure I offer my dessert to her!"

"Fine," Ruth said, feigning anger. "Let her eat cake!"

END NOTE

1. This case is adapted from T. A. Albrecht and B. W. Bach (1997), *Communication in complex organizations: A relational approach* (pp. 194-195). Orlando, FL: Harcourt Brace College Publishers.

FOR FURTHER THOUGHT AND REFLECTION

1. It is said that communication rules help prescribe rules for behavior. What general communication rules do you see operating throughout this case?

2. It is said that communication rules are used to evaluate, justify, correct, predict, and/or explain behavior. How do communication rules in this case function to evaluate, justify, correct, predict and explain behaviors?

3. What implicit (unstated prescriptions for behavior) and explicit (clearly stated prescriptions for behavior) rules did you see? Which appear to have more importance?

4. When is it appropriate to break rules? How were rules broken in this case?

5. Rules of organizational socialization (e.g., learning the ropes of how to behave in a new situation) are discussed in this case. How might the types of socialization rules identified here apply to other situations and contexts?

6. Sororities and other organizations often have relatively formal rules for when and how to communicate. In more casual relationships, rules tend to be less formal, conscious and explicit but equally present. Identify rules that guide how you and others act when your family has dinner, or when you and friends go out to dinner together.

REFERENCES

Albrecht, T. A., & Bach, B. W. (1997). *Communication in complex organizations: A relational approach*. Orlando, FL: Harcourt Brace College Publishers.

Bach, B. W. (1990). Moving up on campus: A qualitative examination of organizational socialization. *Journal of the Northwest Communication Association, 18*, 53-71.

Bullis, C. A., & Bach, B. W. (1989). Socialization turning points: An examination of change in organizational identification. *Western Journal of Speech Communication, 53*, 273-293.

Shiminoff, S. B. (1980). *Communication rules: Theory and research*. Beverly Hills, CA: Sage Publications.

BECOMING A FAMILY

Turning Points and Interaction Patterns in the
Development of a Blended Family

Dawn O. Braithwaite, Leslie A. Baxter

KEY WORDS

■

blended family
family development
turning points
dialectical tensions
rituals

Lonnie[1] was lugging the last trunk of her clothes down the stairs. The brightly colored trunk, adorned with decals from her new college, made a loud "thump!" as she dragged the heavy load down each of the worn steps. "Which of you kids is making all that racket?" her mother, Gail, called brightly. Lonnie smiled to herself. Even though she was 18 years-old and off to college, she still loved to bug her mother. "Here, let me help before you scratch up all the stairs, for goodness sake!" Lonnie smiled and offered her mother one handle of the trunk. "Where are Tim and your sister? I want to get going soon so the baby will sleep while we are on the road." Lonnie pointed out to the driveway where Tim and her sister, Celia, were shooting hoops next to the van packed with Lonnie's treasures. "Thanks, Mom! Go get Emily and let's roll!"

As she stood at the bottom of the stairs, Lonnie felt strangely sad. It didn't seem so long ago that she couldn't wait to get out of this house. Now the day had come, and all Lonnie could do was think back to all the memories she had of life in the old yellow house. In some ways, it was even hard to remember what her life was like before they lived there, but as she stood waiting, she thought back to other moving days and related memories.

Dad Moves Out

Lonnie had known this day was coming. It was just two weeks after her 12th birthday. Her parents, Gail and Gene, had a huge fight the night before, the biggest one Lonnie and her nine year-old sister, Celia, had ever heard. Things had been bad between her parents for some time. Gail seemed especially intent on trying to keep things as normal as possible—for example, trying to keep up a weekly family-dinner-night out. In the early years, these had been happy occasions, as they ate at a casual local diner run by "Flo and Mo." But in recent years, Lonnie could only remember coming back from these dinners and listening to her parents going at each other in the front seat of the car. Things would be good for awhile, and then they would get bad again.

Finally, one warm July night, Gail and Gene called Lonnie and Celia together after dinner to explain that they had tried to work things out, but that "sometimes moms and dads just can't make things work." Their father was moving out. The girls would be best off living with their mom, "in the only house you have ever known." Their dad would only be 20 minutes away; they would have dinner with him on Wednesday nights, and spend every other weekend and part of each summer with him. Lonnie was not unfamiliar with this arrangement. Several friends' parents were divorced, and they had similar schedules.

N O T E S

The Single Years

For the next two years, Lonnie and Celia lived with Gail in their house on Evergreen Avenue. They didn't have much money, and they missed their old family with their mom and dad together. But they were relieved that their parents were no longer fighting. Once their dad got on his feet and bought a condo, the girls shared a huge bedroom there with their own stereo, TV, and VCR. In contrast, things were tight financially at home. They turned their dad's old office into a bedroom for Celia and painted a second-hand bed and dresser for her. Each girl had her own room at least, and Lonnie relished some privacy.

Lonnie was aware that her mom was working hard to support them while going to night school. As the oldest, Lonnie took on a lot of responsibility and learned to cook. She often had a simple dinner waiting when her mom dragged herself home, and they all made it a point to eat together most nights. One of the things the three of them enjoyed was going out for pizza and window shopping on payday. Although they spent a modest amount of money, it felt extravagant. More importantly, they enjoyed these nights out because they got a chance to talk. While they ate and as they walked along looking in the shop windows, their mom asked them about what was going on in their lives, and they shared their concerns and questions. One of their favorite games was to play, "What we would do with a million dollars!" They would fantasize about the wild purchases they would make. For Lonnie, this was the highlight of the week.

Tim Arrives on the Scene

That summer she and Celia had spent a month with their dad and his parents at the lake. It was great to be with Nana and Grampa, but Lonnie missed her mom. When they arrived home, Gail seemed overjoyed to see them. Lonnie noticed that her mom had a new hairstyle and she was wearing new earrings. When she asked about it, Gail blushed and said, "Oh, we'll talk about it at dinner." They went out to Flo and Mo's to celebrate their homecoming and, on the way home, Mom said, "Well, girls, I hope you don't mind, but I am going to the movies later tonight." Lonnie was surprised and asked, "Going out? With Betty?" "No, well, um . . . with Tim." "'Tim the Tool Man' from TV?" laughed Celia. Their mom stammered, "No, Tim Bartino, a man I have been seeing." Lonnie felt sick. "You mean you've been dating someone and you didn't tell us?" "No, Lonnie, well, I . . . I met Tim at school last spring. We had coffee a few times, but the last couple of weeks we have been going out. Don't worry—it's nothing serious." Lonnie and Celia didn't say anything because they didn't want to hurt their mom's feelings, but as the two of them talked that night they shared their anger and disappointment that their mom wasn't home on their first night back.

Over the next few months, "nothing really serious" became "something serious" as Gail and Tim began spending more and more time together. Lonnie and Celia were wary of Tim at first. Unlike their dad, he was a quiet man, a studious engineer who was working on his Masters in Business Administration in night school. He was divorced with two children—Tony, who was a high school junior, and Tina, now 18, who had dropped out of high school in her senior year. Tony and Tina lived three hours away and it was two months before Lonnie even met them.

Tim was spending much more time with them. In fact, he was staying at their house most of the time now. Once they had worked through some of the initial nervousness, like seeing Tim at breakfast, things had fallen into a fairly normal routine. For the first time, life seemed kind of like it was before her parents' divorce, when they had been a family. It felt like kind of a turning point when Lonnie heard herself the first time telling her friend that she had to be home for a "family dinner." It was nice and, well, just normal to have the four of them together, and their mom seemed so happy. At the same time, Lonnie was bothered, too. Had her mom been that unhappy with just the three of them? Was her dad really that replaceable? One evening when Tim asked her what time she would be coming home from a party, she blurted out, "Hey, you're not my dad! I am not ready to trade in dads this year!" He looked very hurt.

On Thanksgiving weekend, Tim gave up his apartment and moved in for good. Her mom called a "family meeting," and the four of them discussed the move. Tim had already spoken with Tina and Tony. He said they "are great with things" and "looking forward to spending our first Christmas together." At first Lonnie felt strange when her mom used the term "family meeting." Were they a *real* family? She really didn't feel the same as she had with her real family, yet, as Tim moved in, it seemed like a new period had started in their lives. Family-like routines had developed, and things began to feel different. As she got to know him, Tim was a little easier to talk to. Lonnie started watching football with him on Sundays; it was one of the times he became truly excited.

Things had changed in their household routines. Whereas Lonnie was used to taking care of her mom and making dinner, often she arrived home to find Tim had already made dinner. She had to admit he was a great cook. Gail would come home and make a huge fuss. "Oh, I am the envy of all my friends!" One of the things that really irked Lonnie was that Tim now went along on their payday dinner and shopping nights. Although they ate at the same old place, the talk around the dinner table was now much different. Celia and Lonnie both talked privately about how they missed talking with just their mom. When

Lonnie brought it up, Gail seemed irritated. "Now, Lon, Tim is just trying to be part of the family. Give him a break!" Lonnie could see her point, but she desperately missed those special times with her mom and the long talks they had shared. Pretty soon they stopped having these nights out altogether.

The Wedding

Spring and the summer after Lonnie's freshman year were a busy and happy time. Gail and Tim announced their engagement in April and were planning an August wedding. Lonnie was glad to see her mom so excited, and she had to admit she genuinely liked Tim and the way the family was going—especially when it was just the four of them. She liked Tony and Tina all right, but things sometimes seemed tense, especially when Tina was around.

Before he asked Gail to marry him, Tim took Celia and Lonnie out to dinner and asked how they felt: "I don't ever intend to replace your dad, but I love your mom and I think we can have a good life together." It meant a lot to Lonnie that Tim respected them enough to consult them. It also showed Lonnie that he was sensitive to the prospect of them dealing with "two dads." Nonetheless, Lonnie had some mixed feelings about it all, and she worried how her dad would feel. She had to admit that she certainly felt much more at home with Tim and Mom than she did with her dad. She knew that she liked Tim a lot, and it would be hard to imagine their little family without him now. The younger Celia didn't seem to be bothered by any of it and was especially excited that all four kids were to serve as attendants at the wedding.

In June, Tim received a promotion at work, and he and Gail began looking for a larger house. Just before the wedding in late August, they bought a big old yellow farmhouse on three acres of land. It was definitely a fixer-upper, but mom was excited about the huge kitchen and told the girls they would finally be able to have a garden and maybe even a horse! The problem was that the house was about 20 miles away from their present home. Lonnie protested. "Mom, this means I will have to leave all my friends and start a new school for my sophomore year! I don't want to attend that stupid South High!" Gail seemed too busy to even hear her concerns.

The day of the wedding finally arrived, and Lonnie felt mixed emotions. How could she feel so happy and so sad at the same time? Gail and Tim were so in love. Last night Lonnie had said to Celia, "You know, Celia, I know this sounds stupid, but I guess till today I always thought mom and dad might get back together." Celia agreed. "I know what you mean. I wish Tim and Mom weren't getting married! And I am not going to call stupid Tony and Tina my brother and sister!" It was a beautiful wedding and, as Tim and Gail exchanged vows, Celia and Lonnie were aware that this was a pivotal moment for them as well. The two girls cried at the wedding—for all they had lost and for all they had gained.

Mom and Tim postponed their honeymoon so that they could move into the new house, which they did the day after the wedding. On Saturday Mom remarried, on Sunday they moved from the only home Lonnie and Celia had ever known, and on Monday, they both started at new schools. These were among the darkest days of Lonnie's life. She missed her friends, and she absolutely hated the "stupid, drafty old house." Most importantly, she resented Tim and her mom's time alone together when she desperately needed her mom's attention and support. While repairs were underway, Lonnie and Celia had to share a room and they fought constantly. The low point was when Tina came for the weekend and slept in their already crowded room.

The First Christmas

By the holidays, things had settled down a lot. The downstairs of the house was shaping up nicely. She had joined the choir at her new school and Josh McEvan had asked her to the Christmas formal. Christmas had always been very special in their household and Gail promised, "I plan to make this a very special Christmas for us all." Her family had always come together on December 24th and decorated the tree with all their family ornaments, stringing popcorn and singing Christmas carols. Then they would go to Christmas Eve mass and spend a quiet Christmas Day at home—just the family—opening gifts and having a huge turkey dinner together.

They made their plans and worked hard to have everything ready for Tony and Tina's arrival the morning of the 24th. When they arrived—late—Tina said, "Geez, it doesn't look much like Christmas around here. Don't you people even have a Christmas tree?" They filled her in on the day's activities, but she did not seem interested. As they decorated the tree, Tim and Tony just sat there for the most part, and Tina was on the phone to her friends. Tim tried to talk them into going to church, but they both begged off. One neat thing was that Tim had gone shopping on his own (and he hated shopping) to buy a special present for each of the four kids. Tina said, "My dad does this every year and comes home with the goofiest stuff," but Lonnie was touched by his efforts and the sweet music box he chose for her.

On Christmas day, Lonnie, Celia, and their mom worked on the traditional Christmas dinner and Tim joined in. Tony and Tina were trying to get everyone to go to the movies and see the new picture opening Christmas Day. "C'mon you guys, let's get out and DO something!" Lonnie tried not to show

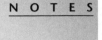

it, but she was really pissed off at those two. "Mom, why can't they just join in and give our traditions a chance?" Gail ran interference, saying to Tony and Tina, "Look why don't you two go on to the movies, and we'll move dinner ahead a couple of hours so we can all eat together, OK?" Lonnie hated to admit it, but she felt much more comfortable when they were gone and just the new family was there.

Settling In

Tim and Gail spent all their free time throughout the winter and spring months working on the house. Tim made a special effort to finish the interior of Lonnie's and Celia's bedrooms first so they could have their own rooms. Tony came to visit much more than Tina did, and he really was a pretty nice guy. He made an effort, while Tina never did, and he took them to some fun places. Tony and Tim had a long-standing routine of watching sports together on Sundays. Unlike mom and Celia, Lonnie had always liked sports, and she would join in the festivities and watch games with Tony and Tim; the three of them went to several professional baseball games together. On these outings they started calling Lonnie "Fred" and "one of the guys." Although she could never bring herself to say it to their faces, she often referred to Tim and Tony as "her dad" and "her brother" to her friends.

Dad Remarries

They also found out that spring that Dad was dating Victoria, a divorced woman with a four year-old son, Connor. Several years later, Lonnie would discover that her dad and Victoria had been seeing each other during the last year of her parents' marriage, which was part of "the last straw" that finally broke their parents up. Gene and Victoria married in a quiet noon ceremony at the courthouse in the late spring. In fact, Lonnie and her sister did not even find out until after the wedding and, although she felt guilty admitting it to herself, Lonnie just could not get all that excited about it.

Dad said that they would now "be a family," but it certainly did not *feel* like a family. Not like what she felt as a child with her mom and dad, and not even close to what she felt with her mom and Tim. In fact, it surprised her to see how strongly she felt about her new family with Tim. Celia, on the other hand, immediately started telling people about "her little brother, Connor." Lonnie just couldn't bring herself to say the word "brother" when it came to the little runt.

Lonnie could not say that she truly disliked Victoria, but she could not say that she *liked* her either. Victoria was a very elegant, formal woman, in contrast to Lonnie's mother, who preferred bare feet to shoes and a picnic in the back yard to a formal dinner in the dining room. Lonnie and Celia were asked to ring the doorbell when they arrived, to leave their shoes by the front door (Victoria had white carpets), and to keep their room at Victoria's house spotless. Their dad also seemed different around Victoria—older and more stuffy.

Dad said they would keep "family dinner night going," and they did try that—for awhile. They would go to Flo and Mo's Diner, and Victoria would look disapprovingly at the menu and inspect the silverware before eating. One Saturday night, Lonnie became irritated and, just to get Victoria's goat, she said, "I love Flo and Mo's because it is my mom's favorite restaurant!" On the way home Victoria announced that she was through going to "that place" and, from now on, "we will have family dinner night at home and I will make a special dinner for us all." True to her word, Victoria cooked elaborate dinners and they ate in the dining room on the good china, but to Lonnie and Celia these gatherings were a huge chore.

As they got older, Lonnie and Celia found reasons to miss these dinners as much as possible. They didn't want to hurt their dad's feelings by telling him how they felt. They still loved him and wanted him to be happy, and missing the dinners meant that they didn't get to see their dad as often—which they didn't like. But they just couldn't take those dinners with Victoria! During the weekends at Victoria and Gene's they missed their mom, and Tim too. Sunday night could not come too soon for them. As the years went on, they found reasons to stay at home, and their visits became shorter and less frequent.

During the summer after her sophomore year, Lonnie went on vacation with Celia, their father, and Victoria to visit Victoria's parents, "Grandma Hinter and Grandpa Hinter" (as they were instructed to call them). They were nice people, but rather formal like Victoria. While they obviously enjoyed playing with little Connor, they did not seem to know what to do with the two sisters. Lonnie was bored and missed her friends and home a lot.

Tina Moves In

Lonnie was almost surprised at how happy she was to get back home, and she looked forward to starting her junior year of high school. What a change from a year ago! She realized how homesick she had been. Mom helped them unpack and said that they were having a family meeting that night. At the meeting, Gail and Tim announced that Tina would be moving in with them for "a while, until her money problems are under control."

While Lonnie dreaded Tina moving in, things went even more badly than she could have imagined. Tina was very rude and demanding. She smoked constantly and got into fights with Lonnie in particular. When Lonnie complained

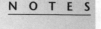

to her mom and Tim, they took Tina's side. "Look, Lonnie, Tina is adjusting to a lot here and has a lot of problems to work through right now. Let's try and keep a lid on things, OK?" Finally, Tina got on her feet financially and was able to move out. Lonnie felt guilty to admit it, but she was really glad Tina was gone and the family was back to normal.

A Second Dad

Things were going pretty smoothly by fall of her senior year. Tony had moved to their city to attend community college and lived in an apartment close by. He spent a lot of time with the family now, and he was a great big brother. School was going well and Lonnie was making college plans. Tim was especially helpful with practical advice and helping her write away for college application materials. The big news was that Gail was pregnant and expecting a baby around Easter! Tim was ecstatic, and Lonnie had to admit that she was surprised at her own reaction—she was really excited! When she was a kid, before her parents' problems, she had always hoped for another baby, and now it was going to happen! Celia was less certain about the whole thing and worried, "They will only have time for the baby. What's going to happen to me?"

The week before the big Homecoming dance, Lonnie was out shopping for shoes to match her dress, when she suddenly felt hot and queasy and had pains in her side. When stabbing pains doubled her over, she called home. Tim answered the phone and told her to "hang on"; he would come and get her right away. It was all she could do not to pass out. Tim took one look at her and said, "Lonnie, we're going to the emergency room." He called Gail on the way to the hospital. Tim held Lonnie's hand as he drove like a wild man. Gail showed up soon thereafter, followed by Tony and Celia. Lonnie's appendix had burst, so she was rushed into emergency surgery. The surgeon said that Tim had gotten Lonnie there not a moment too soon.

Tim barely left Lonnie's side while she was in the hospital. She had never seen this side of him. She had always known he cared about them, but she never realized just how much. Tim had rarely hugged her before and, for the first time, he said he loved her. It made Lonnie cry. Much to her disappointment, Lonnie missed the dance. Gail arranged for her friends to stop by the house on their way to the dance, but it was Tim who touched her the most: He bought Lonnie beautiful pink roses, and attached was a little heart-shaped pin for her. She couldn't believe how sweet he had been. Tim told her friends, "Guys, you better get going soon; my daughter needs her rest." He had never called her that before. Later that evening, as everyone got ready for bed, Lonnie gave Tim a kiss and said, "Thanks, Dad."

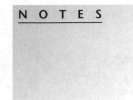

Lonnie was returned to the present by her baby sister's crying as Gail carried Emily downstairs. "Shake a leg, Lonnie, or we'll be late to your college orientation!" Gail said as she scooped up a diaper bag filled to the brim. Tim came and carried the baby to her car seat. Gail turned to Lonnie and gave her a great big hug. "This will always be your home, you know, no matter how far away you are."

END NOTE

1. This case represents a composite of the experiences of members of blended families expressed in research interviews with the authors and their research team. The names of the characters have been changed.

FOR FURTHER THOUGHT AND REFLECTION

1. What makes a group of people a "real family"? In your view, which of the groups in this case study are "real families"? Why so?

2. A theoretical perspective known as *relational dialectics* claims that relationships are organized around opposing tensions, or pulls in opposite directions. What simultaneous dialectical tensions or pulls can you identify in Lonnie's account of the development of her blended families?

3. What are the major turning points, significant points of positive or negative change, in the development of Lonnie's blended families?

4. Lonnie's blended family with Gail and Tim developed differently from her blended family with Gene and Victoria. What factors contribute to the different developmental paths these two blended families experienced?

5. Rituals are recurring interaction events, formalized or informal, that hold importance to their participants. What rituals can you identify in this case study? How did rituals change as Lonnie's families changed? Why were some rituals able to adapt to new circumstances while other rituals were not?

REFERENCES

Amato, P. R. (1993). Children's adjustment to divorce: Theories, hypotheses, and empirical support. *Journal of Marriage and the Family, 55,* 23–38.

Baxter, L. A., & Montgomery, B. M. (1996). *Relating: Dialogues and dialectics.* New York: Guilford.

N O T E S

Baxter L. A., Braithwaite, D. O., & Nicholson, J. (1999). Turning points in the development of blended family relationships. *Journal of Social and Personal Relationships, 16,* 291–293.

Baxter, L. A., & Bullis, C. (1986). Turning points in developing romantic relationships. *Human Communication Research, 18,* 336–363.

Braithwaite, D. O., Baxter, L. A., & Harper, A. (1998). The role of rituals in the management of dialectical tension of "old" and "new" in blended families. *Communication Studies, 48,* 101–120.

Cissna, K. N., Cox, D. E., & Bochner, A. P. (1990). The dialectic of marital and parental relationships within the stepfamily. *Communication Monographs, 57,* 44–61.

Ganong, L., & Coleman, M. (1994). *Remarried family relationships,* Thousand Oaks, CA: Sage.

Imber-Black, E., Roberts, J., & Whiting, R. A. (Eds.). (1988). *Rituals in families and family therapy.* New York: W. W. Norton & Company.

Papernow, P. L. (1993). *Becoming a stepfamily: Patterns of development in remarried families.* San Francisco: Jossey-Bass.

WHEN SEX ISN'T DIRTY

Can We Talk?

Stephanie M. Mechmann, Sheryl Perlmutter Bowen

KEY WORDS

■

disclosure
metaperception
gender expectations
taboo topics
honesty

"Um, can we talk about something, Rich?"

Rich looked at his girlfriend with a puzzled look. *Uh, oh, what did I do now?* he thought to himself. "Sure—fire away."

Sarah started fidgeting with her hands and kept her eyes focused on her lap. She let out a deep sigh. "I think we need to talk again about sleeping together."

Looking very relieved that he wasn't in trouble, Rich smiled and reached for Sarah's hand. "Is that it? I thought we already talked about this and were comfortable with our decision."

Quickly looking up to meet his eye, Sarah responded, "Well, yes and no. I just think we should talk about it some more. I mean, I know we're both not virgins, but it is an important decision. Especially since I know this means more to me than it has before." She thought to herself, *You mean more to me than any other guy before. I don't want to ruin things. I want this to be special, meaningful. I've got to say it just right.*

There was a moment's pause as Rich tried to collect his thoughts and choose his words carefully. He thought, *OK, be careful here. She means a lot to me. I don't want to mess things up. This, this is definitely different from before.* "I thought that we decided that we were ready for this step. We're not seeing anyone else. We haven't since we started dating, and we want to make this commitment." He paused before going on. "I meant it when I said I love you, you know."

Right on his heels, Sarah interrupted, "I know. Me, too. But I just want to make sure. I want this to mean more than it has before. I don't want you to be in the same group as Mike or Jason." *You never were and never can be. How can I make sure you know that?*

"Sarah, I understand. I want this to happen. I care about you so much, but I also don't want to push you. We aren't going to have sex unless we are both comfortable with the decision."

"I am comfortable. I know it's right. I just wanted that extra reassurance from you." She smiled. *I love you,* she thought. "And one more thing. . . ." *How do I ask him about this?*

A smile broke across Rich's face again. "I know what you're thinking. You don't even have to say it. Of course we'll use some kind of protection. Condoms, I'm assuming? I know they're not 100 percent foolproof, but they've always worked well before."

Sarah's entire face relaxed. "How do you know me so well already? It's only been a few months."

Several months pass, and Sarah and Rich are still together . . .

"So, did everything go OK at the doctor's? What did she say?" a concerned Rich asked.

"Yeah, everything looks fine. They did the normal tests, but she said I look good," replied Sarah.

"And what about the pills?"

"Dr. Siegel said that she thinks it's a smart decision on our part and she wrote out a prescription for me for the birth control pills. We talked about the possible side effects, and we picked a brand that will hopefully work well with my body."

"Oh, good. And I promise you, I will pay for half of it each month. This is for both of us, so we don't have to worry as much anymore. How soon can you start using them?"

Sarah smiled. "As soon as I pick them up at the drugstore. But, Rich, don't you realize that they won't be effective for two or three months? I have to wait until the hormones take effect before the Pill is of any use."

"Oh." Rich looked a bit pensive then looked warmly at his girlfriend. "Then we only have to use the condoms for like another two months? That's not bad. We've been using them for five months anyway. Two more months won't kill us."

That night in her dorm, Sarah was watching TV with her two best friends. She had told them about her visit to her gynecologist and the decision to use the Pill for birth control.

Micki leaned over and gave Sarah a huge hug. Actually, tackled is more like it. "Congratulations, babe! You're gonna love it. All you have to do is pop a pill once a day—it's fantastic. Now you don't have to talk about anything or even plan ahead. You and Rich should have done this sooner."

Pushing Micki from on top of her, Sarah laughed. "Sooner? We only began having sex five months ago, and we had been together for a few months at that point. I don't regret it now; I mean, we're exclusive and totally committed. But I had no idea then that we'd still be together, for almost a year now." *I've never gotten along with someone as well as I do with Rich. It sounds dumb, but we complete each other. Yikes, I'm only 20 and I can't believe I'm thinking about the "M" word. But you never know. Trust like this only comes around once in awhile. And I LIKE talking to him; what does Micki mean about not having to talk?*

Sarah continued with Micki. "So you don't have any side effects?" She sounded a bit apprehensive.

With a huge laugh, Micki confidently told Sarah, "No way. It's one of the best things I ever did. My periods are shorter and more regular, plus I don't have to worry about carrying condoms all the time. Whatever happens, happens. What more could you ask for?"

Amanda, who had been unusually quiet, decided to pipe up. "Yeah, but that's not always the case, Mick. My sister was on the Pill—several different types—and had problems with all of them. Horrible mood swings, and she gained like 15 or 20 pounds. Why do you want to screw around with your body's chemistry like that?"

A shadow passed over Sarah's face. Micki turned Sarah to face her. "Don't listen to her. It's great. Trust me."

Amanda grumbled something under her breath and tried once more. "OK. Forget about the problems synthetic hormones can cause to your body. What about STDs?"

"What?" Sarah exclaimed. "Rich and I are monogamous. We don't sleep or even see anyone else."

"Sure. Now you don't. But you haven't been a virgin for awhile, hon. You've slept with how many guys?" Amanda asked.

In her own defense, Sarah sharply answered, "Only three before Rich. What are you implying? That I'm a diseased slut?"

"No, no, no, no! My god, no. I didn't mean that. I'm sorry. Just listen to me," Amanda replied. She took a deep breath and continued. Sarah looked upset, and Micki was watching them like a tennis match. "I'm just saying that because you have slept with other people there's a greater chance of STD infection. Remember my freshman year roommate? She got herpes from the first guy she slept with. And they were together for a while. Now she has a friend for life, with herpes. And Rich has had other partners too, right?"

Sarah nodded her head. "Two besides me."

"OK. So between the two of you, you've had five partners. I'm just saying that the Pill doesn't offer any kind of protection from STDs, including HIV. If you're going to do the Pill, I say either get tested for everything that's out there or keep using the condoms."

Sarah was quiet for awhile. "Thanks. I never thought about that before. I'll have to talk to Rich." *I'm glad I've got my girlfriends to check things out with. Wonder what Micki thinks about this STD thing? Isn't she worried?*

That night, as she was falling asleep, Sarah's mind was working on overdrive. *But I've always been so careful. I've never slept with anyone who was dirty or skeezy. And I always used condoms. Well, almost always. There were those few times. . . . But Rich ? I'm sure he said he always used condoms, too. Yeah, that's what I said, too. I didn't want him to think. . . . Could we have something?*

The next night, as Sarah and Rich were on their way home from dinner and studying, Rich asked Sarah, "Did I do something that I don't realize? What is it?" *Great. What did I do or not do? She hasn't been this quiet for months.* "Come on, talk to me. What's bothering you, hon?"

Sarah looked out the car window and sighed. "I've just had a lot on my mind."

"No way. You're not getting off that easily. Really, what's bothering you? Come on, you know you can say anything to me."

Yeah, but what will you say to this? "Promise you won't get mad? I just think we need to discuss some things." She started fidgeting with her hands, a sign that Rich knew meant it was serious.

"Sarah, you know I won't get mad, whatever it is. We agreed to not ignore important stuff. We can talk about anything. Let me park the car so I can pay attention." Rich pulled the car into the on-campus apartment parking lot and turned the motor off. He turned to Sarah who was still staring out the window. *This has got to be bad, and I don't even know what it is. She's much too serious.*

After a few minutes, Sarah turned around and looked at Rich. "I've just been thinking about going on the Pill and. . . ."

Rich cut in, "You don't want to do it? Why?"

"Rich, please don't interrupt. I've just been thinking about the side effects and implications. I still want to go on it, and hopefully I won't have any bad side effects. But what I'm concerned about is protection."

Rich relaxed a bit. "But the Pill has like a 99 percent effectiveness rating, doesn't it? We'll be protected."

Sarah paused. "That's not what I mean. I mean protection from STDs, even HIV. Before you say anything, let me explain it. I've slept with three other guys in my life. You've slept with two other women. Now, I know we both have said that we always used condoms, but Rich, come on. Even *we* don't always use them. There are always those times when you just don't want to stop. So there's the possibility that one of us could have gotten something."

They were both silent. *Shit. What did I do now?* she thought. *He probably thinks that I don't trust him. But Amanda was right. I'm just trying to protect the two of us.*

"Don't you trust me? Neither one of us has any problems. No symptoms of anything. Do you think that I've slept with dirty girls or something? Well, I haven't. You and I have the best relationship possible, or so I thought. We talk about EVERYTHING, and I love that, mostly. But this is out of line. I'm clean. I thought you were, too. Why can't you trust me? OK, wait, I can't talk any more about this now. I need to think before I begin saying things I don't mean. Let's go home now and talk about this tomorrow."

"Sure." Sarah got out of the car before Rich could see the tears in her eyes. "You don't have to walk me up. I'll see you tomorrow for lunch at 12:30, OK?"

"Sure. Tomorrow."

Rich walked into his apartment and headed straight for his room. He needed to calm down and think. *Damn, did I snap at her? I didn't mean that. She just put me on the defensive. But what am I supposed to think?* There was only one thing to do. He picked up the phone and dialed. "Hi. Shawn?"

A yawn greeted him. "Yeah? Rich?"

"Sorry to wake you. I need to talk. It's about Sarah and me."

The familiar voice sounded more awake. "Sure. Anything, anytime. You know that. What's the problem?"

Rich let out a deep breath and explained the situation to his best friend from high school. No matter what the problem was, especially when it came to women, Shawn could cut right to the chase and make everything seem so clear. *I don't know what I'd do without Shawn. Everyone needs a friend they can really talk to, someone who's not involved in the relationship.*

After Rich finished his lengthy explanation, Shawn paused for a moment. "Rich, what's the real problem here? Now try to keep your defenses down and listen. You both have had other sexual partners, right? Right. Don't even try to answer because I'm talking. You're listening. Now the two of you are being responsible with the whole pregnancy thing by going on the Pill. Good move. But she's right. One of you could have an STD."

Rich snapped back, "I've been damn careful, and you know it."

"Yeah, I know you've been careful. I also know nothing is 100 percent, so why not just have yourself and Sarah checked out to be sure?"

Rich replied, "I'd be embarrassed to go to a doctor for that."

"I'll grant you it's embarrassing, " Shawn agreed, "But it's less embarrassing than having an STD or giving one to a woman you care about. That's what happened to my friend Erik. He caught an STD and didn't know it for awhile. He found out only when his girlfriend developed symptoms. How do you think that made him feel?"

Rich felt himself beginning to see Shawn's point.

Shawn continued, "Don't you realize that she's trying to protect the two of you? And think of it this way: there's a greater risk for her. A lot of STDs don't show up in women until after they've done some considerable damage. Have you two talked about marriage at all?"

"Once or twice. I think we both think about it but are afraid to say anything, you know?"

"OK. So basically this is serious. More serious than anything else?" Shawn probed. "So then it's something worth protecting. Here's my advice. Let her go on the Pill. Keep using the condoms. And get tested so you both can know for sure. If you don't have anything, then you can just use the Pill. This is something you can't mess around with, bud."

Rich started nodding his head. "You're right. You're right. As always. Thanks a mil, Shawn. I'll talk to her tomorrow."

"No way. Not after what you said to her tonight. Go over there, apologize, and get this over with. You're one of the nice guys, Rich, but sometimes you act otherwise."

Rich responded with a laugh. "Thanks. Remember what I said about you being right? I take that back. Go to sleep. I'll call you later. I'm going over there now."

FOR FURTHER THOUGHT AND REFLECTION:

1. Based on what you've learned about their relationship, how would you characterize Rich and Sarah's relationship and their communication? What is likely to happen when Rich goes back to talk to Sarah? Model how the conversation might go.

2. Do you think Shawn is a man or a woman? Why?

3. How open and honest are Sarah, Amanda, and Micki with one other?

4. What concerns do people have when talking about or negotiating sexual limits? What other ways might couples have the initial discussion about safer sex? How do/can people talk about sex when they don't know each other very well?

5. How are Rich and Sarah's discussions shaped by Sarah's disclosures?

6. Are there questions you have about HIV/AIDS/STDs or contraception? What resources can you identify on your campus or in your area to answer these questions?

REFERENCES

Bowen, S. P., & Michal-Johnson, P. (1996). Being sexual in the shadow of AIDS. In J. T. Wood (Ed.), *Gendered Relationships* (pp. 177–196). Mountain View CA: Mayfield.

Cline, R. J. W., Johnson, S. J., & Freeman, K. E. (1992). Talk among sexual partners: Interpersonal communication for risk reduction or risk enhancement. *Health Communication, 4,* 39–56.

Metts, S., & Fitzpatrick, M. A. (1992). Thinking about safer sex: The risky business of "know your partner" advice. In T. Edgar, M. A. Fitzpatrick, & V. S. Freimuth (Eds.), *AIDS: A Communication Perspective* (pp. 1–19). Mahwah, NJ: Lawrence Erlbaum.

Reel, B. W., & Thompson, T. L. (1994). A test of the effectiveness of strategies for talking about AIDS and condom use. *Journal of Applied Communication Research, 22,* 127–140.

PART III

COMMUNICATION PROCESSES IN ESTABLISHED RELATIONSHIPS

THE EMBARRASSMENT OF PRIVATE DISCLOSURES

Newly Married Couples[1]

Sandra Petronio

KEY WORDS

■

privacy
disclosure
embarrassment
rules
boundaries
marital adjustment

On the way over to Matt's parents' home, Jennifer asked, "Matt, why do we go over so often?" "Because my mom likes to see us," said Matt.

"But she is always asking me personal questions about our marriage. Half the time I don't know what to say—I feel embarrassed. And, why does she *insist* that I call her Mom? It makes me feel funny," Jennifer confessed.

"You can say anything to her; she's easy to talk to," Matt said encouragingly. "I think she wants you to feel like you are a part of the family. That is why she told you to call her Mom." Matt got the feeling that Jennifer didn't appreciate his mother, and he was confused about Jennifer's complaints. After all, he felt so pleased when he saw them spending time together.

As Jennifer sat talking to her mother-in-law, Kelly, she realized how uncomfortable she felt. She wasn't used to talking with Kelly about personal things. When she stopped to think about it, she really didn't know Kelly. Jennifer wanted to get close to Matt's mother, but Kelly expected her to act as if they had known each other all their lives. Jennifer was torn. She wanted Kelly to like her, yet she felt that her privacy was always being invaded.

Figuring this out was going to be tough, and Matt was not going to be much help. Matt just didn't see the problem Jennifer was facing. The strangest part was that it was Matt's openness that attracted her. He had no trouble telling her all about his feelings. Now the difference in how they defined privacy was beginning to be a problem.

MATT'S POINT OF VIEW

Matt loved his family. He found Jennifer's reluctance to talk to his parents and brothers difficult to understand. "Jennifer, all my life I have been open with my family, especially my mom. Why can't you just let it go and tell them the things you feel?" "Because they are not *my* parents," Jennifer complained. "Well, they are now," Matt pointed out.

Matt worried about Jennifer from time to time. She seemed so closed sometimes—like the time they moved into the new house after they were married. The bathroom had a separate shower with a clear glass door and large window looking out to the rest of the bathroom. When they picked the house out, Jennifer never said a word about the shower.

Matt remembered the first time they were in the bathroom together getting ready for work. Jennifer was in the shower, and Matt came in to shave. Jennifer yelled at him not to stare at her through the glass. She acted embarrassed—as if it wasn't appropriate even to glance her way. *We're married, for goodness sake,* thought Matt. From then on, Jennifer waited until Matt was out of the way to take her shower. Matt found this behavior hard to understand.

Matt has two brothers, and his parents are still together after twenty-seven years. Matt's parents have always been very open with their children. The brothers all get along reasonably well. They have never expected too much privacy, even when they were living together in their parent's home. When they were growing up, his parents always expected the children to talk to them if they were facing problems. They also really liked "family talk time" around the dinner table. In fact, everyone was expected to be home for dinner and the television had to be turned off during the meal. Matt has fond memories of the way he talked with his family during these times. It wasn't just during dinnertime that the family confided. He remembers one incident that happened with his brother Jamie.

"Say, I really need to talk to everyone about something. Could we meet in the family room after dinner? I need your help," Jamie asked one evening. The family agreed. Matt recalls that they were all curious, wondering what Jamie had to say; but they knew that it was up to him to tell.

Although they were an open family, they had their rules about not pushing someone to talk. Jamie seemed edgy, as if he had the weight of the world on his shoulders. Matt was afraid of what Jamie might say. But he was his brother and would always be there for him, no matter what.

Jamie finally announced to the family that his girlfriend was pregnant. "My stomach dropped out," Matt told Jennifer after they were married. "I thought his life was ruined. Everyone was great, though. I was worried that Mom would go ballistic; but she was just concerned about Jamie, as well as his girlfriend." Matt's family talked it out. Jamie and his girlfriend, Alicia, wanted to keep the baby. He was just finishing college and was looking forward to being on his own and starting a career. Jamie and Alicia decided to get married.

"We always knew that we could come to our family with problems; but after the stuff with Jamie, I was really struck by how open our family really is with each other. Even my Mom and Dad come to us and tell us when they are having some problems. I like the fact that they include us kids in their lives," Matt confessed to Jennifer.

"It gives me a sense of security that I know other kids don't have with their parents. My brothers are always telling me things about their lives, too. I really can depend on my family to listen when I need to talk. That's why I can't see your reluctance to talk to them, Jennifer," Matt complained. "Well, Matt, my family is completely different from yours," stated Jennifer.

JENNIFER'S POINT OF VIEW

Jennifer grew up in a family that didn't believe in talking freely about problems. Her father, Lyle Johnson, always commented that discretion was a valuable lesson to learn in life. Likewise, Jennifer's mother, Kristen Johnson, believed that revealing too much to others would make a person vulnerable. She taught her kids that, even if you are talking to other family members, it is best to keep things to yourself and work them out on your own instead of bothering everyone else with your troubles. Working them out showed strength. Jennifer, her two sisters, and her brother all recognized the merit in keeping some things private, even among themselves.

Jennifer's family respected privacy. When the kids were growing up, they did not pry into each other's business. They did not touch personal property; nobody barged into another's bedroom without knocking; nobody borrowed clothes, bikes, or anything without asking first. They also did not often burden each other with problems.

Jennifer remembers learning a valuable lesson about privacy when she was young. Her mother always warned against going through anyone else's dresser drawers or closets. She especially cautioned the children not to touch a drawer in her bedroom. But, when Jennifer was a child, those warnings made her curious. On one particular afternoon she was home from school, not feeling well. She was supposed to stay in bed, but as a restless seven-year-old, she wandered around the house ending up in her mother's room. Her mother was down in the basement doing the laundry. That drawer captivated Jennifer. She wondered what was in there that would make her mother warn the children so many times never to touch it.

Noticing earlier that her mother had a lot of laundry to do, Jennifer turned toward that secret drawer. She quietly opened it and moved the papers around. "Hum," she thought, "only papers." Then she picked one up that looked kind of old. As she read the words on that paper, they did not make sense to her. She saw that it said "Birth Certificate" on the top. She remembered that she had seen her own birth certificate and it had her whole name on it—"Jennifer Johnson," with her mother's name, "Kristen Johnson," and her father's name, "Lyle Johnson." This paper looked like it was her brother's birth certificate. Yet she was not sure. It said "William," which was her brother's name. But the last name wasn't Johnson. Instead, it said "Cramer." Jennifer didn't know what to make of this discovery. She realized that she had been in the room a long time. She was afraid her mother would find her, so she stuffed the certificate back into the drawer and left the room quickly.

Even at Jennifer's age, her dilemma was clear. She could not ask her parents about the information she found because she knew how much they valued privacy. She was also worried that she would get into trouble for snooping in the dresser. She did not think it was okay to ask her brother. In fact, she wondered if he even knew about this at all. She kept the secret to herself. She wondered at times why her brother's certificate had a different name on it. Jennifer knew, though, that she could never find out from her family. She was reminded of this incident as she thought about Matt's family. They would have discussed this at some length. But she could not really understand how they felt so free to disclose.

Even talking to Matt about Kelly's request to call her "Mom" was hard for Jennifer. Usually she tried to work out a way to handle unpleasant situations like this one. Jennifer was trying to be more like Matt, but it was not easy. "Matt," Jennifer commented, "it is hard for me to tell you about this problem with your family. In my family, we don't complain to each other about things like this. We just try to cope ourselves. So please know that this is very troubling to me."

"Jennifer," said Matt, "I really don't understand the fuss."

INCIDENT WITH MATTHEW'S FAMILY

Why were she and Matt so opposite in the way they thought about privacy? Things kept coming up that made it clear Matt expected Jennifer to be very open. Part of her wanted to make Matt happy; part resisted.

One Sunday afternoon, Matt and Jennifer were visiting his family. As usual, when they finished dinner, the family joined in to clean up amid chatter about nothing and everything. Matt loved this time most when he visited—all the family doing something together and joining in on different conversations that were going simultaneously. They always were kidding and joking with each other. Matt was worried about whether Jennifer would fit into his family. She did not seem to welcome or understand that teasing was his family's way of loving each other. One family motto was "Why tease someone you hate—it is a waste of energy."

Jennifer liked a good laugh as much as anyone did. But, often Matt's family joshed about people she didn't know or made "inside jokes" that were never explained. Many times when they teased her she felt embarrassed. She really didn't like the teasing; it made her feel like they were picking on her. She felt that Matt's family was intentionally trying to embarrass her. This afternoon was especially bad for Jennifer. The whole family was at the parent's house, including Matt's two brothers, Jamie and Ed, Jamie's wife Alicia, and his parents Kelly and Michael. They all sat at the kitchen table talking.

Then Ed started to talk seriously about taking a job in another city. He wanted to change jobs so he could make more money. He also talked about a woman he was interested in and asked for some advice from his parents. Jennifer wondered why someone would seek advice so openly in front of so many people. When the conversation died down about Ed's decision, Kelly turned to Matt and asked how he and Jennifer were getting along. Matt quickly revealed that Jennifer was uncomfortable about having to call her Mom. Kelly asked Jennifer why she felt that way, but Jennifer wasn't sure how to respond. She had told Matt in confidence and thought that he would know not to tell his Mom. Kelly saved Jennifer further embarrassment by telling her not to worry, that she didn't have to call her Mom if she didn't want to. Nevertheless, Jennifer was concerned that Kelly was offended.

Just as she was thinking that she'd have to talk to Matt about disclosing like this and putting her in an awkward position with his family, Matt surprised her even more by confessing that he and Jennifer had another, more serious problem. He told his family that he and Jennifer disagreed about when to have children. Jennifer wanted to pursue a career. She had studied hard and finished her BA degree, and now she was hoping to go to law school. Matt wanted to have children right away. Jennifer knew Matt's family was hoping for grandchildren soon. She was upset that Matt raised this issue without letting her know he was going to tell his family.

Jennifer already felt miserable about Matt telling his mother that she did not want to call her "Mom." Now she wanted to scream and run away, maybe even be swallowed up by a big sink hole. He had told his *whole* family they were having this problem. Jennifer's ears began to ring; she thought that she might become sick on the spot and lose the fine dinner she just enjoyed.

How could he be so insensitive! she thought. *The nerve of him to humiliate me like that!* When Jennifer calmed down enough to hear how the family was responding, she couldn't take any more of it. Every member of the family had an opinion about their problem. Some of his brothers were mad at her for putting a career first. Jennifer tried to explain her feelings but the family was on Matt's side. She felt so humiliated that she ran from the room.

Matt and his family were not sure why Jennifer reacted this way. They were trying to help Matt and Jennifer with their problem. However, Jennifer seemed so unwilling to be helped.

"What's up with Jennifer?" asked Ed. "What is her problem?"

"I don't know exactly. I better go and talk to her," said Matt.

TIME FOR UNDERSTANDING

"Jennifer, why did you run out of the room?" asked Matt later. "My family was only trying to help us with this decision."

"You just don't get it do you, Matt," said Jennifer.

"No," Matt responded, "please help me understand."

"Our private times are not just yours alone to disclose," said Jennifer. "They belong to you *and* me now. Just like if you drew a circle or boundary around them and marked them as ours only. Because we are *both* responsible for our private life, I should have a say in *how* you talk about us, *when* you talk about us, and *with whom* you talk about us.

"You are comfortable with your family—you have known them all your life," pointed out Jennifer. "I, on the other hand, just met them. I don't know them at all; they are strangers to me. My family has rules about not disclosing private information, even to other family members," explained Jennifer. "For me, talking about personal matters even with you is difficult. I have been working on this, but I cannot deal with telling your whole family things that should be kept private between us."

"I still don't get it," said Matt.

"I think it is up to *us* to decide when we have children. Your family should not be involved in the discussion. Tonight I felt embarrassed and like a villain. It was more than I could tolerate. I don't think I can look at your family, never mind have dinner with them any more," said Jennifer.

From Jennifer's point of view, this information is something she and Matt are responsible for and should manage together. That means they have to talk about when it is okay to tell others, how much of their private information can be told to others, and when or where it is told. They need to agree on the way to disclose this information, and to determine when it is and is not okay to make the information public.

Matt is not used to this method of sharing. Although he is very open about his feelings and expects Jennifer to be open as well, jointly agreeing on when to disclose and when to keep something private is unfamiliar to him. His family rule was to be open; that was the rule he had always lived by. Now, he is expected to consult Jennifer before he tells anyone else something about the two of them. This was going to be tough. He didn't know why Jennifer just couldn't change the way she dealt with their problems. To do what Jennifer wanted, he was going to have to learn new ways of dealing with privacy. But, he wondered why he was the one who had to change.

Matt knew it was going to take a real effort on both parts to work this out in a way that would be comfortable for him and for Jennifer. He worried about how this would affect his relationship with his family and he wondered how Jennifer would ever get close to them if she would not open up to them. Nevertheless, he loved Jennifer and they had to figure something out. It was funny, because Matt never thought this kind of thing would be a problem. He was also sure that Jennifer never expected her way to dealing with privacy would be a problem either.

END NOTE

1. This case represents a composite of experiences found in open-ended questions about private disclosures by newly married couples. The names are fictional.

FOR FURTHER THOUGHT AND REFLECTION

1. Why is privacy so important in marriage? What is the relationship between privacy and disclosure? What is the difference between remaining private and lying?

2. Matt and Jennifer grew up with different privacy expectations. How are their expectations different, and how did this difference influence their new marriage?

3. Jennifer and Matt talk about privacy rules. What are the rules according to Communication Boundary Theory of private disclosures? How are the rules changing for this couple?

4. Why does Jennifer feel embarrassed? Would you? Why?

5. Many newly married couples do not talk about the expectations they have for privacy and disclosure. Privacy rules are often assumptions people make without confirming another's point of view. Beside the points raised in this case study, in what other way might Matt and Jennifer have privacy conflicts in the future?

REFERENCES

Cupach, W. R., & Metts, S. (1994). *Facework*. Thousand Oaks, CA: Sage.

Canary, D. J., Cupach, W. R., & Messman, S. J. (1995). *Relationship Conflict*. Thousand Oaks, CA: Sage.

N O T E S

Karpel, M. A. (1980). Family secrets: I. Conceptual and ethical issues in the relational context. II. Ethical and practical considerations in therapeutic management. *Family Process, 19,* 295–306.

Petronio, S. (1991). Communication Boundary Perspective: A model of managing the disclosure of private information between marital couples. *Communication Theory, 4,* 311–332.

Petronio, S., Olson, C., & Dollar, N. (1989). Privacy issues in relational embarrassment: Impact on relational quality and communication satisfaction. *Communication Research Reports, 6,* 216–225.

Shimanoff, S. B. (1987). Types of emotional disclosures and request compliance between spouses. *Communication Monographs, 54,* 85–100.

Steil, J. M. (1997). *Marital Equality.* Thousand Oaks, CA: Sage.

Vangelisti, A. L., & Caughlin, J. P. (1997). Revealing family secrets: The influence of topic, function, and relationships. *Journal of Social and Personal Relationships, 14,* 679–705.

CROSSING THE TRACKS OF FRIENDSHIP AND DATING

Negotiating Tensions Between Certainty–Uncertainty

Walter John Carl

KEY WORDS

■

ambiguity
certainty–uncertainty
contradiction
dialectical tensions
meta-communication
response strategies
relationship labels

NOTES

"Hello?" Anya moaned sleepily as she answered the phone.

"Hey, how are you?"

"Oh, hey, Robert. I was having this really strange dream. It was so weird."

"Really?"

"Whoa, it was really weird."

"Yeah, you said that already. Did I call too late?"

"Well, I was sleeping."

Anya and I cherish our late-night phone conversations. We met eight years ago when her family moved from out west. Because we lived two hours apart, we only saw each other once a week at church services, and phone calls became a common occurrence. Probably the best part of our relationship has been our deep, philosophical talks about life, love, and spirituality. Thinking ourselves mature for our ages—she 21, myself 24—we continually talk about the future. We each have an ideal picture of the perfect companion in our life, unsure if we should hold onto or let go of these fantasy images.

"Hey, I've been doing some thinking," Robert says. "Didn't you say a while ago that you felt as if we don't fit together sometimes?"

"Yeah," Anya agrees, pausing before continuing. "It's awkward between us at times."

"Exactly! I feel as if there is this tension that kind of underlies our relationship. I'm not sure if tension is the right word, maybe that's too strong."

"Hmm."

Robert continues, "At times we have a lot of fun and can relax around each other. And then there are other times when it just doesn't seem we're completely comfortable with each other."

"Yeah, I notice it occasionally. It seems we've been more serious and tense around each other, especially lately. For instance, last time we talked—we never talked about dating before like that. Maybe we're trying to force our relationship."

"I don't think we're forcing it," Robert says. "I thought both of us felt maybe we could make a great couple because we really enjoyed being around each other and doing stuff together."

"Yeah," Anya says. "But we've been so good together just as friends."

When Rob and I first met it was pretty clear that we were going to be close. Both of us were a part of this great circle of friends at church, and we had plenty of fun times together, even though we could only see each other for a short time every week. Our friendship, though, became much more tenuous when we started to hang around just each other.

We began to flirt with romance. Before he left for college, we fooled around a bit physically, mainly kissing and massaging, but never actually sleeping together or having sex. See, for us, there was a lot of ambiguity surrounding the physical and emotional aspects of sex. For so long, we'd said we were "just friends"; but then we started getting more physically involved, and that felt kind of weird. It's as if there's this friendship track and a dating track. We traveled so far down the friendship track together that it makes for some exciting, yet awkward, times when we try to change trains. It's almost as if we live between the two tracks, not fully on either one. We thought that if we're romantically involved we should be dating—at least that's what our church, family, and other friends said—but we also always thought of each other as great friends, almost soul-mates. This uncertainty about being friends versus a dating couple confuses us at times. But at least we can say it never made our relationship stale or too predictable!

"You know, Anya, I thought of something else. Remember when we were sort of flirting and teasing with each other in the basement?"

"Yeah."

"I went to kiss you. . . ."

"Yeah," Anya interrupts. "I wanted to say something about that. It was as if because we'd talked about dating earlier that day you felt that you were entitled to kiss me, that you had automatic permission or something."

"It wasn't about permission," Robert pleads. "In your life right now, you have these boundaries set up about not wanting to get involved with anyone physically."

"Yeah. . . ." Anya agrees.

"And I respect that. But then we can't explore anything about us being physical with each other. We have this certainty about our friendship, hanging out together and doing things. But we're not sure about anything romantic, or sexual. Maybe we don't have those feelings of attraction for each other because we don't allow ourselves to go there. I mean, I respect your decision about our boundaries, and I don't want you to think that by kissing your neck I was trying to disrespect you or your feelings. But how are we supposed to know if that romantic aspect of our relationship is there if we don't try it out? I don't know, . . . well, maybe we're just better off as great friends."

"Yeah, I know. But I did feel a little as if you weren't considering how I felt about getting involved physically. I'm glad you said something. Maybe I'm more traditional than you think. And maybe we're just different that way."

Rob and I grew up in the same church, and part of our attraction toward each other was that we believed in and wanted the same things out of life. It was a constant for us, something we didn't have to worry about. Now that's changed. We sometimes disagree with each other about religion, being involved in a church, and also about being sexual. And even though we maintain many wonderful things in common, we have never had to deal with having such divergent views in our relationship before.

"You know, Rob, regardless of some of our differences, one thing I've always liked about the two of us is that we can talk about our relationship so well. It's not that we have to always talk about *everything;* I mean, that can get old in itself. But it's nice to be so open and direct with each other. I just don't have that in my relationships with other guys so much. I guess that makes it that much more unique, and challenging, for us."

Robert reflects, "True, but in some ways we aren't unique. For example, I notice in the dating relationships I've had, there are two themes: the time in my life and the geography. Either the other person and I live a long distance from each other, or we're at different times in our lives in terms of the type of relationship we're looking for. The aspects just never seem to match up right. Like us—we live in different places, and we have differences in terms of what we're looking for."

"Yeah Rob, duh! Doesn't every relationship happen in a time and a place?"

Robert shoots back, "Yes, there are some observations or truths that are mundane and everyday, but they're still significant."

"Uh huh," laughing. "Nice try."

"But it *is* true!" Robert cries playfully, defending his position.

"You know, Rob, I just want to see you happy. We *are* different. You have needs that I can't fill for you and I have needs you can't fill for me. We're not the best people for each other in terms of dating."

"I can agree with that."

"OK, so we're not going to date!" Anya resolves.

"Good, I'm glad we've taken care of that!" Robert states matter-of-factly, with a little smile.

"You know, there's this other thing with us," Anya adds. "It's almost as if we have this competition about who likes the other more."

"Yeah, Anya, but I think that's more you than me."

"See, there you go again!"

"Me, no, not me. I'm just innocent. I don't flirt," mocking how Anya consistently denies flirting and attracting attention from other men. "You big flirt."

"I am not! You see, there were these guys on the street who came up to me . . ." scurrying to defend herself.

"Yeah, it's always the same story, it's just a different time and place, and the constant is you. See what I mean. Big flirt," Robert says playfully.

"You see how comfortable we are now that we said we're not going to date. We can be loose around each other, and it's not so serious."

"Yeah, I know," Robert concedes. "It's kind of nice."

"See, we can be comfortable again. And then that's exactly what makes us wonder why we're not a couple."

"Well, we were fine until you brought it up again," Robert teases. After a short pause, he continues, "You know, I don't think we've come to anything new here. I think we've been in this same place before, you know—about staying good friends and not dating. But maybe it's just more explicit now since we talked about it."

"Yeah, I guess."

Robert asks, "Can I be honest though?"

"You mean you were lying before?"

"No! No," Robert says. "I mean, I just don't know if you'll like what I'm going to say. It's just that, after all we've said, I noticed something about us. I think there are these two truths in this relationship."

"Yeah?" Anya queries. "What are they?"

"Well, truth one is that it's the best decision of our lives to stay friends, as we just 'agreed' to. And truth two is that it's the best decision of our lives to get more involved romantically and say we're dating. I mean, we like and want so many of the same things in life, even though we have our differences."

"Yeah!" They both laugh.

Robert continues, "And both are true and happening simultaneously. There's this tension between the two. The tension is always there, which is routine for us. We keep coming back to it. And it's always new because it takes us to a new place in our relationship. You know, I can honestly say I feel that we'll have this conversation again. And I'll be just as genuine and sincere about thinking it would be best for us to stay apart, at least romantically, and it would also be best for us to be together."

"It's like we can't have one without the other," Anya adds.

"I don't really understand it, but I'm certain that both are true. I think it makes our relationship special. Some people say the tension is what life is all about."

Anya responds, "It's as if it makes our relationship more attractive and yet more frustrating at the same time! So . . ."

"Sew buttons."

"So, where do we go from here?" Anya says to fill the uncomfortable gap in conversation, a rarity for them both.

After a brief pause, Robert says "I don't know, maybe we don't have to see friendship and romance as excluding each other. Maybe we can have both."

"Maybe, but do you think that would take away the tension?" Anya asks.

"I don't know about that," Robert smiles, "at least not with us. I mean, the tension will probably always be there. And at some level, we probably wouldn't want it to go away. The tension seems to be what keeps us moving along in our relationship."

"You know, Rob, I'm glad you woke me up. I really do want what is best for you and for me, too. What that is exactly, I'm not quite sure. But I do love you."

"I love you, too." Following a moment of silence, Robert states, "I guess it's getting kind of late, and we both need to work in the morning."

"Yeah, I guess so."

"Goodbye, Anya."

"Good night, Rob."

"Sweet dreams."

FOR FURTHER THOUGHT AND REFLECTION

1. How do Anya and Robert cope with the feeling that their relationship overlaps different categories of friends and dating or romantic partners? What role does this ambiguity play? How might relationship labels help or hinder the relationship in this case?

2. Where do you think labels for relationships come from? What functions do you think they serve in everyday relationships?

3. Make a list of the tensions, or relational dialectics, Robert and Anya face in their relationship. How might the tensions be related to one another? Do you think it is possible to feel—as Robert and Anya do— both certainty and uncertainty at the same time? Reflect on this theme of "both/and," and think about the extent to which it is present in your own romantic relationships with same-sex or cross-sex partners.

4. How do Robert and Anya deal with the tensions? How are their responses like or unlike those you might have experienced in your own relationships?

5. How do you think the fact that Robert and Anya talk about their relationship helps manage the tensions that keep it as one or another sort of relationship?

6. When Anya tells Robert "But I do love you" and Robert responds "I love you too," what type of love are they talking about? What is the boundary between "love like a friend" and "love like a lover" that is being negotiated through their talk?

REFERENCES

Baxter, L. A. (1988). In S. Duck (Ed.), A dialectical perspective on communication strategies in relationship development. *Handbook of personal relationships* (pp. 257–273). New York: Wiley.

Baxter, L. A., & Montgomery, B. M. (1996). *Relating: Dialogues and dialectics.* New York: Guilford.

Duck, S. (1994). *Meaningful relationships: Talking, sense, and relating.* Thousand Oaks, CA: Sage.

Rawlins, W. K. (1992). *Friendship matters: Communication, dialectics, and the life course.* New York: Aldine de Gruyter.

Werking, K. J. (1997). Cross-sex friendship research as ideological practice. *Handbook of personal relationships: Theory, research, and interventions* (2nd ed., pp. 391–410). Chichester, UK: Wiley.

DOUBLE JOBS

Balancing Relational, Family, Community, and Job Responsibilities

Jess K. Alberts, Michael K. Rabby

KEY WORDS

■

dialectical tension
compliance-gaining
self-disclosure
relational maintenance
conflict

Friday Evening

Ray glanced at his watch as he gathered up his books, papers to be graded, and lesson plans. Where had the time gone? It was already 5:15 P.M., and he needed to pick up his daughter Maria at her dance class by six. He couldn't be late. He didn't want to keep Miss Kelly waiting, and he simply couldn't bear the look of disappointment on Maria's face if he wasn't there to see the last run-through of the dance for her recital. Just as Ray was ready to make his escape, Principal Tanaka stuck his head in the classroom door.

"Hi Ray. I'm glad I caught you. I was wondering if you're planning to come to tomorrow afternoon's Halloween carnival. You can bring Maria and Chuy."

Ray had completely forgotten about the carnival, and his weekend was already so busy. Maria's dance recital was Saturday night, and his mother's birthday party was Sunday afternoon. And somehow he had to find time to grade a set of papers and prepare Monday's lessons. But how could he explain all of this to his boss? "Well, Tom, I might drop by for a few minutes. I'm not running a booth this year, and we have Maria's recital tomorrow night. We haven't been able to find a sitter, so we'll probably have Chuy with us. He's still a little young for the carnival."

Ray noticed Tom frown a little. "You know how important it is to the kids and their parents to see all of the teachers at school events. It shows that we care and that we support the community we work in; I would really appreciate it if you were there." Ray sighed quietly. "We'll stop by for a little while."

"Then I'll see you tomorrow," Tom said as he headed down the hallway.

Ray looked down at his watch again then hurried out of his classroom. If the traffic wasn't too heavy and he hit all of the traffic lights while they were green, he might make it in time to see the end of Maria's dance rehearsal.

Across town, Shawna was loading her briefcase and saying good-bye to her co-workers. She crowded into the elevator with about eight other employees from Geranios & Jones Investments. Everyone was in a good mood. It was finally Friday, the weather was beautiful, and the whole weekend stretched out before them. Shawna found herself buoyed by her colleagues' energy and happiness. She heard several people discussing where they should go for happy hour.

"Hey Shawna, do you want to go to Bill's Bar with us to have a quick drink while the traffic clears out a little?" someone in the back of the elevator called out. Shawna was tempted. She had just signed another investor and felt like celebrating a little. She knew Mrs. Ortiz wouldn't mind if she were a few minutes late picking up Chuy . . . but she couldn't. Chuy was still being breastfed so she couldn't drink anyway, and he would be getting hungry in just a few minutes. Plus, Ray and Maria would be waiting on her. "No, guys, not tonight. Thanks for asking, but I'll have to take a raincheck," she replied.

As they headed out of the elevator into the parking garage, Shawna's friend Ellie pleaded, "Aw, come on, Shawna. You never go out with us. Can't you stop by just for a little while? It will be fun."

Shawna smiled wistfully as she shook her head and climbed into her car. It *would* be fun, she thought. But it would be good to spend some time with Ray, Maria, and Chuy, too. They didn't have enough time together during the week, so she looked forward to the weekend. She knew they had Maria's dance recital and Ray's mom's birthday, but she hoped she would have time to relax a little, as well. And she needed to find time to make a few phone calls to prospective clients to set up some appointments. She couldn't be lazy if she hoped to be promoted to partner some day. With mixed feelings, Shawna pulled into traffic and drove toward home.

Friday Night

Ray stood looking at Chuy lying asleep in his crib. As he stood in the dark bedroom, Ray could hear Maria and Shawna in the next room deciding what to have for dinner. Maria was holding out for pizza while Shawna was suggesting roasted chicken, corn, and salad. They were all so tired; he just didn't know if he and Shawna had the energy to cook dinner tonight. Pizza sounded like a pretty good idea to him.

Later, as they ate the pizza, Shawna could tell that Maria was tired but excited. She kept leaping up from the table to demonstrate steps from her dance recital. They had trouble getting her to calm down and eat her dinner. Maria talked all through dinner then wanted to play a game. So the three of them played two games of Candyland, and then they began coaxing Maria toward bed. Ray and Shawna needed some time together, too. After brushing her teeth, reading two stories, and drinking a glass of water, Maria finally fell asleep.

While Shawna was putting Maria to bed, Ray had built a fire in the den. They sat next to each other on the couch and stared into the fire. During the week they were so busy taking care of the children, working, and trying to keep the house from turning into a disaster area. They simply didn't have enough time together. Since Chuy was born, Shawna had noticed how much harder it was for Ray and her to stay connected. She loved her husband, but sometimes she felt distant from him. They didn't have enough time to talk, and she often didn't know what was going on in his life or how he was feeling. She remembered with longing how Friday nights used to be. They would have a romantic dinner and talk for hours about their work and their hopes and dreams.

Ray broke into her reverie. "I guess we'd better make plans for this weekend. As you know, we have Maria's dance recital at 6 P.M. tomorrow, and Mom's birthday party is Sunday afternoon." Shawna looked up. "I know. And somehow we need to find time to get the laundry done and some groceries bought. I was really hoping to go to an aerobics class tomorrow morning, too."

Ray continued, "Yeah, and I just found out this afternoon that Tom expects me to show up at the Halloween carnival tomorrow afternoon. I should probably go for at least a couple of hours." Shawna was dismayed. How were they going to accomplish everything? She *had* to find time to make some phone calls tomorrow, and she was sure that Ray had school work he needed to do, as well.

"Ray, how are we going to get it all done? I need to work for a few hours, and I am sure that you do too. Do you really have to go to the carnival?" Ray sat quietly for a few minutes looking into the fire. "We can work it out. Why don't I take Maria with me to the carnival while Chuy is napping, and you can make your phone calls? Then we'll come back and pick you and Chuy up on the way to the recital."

"That should work. And if you will watch the kids while I exercise tomorrow morning, I will take them shopping while you work on your classes. Will a couple of hours be enough?" Shawna asked. Ray replied, "I think so. It is going to be a busy weekend, but I think we can fit it all in."

Shawna leaned back into Ray's arms; she was just getting comfortable when she heard Chuy crying. "I'd better go feed him again," she said, "but don't you go anywhere! I'll be right back, and we can pick up where we left off." But it took longer than she expected to get Chuy back to sleep, and when she returned to the den, she found Ray snoring gently in front of the fire.

Saturday Morning

Saturday morning was hectic as usual. Ray and Shawna fed the children and Shawna was heading out the door for her aerobics class when Maria started crying. She didn't want her mother to leave; she wanted Shawna to stay and help her practice for her recital. Shawna was torn. Maria seemed truly upset, but Shawna had been looking forward to her exercise class. She didn't just enjoy the class; she found that exercising helped her manage her stress, and it gave her some much needed time alone. She wondered if she would ever be able to do anything for herself again and not feel guilty.

Ray insisted that Shawna go to her aerobics class. He reassured Maria that he was a pretty good dancer himself and that Shawna could look over their efforts when she returned. After all, she was going to be gone for less than two hours. Finally Maria stopped crying, and Shawna hurried out the door before a new crisis could erupt.

While Shawna was gone, Ray picked up the kitchen, started a load of dishes and encouraged Maria as she practiced her dance steps. Chuy sat contentedly on the floor playing with a set of measuring cups and a wooden spoon. While Ray was applauding Maria's efforts, the phone rang. He wasn't surprised to hear his mother's voice on the phone. Since his father had died, his mother called all of her children more frequently. They chatted for a while about family and the party scheduled for the next day.

"Raymos," his mother said, "I was wondering if you could do me a favor." Ray replied, "Sure, Mom. Anything for you." Later he wished he hadn't agreed so quickly. "I noticed this morning that the yard is too long, and there are weeds in the flower bed. It won't look good for the party tomorrow. Could you come over and mow the lawn?" she asked. Ray didn't know what to say. How could he find time to do one more thing today?

"Mom, Shawna's gone right now, and I need to stay here with Maria and Chuy. Could Roberto do your lawn?" he asked hopefully. But, no, his brother Roberto was not home, and his mother needed him. "I tell you what I can do," Ray told her. "I'll call Mr. Martin to do your lawn for you. And if he's too busy, I'll bring the kids over, and you can visit with them while I do the lawn. Okay?" "Sure," she replied. "I guess if you're too busy Mr. Martin can do the lawn. But call me if you're coming over. I'd love to see my grandchildren."

Ray felt bad. He tried to help his mother out, and he knew she enjoyed seeing his children. But today was just too hectic already. He could only do so much. Just then he heard Shawna's car pull in the driveway, and Maria raced to the door to greet her mother.

Saturday Afternoon and Evening

Shawna waved as Ray and Maria left for the Halloween carnival. Maria had wanted to wear her lamb dance-recital costume to the carnival, but Shawna and Ray had finally convinced her to wear her Mulan outfit instead. Shawna wished she could go to the carnival, too; she would like to see all of the other teachers and Ray's students. Instead, she put Chuy in his walker and picked up the phone. She had a list of ten prospects to call. She just hoped that some of them were home.

An hour and a half later, Shawna had left four messages, was told "I'm not interested" three times, had one "no answer," and talked to one prospect who wanted a call-back the next week. Chuy was still sleeping, so she made her last phone call.

Bingo! Finally, someone wanted to meet to discuss her handling their financial investments. She was thrilled until she discovered they wanted to meet on Sunday afternoon. For a moment, Shawna didn't know what to do. She wanted to sign these new clients; it would be great for her career. But tomorrow afternoon was her mother-in-law's birthday party. What should she do? Finally, she said "I am free to meet at one o'clock, but I do have another engagement on Sunday afternoon. Is that time okay with you?" They agreed, and she hoped that Ray would understand.

Ray and Maria arrived home shortly after her phone call, and Shawna hurried to get Chuy ready for the recital. They had all climbed into the car when Ray remembered the camcorder. Shawna rushed inside. Maria was so excited she could hardly sit still. Ray crossed his fingers and hoped that she was not too excited to remember her dance.

Saturday Night

The recital was a success. All of the parents had a great time, and the children were so proud of themselves. After pictures were taken, cookies eaten, and the punch consumed, they finally went home. Maria was exhausted from the carnival and the recital, so she went to bed easily.

Ray and Shawna finally had a chance to sit down to eat dinner and talk. Ray told her about the carnival. His students were pleased to see him, and many of the parents came over to talk to him. He helped run the Haunted House for a while, and Maria had a good time, although Ray figured she had eaten too much candy. He told Shawna how much he had missed her and that he wished she could have come.

Shawna told him her good news—it looked like she might get another client. At first Ray was pleased. He was happy for her success, and he knew their lives would be a little easier once Shawna was made partner in her firm. But when she told him about her appointment, he became upset. "Shawna, you know Mom's birthday party is at three," he reminded her. "I know, I know. I promise I won't be late," she assured him.

"That's fine, but you also promised that you would take the kids grocery shopping tomorrow so I could work," Ray said. "Oh, no. I completely forgot!" Shawna cried. "I don't know what to do. I hate to call up new clients and cancel on them." Shawna knew Ray needed time to work, but wasn't her job just as important?

Ray found himself getting angry. "Well, you're just going to have to call. I need this time to work. You are always putting your career ahead of me and the children. This time you're going to have to change your plans."

Shawna could feel herself becoming defensive. She knew that Ray was right—she had promised. But she did *not* put her career first, and all of the work she did was *for* the family. Why couldn't he understand that? She replied, "I do not 'always' put my career ahead of the family. I work hard at my job and at being a wife and mother. You're just jealous of my success."

Now Ray found himself becoming very angry. "That is not true, and you know it." He was tired, he felt overwhelmed, and he could not believe the way Shawna was behaving. He hated to fight, but Shawna was completely wrong this time.

At the same time, Shawna realized that she wasn't being fair to Ray. He really did need her to be home on Sunday, and he had given her the time she needed to make her phone calls. So she said, "Ray, I'm sorry. You're right. I did promise. Sometimes I get too focused on making money and being successful. I'll call and reschedule the appointment for the morning. Please don't be angry. Why don't we just relax and watch a movie for the rest of the evening?"

At first Ray wasn't ready to stop arguing. He was still angry. It always took him longer to recover from an argument than it did Shawna. It took some effort, but he finally calmed down. As an act of conciliation, Shawna agreed to watch a film she knew Ray wanted to see. By the end of the evening, Ray wasn't angry at all, and he and Shawna had completely made up. Ray hated conflict, but he guessed it was inevitable.

Sunday Morning and Afternoon

After church, Shawna and Ray took the children out for lunch. Then it was home for a quick nap while Shawna wrapped presents and Ray began working on his lesson plans for the week. Shawna made a grocery list and woke Chuy and Maria up to take them with her to the grocery store.

At the grocery store, Maria tried to persuade her mother to buy sugar-coated cereal, soft drinks and cookies while Shawna tried to persuade her daughter of the value of fresh fruit, broccoli, and juice. As she waited in line to check out, Shawna was struck by the number of families grocery shopping on Sunday afternoon. When Shawna was a little girl, most grocery stores were closed on Sundays. Times certainly had changed. Now instead of taking their children on picnics or to the zoo on the weekend, many parents bought groceries and spent time on work they brought home from the office. It made her a little grumpy just to think of it. Shawna buckled her children into their safety seats, loaded the groceries into the trunk, and drove home thinking about Sundays at the zoo.

Sunday Evening and Night

Ray had finished his lessons plans before it was time to go to his mother's birthday party, but he was going to have to grade papers before he went to bed. He,

Shawna, and the children had really enjoyed the birthday party, and his mother loved the presents they had bought for her.

He liked being with his family. It was noisy but fun. All of his nieces and nephews played outside while he got a chance to visit with his brothers and sisters. He especially liked sitting around the kitchen table telling stories with his mother, his siblings, and their spouses. He hadn't seen his mother so happy since his father had died. He really wished he had more time to spend with her. He told himself that when the children were a little older and Shawna had made partner things would be different. They would have more time for his mother, and for each other.

Shawna tucked Chuy into his crib then went to Maria's room to hear her prayers. Ray was already in her room reading her a bedtime story. She stood at the door and watched them giggling together. These were among the best moments of the day. For a few minutes she would not think about work or the laundry that still needed to be done. She would just listen to her family and remember how lucky she was to have such a wonderful husband and healthy children. This time of their lives was really busy. She could hardly keep up with all of the responsibilities they had, but still she was fortunate. She looked forward to when they would have more time, fewer responsibilities. She didn't know when that time would come, but she held out hope.

Ray joined her in the doorway, and they listened to Maria say her prayers. There were still dishes to wash, laundry to do, and papers to grade. But, for a few moments, all of that could wait.

FOR FURTHER THOUGHT AND REFLECTION

1. A theoretical perspective known as *relational dialectics* suggests that people have to manage opposing tensions or pulls in opposite directions in their relationships. What dialectical tensions or pulls do Ray and Shawna have to manage in their relationship with each other? In their relationships with their children? In other relationships?

2. Communication researchers argue that self-disclosure—revealing to others information about yourself that they would not otherwise know—is essential in developing close relationships. How does Shawna feel about the level of self-disclosure in her marriage at this time? When do Shawna and Ray self-disclose to each other? Does it always have a positive effect on their feelings for each other?

3. Compliance-gaining, or persuasion, occurs whenever we try to convince someone to believe as we do or do as we would like. Who engages in compliance-gaining in this case study? In how many different contexts does compliance-gaining occur? How frequently do the various characters engage in compliance-gaining?

4. The study of relational maintenance focuses on the communication and behaviors people use to stay together. What do Shawna and Ray do in order to remain close as a couple? What external factors are in place that help keep them together as a couple?

5. As Ray suggests, conflict is inevitable. What do Ray and Shawna have conflict over? What negative communication behaviors do they engage in? What positive behaviors do they use? Why do you think it took Ray longer to recover from their argument?

REFERENCES

Alberts, J. K. (1988). An analysis of couples' conversational complaints. *Communication Monographs, 55*, 184–197.

Baxter, L. A. (1993). The social side of personal relationships: A dialectical perspective. In S. W. Duck (Ed.), *Social context and relationships* (pp. 139-165). Newbury Park, CA: Sage.

Jones, E., & Gallos, C. (1989). Spouses' impressions of rules for communication in public and private marital conflicts. *Journal of Marriage and Family, 51*, 957–967.

Markman, H., Stanley, S., & Blumberg, S. L. (1994). The differences between men and women in conflict. *Fighting for your marriage*. San Francisco, CA: Jossey Bass.

Murstein, B. I., & Adler, E. R.. (1995). Gender difference and power in self-disclosure in dating and married couples. *Personal Relationships, 2*, 199–209.

Ragsdale, J. D. (1996). Gender, satisfaction level, and the use of relational maintenance strategies in marriage. *Communication Monographs, 63*, 354–371.

Rosenfeld, L. B., & Bowen, G. L. (1991). Marital disclosure and marital satisfaction: Direct-effect versus interaction-effect models. *Western Journal of Speech Communication, 55*, 69–84.

YARD SALES AND YELLOW ROSES

Rituals in Enduring Relationships

Carol Bruess

KEY WORDS

■

relational culture
rituals
intimate play
private language

The back and forth motion of the porch swing was a comfort to Martha. It was two nights before their annual family yard sale, and she and her husband Jack sat swaying on their front porch swing. She enjoyed the repetitive motion and the memories it prompted of the little house she and Jack had rented while in graduate school.

It had been 26 years since they had gotten married and sat on a porch swing similar to the one that now greeted visitors to their home. Back when they were first married, they would regularly sit on the swing, late in the evening after a long day of studying. It was time to talk about the day and about their lives, and to dream out loud about their future together. In their current lives, Martha and Jack did a similar thing, often using "porch-swing time" as a moment to reflect on their past and their three children, and to dream about their future together.

Porch-swing time, Martha would tell you, had many important components. It was not just about talking and swinging—it was about popcorn. Martha and Jack have always shared a love of popcorn. When they were dating in college, they used to order the biggest bucket possible at the Buckman Theatre and wrestle each other for the last kernel. During that period of their lives, as they prepared for their weekly (sometimes daily) sitting, they would make a big panful on the green enamel antique stove their landlady had fortunately left for them in their tiny kitchen. Jack always insisted on a mountain of salt. With the popcorn, they sipped red wine from cheap wine glasses, a wedding gift from a distant family friend.

"Those were the days, weren't they, Jack?" Martha asked as they sat together this warm summer night on the swing on the porch of their beautiful two and one-half-story Victorian home. They used to talk about owning the very home they now owned. Jack knew Martha would begin talking about their lives together that evening; she often became reflective when one of their children called home with some important news. Their younger daughter Jill, now 23, had just called an hour earlier to share some news. She had been selected for a new job that would take her to Japan to teach. Jill had been the last of their children to move out, living with them for the last time two years ago when she was finishing college.

Jenny, 29, is their older daughter. She had received a degree in elementary education and now lives in Green Bay, Wisconsin, where she teaches 4th grade health and physical education. Their middle child, Chad—28—was just recently married and is living in a small town in Ohio with his wife. They hope to have many children.

Although Martha and Jack love their three children dearly, they both openly admit that this "empty nest" they are experiencing is heavenly. They have begun to do things that they hadn't since they were newlyweds. Weekday mornings, for instance, were very different without kids around. They were certainly more relaxed. When the children were in school, life always seemed too rushed in the morning. Martha would be running frantically about the house—packing lunches, filling bowls with Cheerios, making beds, and persuading the kids to brush their teeth. Jack usually left the house shortly after the kids awoke, avoiding most of the morning hustle. He and Martha rarely had a chance to even speak in the morning. Now Jack started each day by rising early and making fresh-ground coffee for Martha and himself. When she awoke a few hours later, they would sit in the early morning quiet together and read the daily news. Often after work, because they had no kids to meet at home, no soccer game to attend, and no dance recital to observe, they would meet for happy hour at a nearby bar, go grocery shopping, or do whatever they wanted. They enjoyed those daily outings and the freedoms that went with being parents without children (at home!). They even began to enjoy a daily phone-calling ritual. Sometime before 2:00 P.M., one or the other would call at work just to say "hi" or to find out the plans for after work. If the 2:00 P.M. time passed without a call, they both admitted feeling a little strange. "It's just kind of something we do now," Martha explained.

Jack nodded in agreement with Martha's earlier statement: "Those *were* the days. But it's hard to remember life before the children."

"Where has the time gone?" Martha pondered.

It was almost always that statement that jump-started the conversation where Jack and Martha relived some of their favorite memories. Tonight, as usual, they did so as they inched their way to the bottom of the popcorn bowl. Neither of them ever really said anything explicitly, but they each quietly knew of the symbolic comfort that the swing and the bowl of popcorn gave them: a reminder of where their lives began together. The trip down "memory lane" this evening was inspired by their annual yard sale, just two days away.

"Remember our yard sale the year we lived in Kettering?" Martha asked. "How could I forget?" Jack laughed. That year, which was the 19th year in a row they had an annual yard sale, they were robbed the night before the sale was to happen. The thieves took almost everything *except* what was to be sold at the yard sale. Still, yard sales are as much a part of Jack and Martha's marriage as their common last name and their three grown children. Even thieves couldn't dampen their enthusiasm for this annual tradition.

Each year since they were married, Martha began planning the spring yard sale in March. Despite the fact that some years there wasn't really much to sell, the whole process was routine and predictable. It went something like this:

"Hey Jack, I was thinking that this year we should sell the old twin beds downstairs at this spring's yard sale." (Each year it's a different household item she inserts; but each year Jack would argue it is precisely the same sentence.)

Jack almost always replies with the same moan: "Do we *really* need to have another garage sale this year?" Martha consistently ignores his insincere grumbling; she knows fully that when the day arrives, Jack gets more into selling silly, useless items for "Low, Low Prices at the Formans' today! . . . . Only 10 cents for this entire box! . . . . We'll throw that tire in for free. . . . Buy one tie and get a dog kennel for half price!" Jack loves yard-sale day, despite what he says. It's something they share, something that has a long history in their family.

Martha yelled down to the basement from the top of the stairs: "Hurry up, Jack. . . . What's taking you so long?" After a pause she thought to herself *Why ask?* She knew exactly what it was. He had run across some old letter or tool or photo and had been captivated by studying it again. Sure enough, as Martha rounded the corner of the basement storage room, she found Jack sitting cross-legged on the floor surrounded by college photos and yearbooks, and reading an essay exam he had written for Fr. Murray's Christian Ethics class. He had gotten an "A." "One of the few from your college days. . . ." Martha chided him. "I can pull out a few of yours if you'd like, Miss Martha Betcher." (Jack often used Martha's maiden name when he kidded her about issues of her "smarts.")

Martha was a very bright and talented woman, having earned a Ph.D. in history from the University of Michigan, where Jack also earned a Ph.D. in educational administration. She kind of liked it when Jack would call her Martha Betcher, because it was his subtle way of saying "I love everything about who you are." Martha had nicknames and special phrases she used privately for Jack, too. The most common was to call him "Fuzz." Its origins lay in a private, playful part of Martha and Jack's relationship. Earlier in their marriage, they had a game they routinely played called the "belly button game." They often revisit this game even now, after 26 years of marriage. Martha explains: "I would check Jack's belly button for fuzz on a daily basis at bedtime. It originated when I noticed some blanket fuzz in his belly button one day and thought it was funny. We both found it fun and teased often about the fuzz. If there wasn't any fuzz for a few days, Jack would put some in his belly button for me to find." None of their friends or family know of the belly button fuzz game, so the nickname "Fuzz" is used publicly while maintaining a symbolic, private meaning for Jack and Martha.

"This stuff is hilarious, Martha. Check out this photo of us with the kids on our annual trip to the beach," Jack pointed to the image of their three young children and to his and Martha's young faces and outdated hairdos. "Remember how we could spend 13 hours on the beach and not even know we'd been gone an hour? Those were such great times. And look at this one of us on our honeymoon. Why is *this* in this box of junk?" Jack quipped.

Martha always got irritated when Jack would complain about "disorganization" or describe things as "junked up." An ongoing argument in their marriage was about who was responsible for the daily tasks and managing the house—cleaning, organizing, purchasing household items, and getting rid of old stuff. Martha would say she is overburdened in this area of their marriage, while Jack would say that he "pitches in quite a bit."

For their entire marriage, except a few years when their three children were very young, both Martha and Jack worked full-time—she as a professor at the local university and he as a high school principal. Despite the fact that they both worked full-time, Martha—like most women in dual-career marriages—did and continues to do the lion's share of work in their home. So when Jack asks these kinds of "organization" questions, she often gets irritated. "It's in that box because you probably put it there, Mr. Organization, Mr. I-never-put-anything-away-that-would-take-some-time-and-effort! . . . Mr-I-don't-know-what-it . . ." It was then that Jack interrupted.

He wasn't in the mood to get in the same old argument they'd had at least a thousand times before. He was having such a great time looking at the old memories in the boxes. "Was that 93 cents or 96 cents?" he asked. Martha shot him a big smile.

This question "Was that 93 cents or 96 cents?" had a very important meaning in the history of their relationship. Jack's parents used to constantly correct one another and bicker over the most trivial details of everything. Once Jack and Martha watched them spend an entire evening arguing whether something had cost 93 cents or 96 cents. It was a question that had always worked for Martha and Jack over the years to help them gain perspective and laugh at themselves when they were on the verge of bickering or losing sight of important issues. It had helped them ward off many unnecessary conflicts in their marriage. And it worked again today.

Directing their attention back to the honeymoon photo Jack had uncovered, Martha observed: "We look so young! That was such a great time of. . . . Oh!" Martha interrupted herself. She had begun to dig further into the box of old stuff that she had thought was lost forever. She pulled out the ribbon from her wedding bouquet. It was yellow, just like the roses that made up her bouquet. "Ugh" said Jack. "That's looking kind of moldy." Martha agreed. But it was still a very special ribbon. For the past 26 years of their marriage, Jack had remembered how special those roses in that bouquet were to Martha. In fact, each year on their anniversary he sends her one yellow rose. One year Jack had driven to 16 flower stores before he was able to locate a yellow rose. But he finally was successful. Martha expects the rose every year on their anniversary, and she says "It reminds me, every year, how much we love each other. It's very sweet."

Martha's attention was quickly transferred from the roses to the box full of their kids' stuff. Without their knowledge, Martha has been collecting items that represent important times in their kids' lives. She glanced in the box labeled "Jill." "Remember the year that Jill had an absolute fit when she found her 'Wubby' doll in the garage-sale pile?" Jack's laugh echoed from inside another box he was exploring. "I thought she'd never get over the trauma. Worse yet, I thought she'd never speak to either of us again." When Jill was just a toddler, she had had a secure attraction to the doll she called "Wubby." No one is quite sure how the doll acquired such a name, but it was well-loved by Jill. Wubby gradually lost Jill's attention when she entered grade school. No one saw or even heard a word about Wubby for over 4 years. So, when Martha ran across Wubby in the bottom of a box of "junk" in the basement, she assumed it would be a perfect yard sale item. "The look on Jill's face when she walked into the garage that Saturday morning and saw Wubby with a 50 cent price tag stuck to her front!" Martha smiled heartily as she remembered the over-exaggerated lecture they received from their 9-year-old daughter about "respecting her property." "How could you do such a thing?!" Jill had cried. Before Martha could recount another word of the Wubby incident, Jack was on to another box.

"Look at this photo of me and 'the guys' at 456!" Jack had found another amazing photo, this one of him and his college roommates surrounded by pink flamingo lawn art in front of the house they rented at 456 Western Avenue. "What a great memory," Jack laughed. Since college, most of "the guys" had moved around the country. One of Jack's best friends was Tim, a kind of soulmate of Jack's through college. Tim and Jack had shared a room in that overcrowded, run-down house at 456 Western, where they had also shared many intimate thoughts. It was in that very room they shared that Tim "came out" to Jack, telling him that he was gay.

Until that time, almost no one in Tim's life knew his secret. He hadn't really known himself until he was about 14. It was one night during college that Tim had decided that he needed to start telling people, to let them know who he was. Jack helped Tim through some of the toughest days of his life—when he finally told his parents and family he was gay; when his parents wouldn't speak to him or visit for over a year during his last year of college; when he began to experience some unthinkable, hateful actions and words from students and others at the college; when he had seriously thought about dropping out of school. It was during that time, their last year of college, when Jack and Tim became the closest of friends.

"By the way," Jack said, interrupting his own wandering thoughts. "Tim called the other night and wants to add a few items to the yard sale. He said they have lots of junk to get rid of after the move." Martha was always pleased to add others' stuff to their yard sale. "The more the better" was Martha's yard-sale philosophy. "He's going to drop it off Friday night. He said it would all be priced."

Since Tim moved back to town, Jack had been very happy. Tim and his partner Bart had decided to move back to the city where Martha and Jack now lived and had raised their children. It was close to where Jack and Tim had gone to college. Tim and Bart were both exploring career transitions and had managed to land desirable jobs.

If Jack said it once, he had said a hundred times: "It's so great having Rock back in the city." (Rock was the nickname he had given Tim in college. He didn't use it very frequently anymore, but it still had a special place in their friendship. It represented Tim's inner strength, something Jack always admired. Tim called Jack "Doughboy" because of his pasty white skin and blonde hair. Tim was the only one who could call Jack that without offending him.) Martha agreed wholeheartedly about Tim being back in town. She really loved Tim, too, like a brother. They had all grown close over the years and shared a history that was missing from some of their other friendships.

So being back in town meant some interesting changes in their friendship. Before living so close, Jack and Tim maintained a weekly calling ritual. Throughout graduate school, even after Martha and Jack moved 600 miles away, Jack and Tim talked on the phone every Sunday night. If it wasn't on Sunday night, it was Monday for sure. Now they traded the calling for a monthly (sometimes weekly) dinner ritual, which most often included their partners, Martha and Bart. The four friends loved the evenings they spent together reuniting, reminiscing, and getting to know one another's families and interests. There was one particular Italian restaurant, Camillio's, they liked best. Every week for about a year, they met at this same restaurant for dinner and coffee. It was the perfect location. They could sit in the same booth all night long and chat and laugh. They often did. The conversation vacillated between serious and silly, light and significant. Most often, it was just "talk." But that's what they enjoyed.

After every one of these dinners, on the drive home, Martha and Jack had a similar conversation. "We're so lucky to have such wonderful friends." It didn't matter who said it, but it was almost always said. And both felt it deeply in their hearts. They couldn't remember what life was like before Tim came back into it.

Tim also had a way of making life interesting, for instance with lawn art (of the pink flamingo variety). About a year after Tim moved to town, Martha and Jack had returned from a two-week canoe trip to the boundary waters of Northern Minnesota to find about 100 pink flamingos stuck in their lawn. They laughed so hard they thought they'd never stop. "Tim!" Jack yelled into the phone. "We'll get you back! And paybacks are hell!"

So it began. Every so often, when not expected, the plastic pink flamingos on wire spokes would show up in either Tim or Jack's yard. Sometimes they dangled from the roof. They looked particularly funny on Tim's snow-covered lawn last February. As the prank developed, local friends and neighbors joined in. They borrowed the collection of pink plastic flamingos for placement in a particular yard and they added their own plastic items (twirling plastic daisies, the rear-view of a female gardener, and bright green bugs with waving wings) to create a veritable and ever-growing plastic farm.

When the prank began, Tim and Jack were the talk of the city. They even got a photo of their lawn art on the front page of the Variety section of the local newspaper. The caption read: "Friendship prank turns pink."

Looking back at the college photo, Jack laughed: "Who would have thought that the flamingos in this picture would have any significance to us today!" They laughed. "Maybe we should sell them at the yard sale tomorrow?" Martha half-seriously questioned. "You're nuts, Marty. Those things will be around until I die. Or if Tim goes first, we can use them at his funeral!" Martha shot Jack a disgusted look. She didn't think it was funny to joke about death.

"We'd better stop this puttering and start moving this stuff up to the garage" Martha said, and she began to move an old rusty fan and a box of her mother's old linens toward the steps. "It's already 5 o'clock, and we don't even have prices on things yet." Jack agreed, although he felt kind of glued to the floor. "I'm hungry, Marty. What do ya say we go over and grab a burger at the counter first, and then we'll come back to finish the tagging?"

Martha couldn't resist an invitation to "the counter." It was a little malt shop just down the street from their house. Since the kids had moved out, a burger had become a frequent Friday evening meal for Jack and Martha. The place reminded Martha of the Woolworth's counter where she and her dad used to go on Saturday afternoons. She and Jack liked it also because it reminded them of a little soda fountain where they went when they first dated. (Sodas were a nickel then! Lime was Martha's favorite flavor, and Jack liked Cherry Coke.) Suppressing her urge to keep working on the yard sale now, she said "Great idea."

Martha could almost taste the burgers they used to eat as the porch swing slowly rocked her and Jack back and forth, back and forth. She loved these "porch-swing" moments more and more as the years drifted by, as their children grew older, and as their relationship grew stronger and stronger. It wasn't that either of them thought they hadn't had a strong relationship from the start, but each session of remembering that they shared on the swing—of memories, of yard sales, of nicknames, of shared friendships, of photos, of stories, and of burgers and popcorn—further clarified the way their years together gave them a history that no one in the world could replace.

Bzzzzzzzzzzz. "Ouch" snapped Jack. "I hate these darn mosquitoes. They're out in force this summer. I'm heading in the house." Bzzzzzz. "Meet you inside," Martha responded as she gathered the empty popcorn bowl and the two glasses with tiny red rings at the bottom where the last drops of wine had settled. She glanced back with a peaceful smile as the swing slowly came to a halt.

END NOTE

1. This case represents a composite of experiences from couples participating in a research study conducted by the author and her co-researcher, Dr. Judy Pearson. The names and identifying details have been changed.

FOR FURTHER THOUGHT AND REFLECTION

1. Rituals are defined as recurring interaction patterns that have importance to the people in a relationship. What kinds of rituals, mundane or formal, were you able to identify in the relationships in this case study? Describe what Jack and Martha's relationship would be like if *none* of these rituals existed. Would it be any different? Explain.

2. Daily, mundane rituals serve a multitude of functions. What functions did they serve for Martha and Jack? For Jack and Tim? As you answer, think about the last part of the question in #1. (Would these relationships be any different without rituals?)

3. Researchers have found that developing nicknames or a "private language" serves a number of functions in our personal relationships. What private language did Martha and Jack use? What function did you believe it served in the relationships in this case? List some examples of nicknames or other private codes you use in your family or friendships. What functions do they serve in your relationships?

4. Do you have rituals in your friendships or personal relationships? In your family? Make a log of the rituals in one of these relationships. After looking at the list, identify how they are important to you and to your relationship. How did they develop?

5. Researchers have shown that people in a relationship often develop their own "relationship culture," the subjective reality that participants in a relationship create. It often weaves partners together, not in the activities or interactions themselves, but in the meanings partners assign to these activities and interactions. How would you describe Martha and Jack's relationship culture to someone who had not read this case? How would you describe the relational culture of one of your own relationships? Compare the two.

6. Although some rituals remain stable, many rituals change (even disappear) over the life of a relationship. After reading the case, identify and reflect on the way certain rituals faded and new rituals emerged, and on the way certain rituals remained relatively unchanged over the life of the relationships. Identify the circumstances that seem to cause ritual changes. Do you see any difference in the kinds of rituals that faded or changed, and those that remained about the same? Reflect on the rituals in your own family or personal relationships. Think of rituals that have changed over time, rituals that have remained relatively the same over time, and rituals that had only a short life in your relationship(s). Were the circumstances similar or different to those of Martha, Jack, and their friends?

REFERENCES

Braithwaite, D. O., Baxter, L. A., & Harper, A. (1998). The role of rituals in the management of dialectical tension of "old" and "new" in blended families. *Communication Studies, 48,* 101–120.

Bruess C., & Pearson, J. (1997). Interpersonal rituals in marriage and adult friendship. *Communication Monographs, 64,* 25–46.

Cheal, D. (1988). The ritualization of family ties. *American Behavioral Scientist, 31,* 632–643.

Schvaneveldt, J., & Lee, T. (1983). The emergence and practice of ritual in the American family. *Family Perspectives, 17,* 137–143.

Wolin, S. J., & Bennett, L. A. (1984). Family Rituals. *Family Process, 23,* 401–420.

CAN WE TALK ABOUT US?

Talking about the Relationship

Linda K. Acitelli

KEY WORDS

■

marriage
relationship awareness
relationship beliefs
relationship talk
gender-roles

Six weeks after the wedding, Stevie was sitting at home alone, already thinking they'd made a mistake. Stevie and Glen had each been married before. They were both in their mid-30s and both a little gun-shy about taking that big step again. Stevie's first marriage had been to a man who would never talk about their relationship, He told Stevie that whenever she said, "We need to talk about our relationship," it made his boots squeak. Glen said his first wife was so hostile that she made a sport out of humiliating him in public. Anyone could see why it made sense not to rush into another marriage. So Stevie and Glen had been a couple for three years before getting married; they were engaged for two years, making sure they really knew one another. They talked about everything. They talked about airing problems right away so they wouldn't build up over time; they talked about having an egalitarian relationship where they had to negotiate the rules—no assumed gender roles or responsibilities, such as she cooks dinner and he takes out the garbage, or she pays more attention to their relationship and he pays more attention to himself.

Stevie was an architect and Glen was a computer-game designer; each valued being a separate individual as well as being a couple. They joked about how their names confused people about who was the man and who was the woman. They secretly enjoyed being the couple everyone saw as different and special. Glen and Stevie realized that others looked up to them as an ideal relationship. They lived together for a year before the wedding. That way everything would work smoothly and there wouldn't be any surprises, right? Wrong. It wasn't that Glen was acting as if there was no relationship, he was acting as if she wasn't even there! What had happened?

Stevie was so worried she started thinking back to see if there were any signs that might have foretold such a disappointing turn of events. All she could remember were the good things. Glen was the first one to start talking about the relationship. That's what impressed Stevie right away. She remembered the cool summer evening she and Glen were having dinner on the outdoor patio of Bicycle Jim's, a local hangout. They had met only a month before, but he said, "I'm hoping we can consider this relationship to be a monogamous one." Whoa, Stevie thought, a man who talks about the relationship!? Even initiates it? Well, she knew she was attracted to him, that's for sure. He had an interesting job, was a rock-climber for fun, went swimming for exercise, was funny, smart, and good-looking, and they could talk on and on about everything, even the relationship! So why not? Stevie was so flabbergasted, all she could say was, "I'd like that; sounds good to me."

Was that a mistake? Did they rush into things too quickly? Take a deep breath, Stevie told herself; of course they didn't rush into anything. That was why they waited three years before they got married! So why was he not coming home for dinner, and not letting her know? Why did he now start making plans that didn't include her? Why were they together less now than before they got married? And it was only six weeks ago that they took their vows! Glen loved being with her; at least that's what he told her. Stevie recalled one day, about a year after they'd started seeing each other—when they were driving along the highway with Glen on the way to the big outlet mall. They stopped to take pictures of ducks on a pond. The mama duck was leading the way, and three yellow ducklings were lined up behind her. Out of the blue, Glen said, "I really love the way we are together. I love this relationship." Now most men tell you they love you, she thought, and yes, he had done that many times; but this is different. He is telling me how good our relationship is. It was thrilling. So it's not like I ever forced him to talk about it, or that we had to talk about it only when there was a problem, and maybe he even talked about it more than I did. Could that be it? That I didn't talk about it enough? A little voice inside of her said, "Get real."

In the meantime, Glen is in his office, feeling overwhelmed with work. He's thinking that he has just got one more idea that he needs to promote, one more job to finish, and then he'll start getting home earlier, but there is such pressure now. Not to mention the after-work social obligations of the business. And there are all these rock-climbing opportunities that have just come up. He thinks it's a good thing that Stevie isn't the clingy type and doesn't smother him. Thank goodness she has her own career and even makes it known that she wants her independence, too. Glen did notice she seemed a bit tense lately, but he wasn't too worried about it. Being an architect is a high pressure job, too, so she probably felt pressured at work. Besides, Glen thinks, I know the rules. If something is wrong with the relationship, she'll let me know right away.

Now if I could only find the right angle for the story of this game, one that would hook people. I know I've got a real winner here, if only I could figure out a way to get the Princess out of the dungeon without making it look as though she needs the Prince to save her. That's old hat. Hmm. That's it! The Princess needs to be given more stuff to do. Maybe more control over her own fate. Women and girls don't buy computer games as much as men and boys do, but we must tap into that market. I can't imagine they'd want computer games all about male warriors who end up saving everybody, including the women—if there are any women in the first place. But what do they want? Should the Princess even be in the dungeon in the first place? Should the Prince be in the dungeon and the Princess be the one to save him? Nah, I don't want to make it so obvious that the viewers say, "How clever, a role-reversal," and then yawn and go on to the next game. Otherwise it would be the same old story in reverse. Nothing new about the plot, just the characters playing different parts. This has got to have a new storyline altogether. A new creation. Like Stevie says, we need to create what we want our relationship to be, I can have these characters create their storyline together! Hey, maybe that's it! Now if only I could figure out the best way to start.

Stevie is pacing the floor. She has decided that she has been patient for too long. It's time to talk about this problem. She knows they agreed that independence was something they both needed, but not to the exclusion of each other. Besides, it wasn't the fact of Glen's not being at home that hurt, it was that he was being inconsiderate by not letting her know his plans ahead of time, as if she had nothing else in her life that could be planned when he wasn't around. He was always considerate before they got married. Now all of a sudden he seems like another person. How could she be so blind?

Stevie heard the garage door open, and she froze. How should I start? What should I say first? I can't believe I'm even worrying about all this considering how much we've been able to talk about in the past! So as soon as Glen walked in the door, she blurted out, "We've got to talk about our relationship!" Taken aback, Glen said hesitantly, "Okay. . . . really? I mean, um, I didn't know there was a problem." "Well, there is," Stevie said forcefully, surprising herself with her own anger. Now Glen looked really worried and confused. He wasn't sure what was happening, but something in the back of his mind told him he was angry, too. Stevie seemed to know so much more about relationships than he did, and she made sense, too. But sometimes it felt like he just let her decide how the relationship was going to be, even when it came to rearranging furniture in what used to be his home. Whatever was bugging her now, he was going to stand firm and not let her rule the roost like his first wife did.

So they sat down on the old couch in the living room that was crowded with all kinds of things from his and her past lives. It seemed a bit too crowded, in fact, because it was meant only to be Glen's place as a single guy. Then Stevie moved in and brought all her things, and it didn't seem the same any more. Stevie wondered if Glen could be thinking he lost his freedom. After being with her for three years, why would it hit him now?

Glen said, "Well, what is it?" "I don't know where to start, so I hope you can be patient with me," Stevie replied. "Okay, I'll listen," said Glen. Stevie began to pour out thoughts that at first didn't make any sense. She talked about his not coming home, her feeling more alone than when she lived alone, her feeling that he's changed, until finally she came to what seemed like a conclusion. "I feel like you don't want to be married," she said. "What!?" Glen asked incredulously. "Why do you say that?"

"Well, ever since we got married you have more and more things to do and seem to find more and more excuses to stay out of the house and shut me out of your life."

"But you always said we should have our separate identities, didn't you?"

"Yes, but not to the point where you pretend the other person doesn't exist!"

"What do you mean, doesn't exist? We see each other every night when I get home."

"Yeah, but that's only when it's convenient for you. I'm not even talking about the amount of time we spend together, even though that might be part of it. I'm talking about the way you seem to be doing things without even letting me know first. I don't want to be some ball and chain. And although we both enjoy our freedom during the day, I at least want to know when you're going to be home so I know whether I can expect to eat a meal with you or spend some time with you in the evening. Otherwise, I worry that something bad must have happened, because you always used to be so considerate in letting me know what you were doing. Something has changed, and we need to figure out what it is."

"Well, I have been really pressured at work lately," Glen said, "but I bet that excuse won't satisfy you, will it? It doesn't feel right to me either. . . . Hmmm. . . . I guess, I feel stifled somehow."

"Stifled?" asked Stevie, with obvious irritation in her voice. "What have I done to stifle you? We've been together three years, and now you feel stifled? What have I done? What's changed?"

"I, uh, well, let's see. More people are making demands on my time now, but, well, I guess that doesn't account for not calling you, does it? I admit there is something going on, but I can't put my finger on it. I am feeling some resentment or something. Maybe I feel like you always have the right words to say when I don't, or that you seem to have some kind of radar that zeroes in on any little tension in the relationship. Maybe I resent that." Glen thought he might be close, but he still didn't feel that he had it right yet.

"It's weird," said Stevie, "There is nothing you've said about me that is any different from the way I've been all along. You even said you liked the fact that we could talk about things as they came up, and that it felt freer to have no hidden baggage of tension dragging you down. The only thing I can see that is different from six weeks ago is that we got married."

Then Glen's face turned red. His thoughts felt jumbled. Was that it? It couldn't be. They had been in a committed relationship for quite some time. So how could that piece of paper change things so much that she thinks I'm a different person, that I don't want to be married to her? Stevie saw the look on Glen's face. "That's it, isn't it?" she asked. "There's something about marriage."

They sat in silence for a while, a bit stunned. Here they were, the "perfect" couple feeling bad about marriage! "You know," Glen said, "I bet there's something about marriage that none of us can ever really escape." "What's that?" asked Stevie. "It is such an ingrained part of our culture that everyone has some idea about what it is supposed to mean," said Glen. "Now I'm not sure if that has anything to do with our problem, but I do know that we can't help but think we know what marriage means."

"Yes, that's it!" Stevie said, excitedly. "If we each assume we know what it means, we don't even talk to each other about it. We think we know what the other thinks it means. We assume we have the same ideas about marriage because everybody does! Then that unspoken knowledge makes us feel as if we know what the other is supposed to do. Oh, man, I can't believe we have new things to talk about after all this time. I can't believe I am asking you this for the first time. What does being married mean to you?"

They looked at one another half-laughing, half-crying, and hugged one another until they realized that hugging wasn't the answer (although it sure felt good!). Finally, and reluctantly, Glen said. "I thought marriage meant I had no freedom to be who I wanted to be. I thought that, in spite of the fact that my relationship with you had shown me that I could be part of a couple and an individual, too." "So, instead of behaving as always," Stevie said, "do you think that being married meant you had to prove you were free, regardless of how you felt about us?"

"I guess so," said Glen. "Maybe that is why I felt so pressured but didn't know why. I hadn't thought about how much power the institution of marriage would have to negate all that we had built up and put us into a trap that I'm sure lots of couples get into. I can't believe we did this. I thought we had the perfect relationship." Glen laughed at how silly the word "perfect" sounded, even to him.

"But it's really not the institution of marriage, is it? I mean, the institution isn't making us do anything. It's our own 'idea' of marriage. Maybe we should think about this—just because everyone else has an idea of what marriage is supposed to be, that doesn't mean we have to have the same idea, does it? First off, we need to find out what each of us thinks marriage means. Then we can come to some agreement about what it will mean for us, okay?" Stevie asked, knowing that this would work out, just like all of the other issues they had worked on before. Besides, Glen loved solving problems and creating new storylines. Here was one they could create together.

"Well, sure, but I have to say something else first. I am not the only one who seems to have changed," said Glen, surprising the heck out of Stevie. "What, what do you mean?" she asked. He said, "What about that rule we agreed upon, that we would bring up stuff as it comes up, no matter how big or small? No baggage, remember? I was amazed at how good you were at that even though you admitted it frightened you. So what happened this time? Why did it take weeks?"

Now Stevie turned red, thinking to herself, I've got my own lessons to learn. Relationship problems always involve at least two people, not just one. "Okay, you caught me off guard here. . . . Why didn't I speak up right away? . . . Well, we had just gotten married, and, well, um, I didn't want to rock the boat." Glen looked at her and said, "You've got to admit that that's a lame excuse, given all we've just talked about." "Okay take it easy on me, I'm still trying to figure it out myself," Stevie said, holding her hands up as if to protect herself. Perhaps she needed to ask herself the same question, what did marriage mean to her? The only marriages she'd seen up close (including her parents') had ended in divorce. All of a sudden she found herself crying. " I guess I was worried that you'd leave me if I started complaining."

Glen put his arm around her, realizing they were treading on vulnerable territory, and he said, "Now why would I do that? Think back in the three years we've known each other and how many times you brought up things that bothered you. How did I handle those times?" "You were amazing," she said. "You'd listen and keep asking me to tell you more about it, even if it was only a little thing such as how the dishes were put in the dishwasher, or how you shrunk my sweater in the dryer. You'd ask if there was anything else, and then we'd work on it, and I always felt better afterwards." So now the power of the idea of marriage hit her, too. "Wow, I can't believe I let my childhood idea of marriage take over like that after all we had done to make our relationship unique. My problem is that I don't really have any models of good marriages, so I really only know what marriage isn't supposed to be. Perhaps that is why I am so eager for us to create our own marriage based on what we want. I guess we still have some things to talk about. It never ends, does it?"

"Just as it should be," Glen smiled.

FOR FURTHER THOUGHT AND REFLECTION

1. While Glen's idea of marriage made him want to flee, Stevie's idea made her believe that all men wanted to escape. As a result, their behaviors did not correspond to their feelings about each other, but instead reflected their unspoken fears and beliefs about being married. How might various contextual factors (culture, ethnicity, religion, income, social network, family, children, etc.) modify this story?

2. Is talking about the relationship only valuable when it is intended to solve a problem? What about when things are going well? When might it be detrimental to talk about the relationship?

3. What is the difference between saying *I love you* and saying *I love the relationship?* What implications does this distinction have for the consequences of talking about the relationship? How might this distinction become important in various problem-solving or conflict situations?

4. Are there gender differences in how much people engage in and value talking about the relationship? Why, or why not?

5. What role does thinking about the relationship have on the relationship? What would it be like if Glen and Stevie had all of these thoughts and never expressed them?

6. How can Glen and Stevie be this calm? Are they for real? Do people really talk this way about relationships? Or does this seem to be an intellectual exercise that happens only in textbooks?

7. How would the value and function of thinking and talking about relationships differ in other types of relationships (e.g., parent-child, sibling, friends, same-sex couples, co-workers)?

REFERENCES

Acitelli, L. K. (1988). When spouses talk to each other about their relationship. *Journal of Social and Personal Relationships, 5,* 185–199.

Acitelli, L. K. (1992). Gender differences in relationship awareness and marital satisfaction among young married couples. *Personality and Social Psychology Bulletin, 18* (1), 102–110.

Acitelli, L. K. (1993). You, me, and us: Perspectives on relationship awareness. In S. W. Duck (Ed.), *Understanding relationship processes 1: Individuals and relationships* (pp. 144–174). London: Sage Publications.

Acitelli, L. K., & Young, A.M. (1996). Gender and thought in relationships. In G. Fletcher and J. Fitness, *Knowledge structures and interactions in close relationships: A social psychological approach* (pp. 147–168). Mahwah, NJ: Lawrence Erlbaum.

Baxter L. A., & Wilmot, W. W. (1984). *'Secret tests'*: Social strategies for acquiring information about the state of the relationship. *Human Communication Research, 11,* 171–202.

Bernal & Baker (1979). Toward a metacommunicational framework of couple interaction. *Family Process, 18,* 293–302.

Knee, C. R. (1998). Implicit theories of relationships: Assessment and prediction of romantic relationship initiation, coping, and longevity. *Journal of Personality and Social Psychology, 74,* 360–370.

Wood, J. T. (2000). *Relational Communication: Continuity and Change in Personal Relationships.* 2nd ed. Belmont, CA; Wadsworth.

Wood, J. T., & Inman, C. (1993). In a different mode: Masculine styles of communicating closeness. *Journal of Applied Communication Research, 21,* 279–295.

SHALLOW TALK AND SEPARATE SPACES

Dealing with Relational Conflict

Sandra Metts

KEY WORDS

■

latent conflict
conflict strategies
rules for managing conflict

N O T E S

arah was frustrated as she drove home from work. Always too much to do and never enough time. She was working way too much and she knew it. But she didn't know how to say no when asked to do more. She was still not finished with the midyear report and, to make matters worse, tomorrow night she was facing an exam in the course she was taking for her Master's degree. She was tired and hungry and hoped that Russell had started dinner. She turned the corner onto the driveway and pushed the automatic opener for the garage door. By the time it was halfway up she saw that Russell's car was not there. "Well, I guess Russell won't be helping with dinner again," she muttered half out loud. "Why is everything my responsibility?"

As Sarah entered the kitchen she saw the message light flashing on the answering machine. "Hi, Hon," said Russell's voice. "It's just me. Wanted to let you know that I will be a little late getting home. Hope your day was good. See you soon."

Sarah felt her mood darken even more. It was already 5:30, and she didn't feel like cooking or waiting to eat. But she looked through the refrigerator until she found the makings of a salad, leftover pork chops, and some aging potatoes. She washed the breakfast dishes in the sink as she prepared dinner. "Geez, he can't even do the dishes when he knows that I am under such pressure," she thought to herself. "Tonight after dinner I am going to ask him to give me a little help around the house, at least until the end of the semester—maybe take care of dinner and dishes during the week and laundry on Saturday."

A short time later Russell pulled into the garage. Sarah was putting dinner on the table when he came into the kitchen. He too was tired and the residue of his stressful day lingered. "Ugh, what a day," he said. "I thought James and Mark would never get out of my office. Get this, they want me to do a survey of the entire county by the end of the month."

"Well, at least you don't have the same stupid report from last week still hanging around your neck like an albatross, and an exam coming up that you haven't even studied for."

"Of course I don't. But then I wouldn't let anyone walk all over me like you let those folks at C & G do to you."

Sarah bristled. "I can't help it," she said.

"Well, you *can*, but you *won't*," Russell responded. Then, looking at the table, he remarked, "Pork chops? We had pork chops last night. And Sunday on the grill."

Sarah tried very hard to control her anger, but her voice was sharp. "Yes, we are having pork chops. If you want something else, you can fix it."

Russell answered without thinking, "Let's just go out for dinner."

"Go out?" Sarah snapped, "after I made dinner? Since when can we afford to throw away food? Or is it that my cooking is just too awful."

"I never said your cooking was awful; I just don't feel like pork chops. Lighten up."

"Lighten up? Easy for you to say. You don't have to work full time, take care of the house, do all the shopping, and work on your Master's degree."

Russell felt his fatigue turning into anger. "Oh, no, it's the poor-me-routine; you give and give and I do nothing. I don't mow the lawn, pay the bills, buy the groceries, cook as often as you do, and clean the house every Saturday."

"Oh? Since when? You never do anything around the house; it's work all week and golf all weekend."

"Oh, so it's my fault that nothing gets done? Maybe I do my work all week because I am not allowed to make noise in this precious house. All I ever hear from you is 'Please be quiet; I'm studying. You know, my Master's degree, my Master's degree.' It's your excuse for everything. 'I don't have time to shop, my Master's degree. Can't watch TV, I have homework. Can't go out, I have an exam. Can't have sex anymore, gotta work on my Master's degree.' At least I get a little peace and companionship on the golf course."

"Oh, you're exaggerating, as usual. I do not make you be quiet, I do more than my share around here, and we . . . we have sex. You're making me out to be a monster."

"Well, frankly, Sarah, that's about it. You have the patience of a gnat, and you're just about as much fun. We have sex when the moon is full, and we never make love any more. I practically have to beg you to come to bed, and a man gets pretty tired of begging for something from his wife that other women offer freely."

"What's that supposed to mean? Are you looking at other women now?" Sarah felt resentful. She knew that there were problems in the bedroom and that she was partly to blame. But she resented Russell making her feel so guilty; it was certainly not all her fault. "Why are you saying this? I can't help it if I'm tired. Maybe if I got some help around here I'd have more energy. I'm carrying a heavy load here. You knew I was going to continue my education when we got married."

"Oh, yes, but I didn't know that it would consume your life and our marriage. Now I have to worship at the altar of the Heavy Load. The pressures of work and, oh, the pressures of that blessed Master's degree. All bow in honor to the Heavy Load."

Sarah felt pushed into a corner. She felt that Russell was attacking the very core of who she was—a good student, a high achiever. "Well, at least I'm capable of getting a Master's degree. I don't see you in college Mr. Einstein. In fact, you barely got out with a bachelor's degree. We had to drag you off the golf course for graduation—or did you even graduate? I can't quite remember."

Russell stood up so abruptly that Sarah was startled. "I know you don't think I'm very smart. Certainly I'll never meet your standards. I don't know why you married such a stupid guy. But I'll tell you, Sarah, I'm a good man with or without an advanced degree! I don't need a piece of paper to prove I'm worth something, but you sure do. We've been married almost two years and you're still not a wife. When are you going to grow up?"

He moved to the door before Sarah could respond. "I'm going out to eat," he said, "and to enjoy my own ignorant company."

"Well, good," Sarah yelled back, "you are the only one who can!" Sarah was agitated as she picked up the dishes and tossed the uneaten food in the trash. As she cleaned the kitchen, she fought back tears. *Why does this always happen. I promise myself I will be rational, but I get defensive and, bang, we are on the downward slope. I didn't think marriage would be like this. Why can't he be a little more supportive of what I'm going through? "Still not a wife"? What kind of crack is that? I'm more grown up than he will ever be.*

Later that evening, Sarah was working at the computer when Russell returned. She heard him click on the television downstairs and she thought about going down to talk to him. Instead, she decided that if he wanted to talk he could just as easily come up to see her. *But he probably won't*, she thought; *he's too stubborn. Besides he said some hurtful things and he owed her an apology.*

Russell stared mindlessly at the television. He knew that he and Sarah needed to talk, but he just couldn't endure another heated argument. He knew that he shouldn't have brought up the sex thing again but she was never "in the mood" anymore. Every night was a struggle just to get her to turn off that darn computer and come to bed. She seemed to think that Master's degree was more important than he was. She was always so serious, about everything. Heaven forbid that a smile should cross her face. And then, oh that remark about his grades! Maybe he wasn't the best student in the world, but he graduated and got a good job. And he was doing well. Why didn't she ever acknowledge that? Better to sit here, he thought, and keep his ego intact than to try another discussion. He loved his wife, but lately all they seemed to do was argue. *I just can't deal with this any more*, he decided. *Maybe if I just don't say anything about anything for awhile, things will settle down.* Russell fell asleep in the recliner and woke up some time after midnight. He found Sarah already in bed asleep. As quietly as he could, he slipped under the covers. Sarah was awakened by his movements and thought about apologizing. But the last thing she needed to hear was how selfish she was. He didn't even seem to care about her needs, only his own—sex, sex, sex. Sarah lay there in the darkness very still, pretending to be asleep. Both lay awake for some time—feeling frustrated, rejected, angry and hurt.

So it continued for several days. Sarah got through her exam and finished her report. Russell got caught up at work and tried to be more helpful around the house, but only when he didn't need to be in the same room as Sarah. The distance between them was chilling. Shallow talk and separate spaces. Neither one brought up an issue that might cause conflict. They showed no affection and closed each other out. Both were beginning to feel the strain in their relationship.

On Sunday afternoon, Russell was golfing and Sarah was working on her studies. The telephone rang. Her older sister, Betty, was in a good mood and began chatting about her family. The kids were doing this and that; Fred was refinishing some furniture. After a few minutes she paused. "Is something wrong? You seem sort of down?"

"Yeah, I guess I am," Sarah replied. "Russell and I had another fight."

"Oh, dear. What about this time?"

"I don't know. Just the same old stuff. He won't help around the house, but when I bring it up, he gets defensive about my Master's degree and starts complaining that we never have sex anymore. How am I supposed to feel sexy when I have to do everything around here? Besides, even when I am willing to have sex, he still complains because we aren't "making love"—whatever that means. We just can't seem to discuss anything without a big fight."

"Oh, I know how that is."

"You do? But you and Fred never fight."

"Au contraire, sister dear. Fred and I used to fight a lot, and we still have conflict but we learned how to "fight fair."

"What do you mean by that?"

"Well, it seemed that most of our arguments began when we were tired. I would complain about something and instead of just saying, yeah, you're right, Fred would complain about something I did. Then I would get defensive and say he was wrong. Then he would say I was too sensitive, and I would say he was selfish. I don't know why, but we just got into these dueling matches that accomplished nothing but hurt feelings. So now, we try to take turns. If I have a complaint, we deal with that complaint and put it to rest. If Fred has a complaint, we wait and deal with it later. We try not to get the issues confused, and we try not to hit below the belt. To call each other stupid or sarcastic or selfish solved nothing. It made us both feel hurt or angry but did nothing to help the situation."

"Yeah, that's pretty much what happens around here," Sarah said. "Maybe we need some ground rules for our conflict. Thanks for listening. Well, I need to get going. Tell the family 'hi' for me."

"Sure, will do. And good luck," said Betty as she hung up.

Later that afternoon, Russell returned home from his golf game, a bit more relaxed than when he left, but still dreading the cold shoulder he was expecting from Sarah. He placed his golf clubs in the closet and decided he had best find Sarah and offer to help with dinner. He expected some kind of vague or curt reply, but he wanted to get it over with. "Sarah," he called. "Are you upstairs?"

Sarah answered from the kitchen. She had already made dinner and Russell noticed that it wasn't pork chops. He wanted to smile at the thought of pork chops, but didn't dare risk it. He expected her to criticize him for playing golf instead of staying home to do the cooking. So, without saying anything, he just began setting the table. During dinner, Sarah seemed particularly nice and even asked about his golf game. "It wasn't bad," he said. "I actually think I'm getting better with my putts. I didn't squirrel to the right so much." Sarah considered for a moment how much pride Russell took in his golf game. Not really very different from the pride she took in her academic accomplishments.

After dinner, Russell began to clear the table. But Sarah stopped him and asked him to sit with her for a few minutes and talk. "I want to apologize to you for my comment the other night about you not being capable of getting a Master's degree. I know you could if you wanted to. I was just angry and lashed out. But I really don't understand why you are so resentful of my efforts to get an education."

Russell's first impulse was to list again the zillion times that her studies intruded on his plans, his needs, and his pleasures. But he paused and said instead, "I guess I just feel left out sometimes. I need time with you, too. All I ever hear is you're so tired and so busy."

Sarah didn't respond immediately, but when she did, she chose her words carefully. "You're right. I have been complaining a lot lately about my pressures at work and school. I realize that I tend to close you out when I'm busy, and I'm sorry for that. But I need your support, not your resentment."

"Oh, Sarah, I'm just not as good with words as you are. I don't resent you, I'm proud of you. I suppose I should tell you that more often. I guess I just want to know there is some line that you can draw for us, some period to be placed at the end of the work day when you put it all away and relax. If that's not possible during the week, at least on the weekend. I want to be supportive, but I feel disconnected from you sometimes, like everything else in your life is more important than me. I have a job too, and I'm doing pretty well at it. I would like to know you are proud of me too, that my life matters, that I mean something more to you than a roommate who helps around the house."

Sarah was struck by the sadness in Russell's voice, and she realized that the burden had not been hers alone. She had not been physically or emotionally available to him for quite a while. She always expected that being in a relationship meant she would have to give up some of her autonomy, but she hadn't realized how careless she had been about sharing her time. Perhaps more important, she had stopped showing how much she respected Russell, how much she enjoyed his wit, his energy, his accomplishments, and his ability to keep work and play in proportion—all the things that had attracted her to him in the first place. She had become much more likely to find fault than to tell him how much she valued him as her friend, her companion, her lover, and her husband. Impulsively, she leaned across the table and kissed him. "What do you say to this? What if we agree that when we have a complaint, we try to keep it focused on behavior, not personality, and that we really try to listen and be supportive even when we are getting very angry? And let's try to stick to one person's complaint at a time. We just keep dumping our own agendas on the table without listening to the other person's concerns."

"Well, that sounds good, but it won't be easy."

"I know, but I think we have to try."

"You're right. And how about apologizing when we are wrong instead of going on the attack?"

"You got it. Now how about helping me with these dishes and then maybe we can work out something so I can have more free time for us?"

"Ugh, I guess that means making a list of household chores and dividing them up, huh?"

"Yeah, but this time, we'll have three lists: household tasks, our own tasks, and things we want to do together."

Russell would have preferred that their life be a bit more spontaneous, especially where sex was concerned, but Sarah was such a planner. Oh well, he thought, maybe that was a good thing right now, given the challenges of being a dual-career couple. He had his doubts, but he decided that he could at least try it her way and see what happened.

FOR FURTHER THOUGHT AND REFLECTION

1. Sarah seems to have good intentions when she first decides to ask Russell for more help around the house. However, several factors seem to derail her original intention. What are some of those factors? Which might be attributed to the situation, and which might be attributed to the interaction?

2. John Gottman (1994) describes four phases of dysfunctional conflict that characterize unhappy couples. *Criticism* is attacking a partner's personality

or character, rather than his or her behavior. *Contempt* is insulting and psychologically abusing a partner's sense of self. *Defensiveness* is the refusal to accept responsibility for one's actions, often done by meeting partner's complaint with a counter complaint. *Stonewalling* is characterized by withdrawing from interaction and keeping an icy distance. What signs of these patterns do you see beginning to show in the conflict between Sarah and Russell? Explain.

3. Sarah and Russell come up with some rules to help them manage their conflict. What are these rules? Do you think their rules are good ones? Are there other rules you believe they should add to guide their conflict, either before it starts or after it is underway?

4. What do you see in the future for Sarah and Russell? In other words, do you believe they have resolved all of the important issues? Do you think there is any "latent" conflict (unresolved issues) that might influence future interactions. If so, describe the issues that might linger as problems in their relationship.

REFERENCES

Alberts, J. K., & Driscoll, G. (1992). Containment versus escalation: The trajectory of couples' conversation complaints. *Western Journal of Communication, 56,* 394–412.

Canary, D. J., Cupach, W. R., & Messman, S. J. (1995). *Relationship conflict.* Thousand Oaks, CA: Sage.

Cloven, D. H., & Roloff, M. E. (1993). The chilling effect of aggressive potential on the expression of complaints in intimate relationships. *Communication Monographs, 60,* 199–219.

Gottman, J. (1994). *Why marriages succeed or fail.* New York: Simon & Schuster.

Honeycutt, J. M., Woods, B. L., & Fontenot, K. (1993). The endorsement of communication conflict rules as a function of engagement, marriage and marital ideology. *Journal of Social and Personal Relationships, 10,* 285–304.

Metts, S. (1997). Face and facework: Implications for the study of personal relationships. In S. Duck (Ed.), *Handbook of personal relationships.* London: Guilford.

Sagrestano, L. M., Christensen, A., & Heavey, C. L. (1998). Social influence techniques during marital conflict. *Personal Relationships, 5,* 75–89.

PART IV

SERIOUS CHALLENGES IN RELATIONSHIPS

BETRAYAL

The Case of Chris and Sandy

Steve Duck

KEY WORDS

■

betrayal
trust
gossip
uncertainty reduction
relationship dissolution

Sandy and Chris had been friends at Whitby High since long before I ever knew them. They were always there for each other, always supported each other, always *had* loyally supported each other since they became friends in grade school. They would do things like standing up for each other if other people were talking bad about the other one. You know how teenagers like to talk behind someone's back. But they stood above it and protected each other faithfully, even when there were all those rumors about the Bistarsky High football team and what had happened at the party after the game. You know the sort of thing. Some people said they had heard about it from the folks at Bistarsky High, but no one else from our school had been there at the time. And Sandy never let on.

There was plenty of gossip about the two of them as individuals, too (and of course, later, about their relationship). Sandy was regularly teased for crazy hair styles and Chris was suspected of doing drugs. Actually that probably wasn't true because I never saw Chris do anything like pot or shrooms, though I personally didn't like Sandy's hair either or the tendency to act big in class. You know, always looking to be the one who knew it all, trying to get a rise out of the teacher by saying outrageous things and coming back with cute answers. But I have to admit that I had a secret admiration for that kind of quick-fire comeback.

Anyone could see that Sandy and Chris liked each other a lot. You know how you can always tell things, not only from the words but also from the way they acted—the nonverbal communication, as I have now learned to call it in my interpersonal communication classes. They used to sit by each other a lot, look into each other's eyes, and laugh together all the time. I don't think I was really conscious of all this until I took the interpersonal communication class. Well, perhaps I did notice, but I didn't give it a label. Anyway, whatever it was, you could tell just by watching them, even when you couldn't hear what they were saying. You just *knew* they really liked each other.

And they had always been very loyal friends. Sandy would often tell a story about when Chris was called to the Vice-Principal's Office and questioned for a long time about someone saying Chris had smoked pot at the football game. Sandy voluntarily went in and claimed to have been with Chris at the game and hadn't seen anything. In fact Sandy told the Vice-Principal it was someone else—from Bistarsky—who looked like Chris. Sandy had to say they'd both been drinking some beer, though, smuggled into the game in coke cans, so they could not have been where the other people had said they were at the time. Sandy and Chris both got into some trouble over that, of course, but not as much as if they'd been caught with pot. Sandy basically took half the blame, instead of Chris getting all of it. That was the sort of thing they did for each other. As to whether Chris really smoked at the game, I don't know what was true. It's just what people said. Anyway, if it hadn't been for Sandy, Chris could have been in huge trouble and really owed Sandy bigtime.

Sandy once said Chris was a *real* help when it came to leaving Whitby to go to college. That can be kinda scary, as you know, but Chris had helped with the move physically, then was "there" psychologically, too—always thinking of reasons to drop by the dorm and check to make sure that Sandy was doing OK. If one thing was obvious about the two of them, it was the level of trust they had in each other. We all used to talk about it. Again, it wasn't as if they kept talking to everyone saying "I really trust Sandy (or Chris)" or whatever; but you could tell from the way they told stories about stuff they did, and how they could tell each other anything, and they just obviously knew a lot about the other person's "history" and emotions and inner feelings. Some of us tried to copy their friendship—or at least we hoped we'd have friends like that one day. That kind of trust and loyalty are hard to find these days when everyone is so superficial. You can talk and talk and talk, but you never feel as if you truly *know* the person.

I like both of them. Not only as individuals but as two really decent people. Sure, they do some of the dumb things we all do, and people like to talk about those things. But they were both cool, and everyone respected them. I got friendly with each of them, and we were all very close at one time.

I suppose that was part of the problem. It's always harder for three people to be close than it is for two, you know? You get "triangulated" when there's three—you know, two against one. One complains to one of the others about some gripe about the third one and wants you to referee, or more likely be on their side. You get to hear a lot of BS, of course. Well, who doesn't *whine* once in a while when they can talk to someone they trust? Sometimes you have to act as a counselor or a go-between for people then. When you get close to someone, you get to know some of their secret fears, thoughts, hopes and opinions about other people. And when there's three of you, some of those hopes and fears are about "the other one." But Sandy and Chris were always close. I expect they talked about me, too. It's only natural. You just hope that no-one says anything too embarrassing!! No one wants a bad reputation, whether at high school or college. I think it's worse at high school though and people were forever talking about who's doing who, and which boys are just out to get on the most girls, and which girls are "sluts." Nobody really talked about Sandy and Chris that way, though.

Then Chris started talking about Sandy in ways I couldn't believe. I mean, when you know both of them and one's telling you they suspect the other is doing it with some scanky person, what can you do? You can't go around telling people what's said behind their back. On the other hand, if you don't and you know that Chris is partly concerned for Sandy, partly worried that it might be true, and partly hoping you'll say you have heard it's not true, should you tell

Sandy or not? Or more precisely, how much should you tell Sandy about the suspicions Chris is mentioning? Or Chris for that matter? How much should you tell Chris that is really true, if you happen to know? You owe something to each of them, but if you keep one person's secret, you let the other person down. If you actually reveal what you know, then you're letting a different one of them down! You're caught right in the middle!

It was harder because I really *knew* the truth for sure. It was a real dilemma, a big one. I guess I see how important it was to a friend like Chris to be able to continue to trust Sandy completely and—given what they'd been through together—Chris had come to expect Sandy to be absolutely honest and above board. A rock, really. You have to be able to rely on your friends, so in this situation it was probably even harder. I mean, given what I know now about their real relationship.

If Chris had suspected a one-off, a one-nighter, a one-time thing and everyone was trashed or something, I think it would all have been easier to deal with. But it wasn't like that. Fact is, the new secret relationship really *mattered* to Sandy, and it looked as if it could turn into something serious. Sandy had found something that could become a real "relationship," and that would mean seeing less of Chris. You know how *that* goes. You get involved with someone, and you start to see less of your friends so you can be with the new person and stuff. Or you get used to hanging out with a friend, and all of a sudden they meet someone special and now they've got no time for you because they are off mackin' with The New Love Interest. Chris obviously suspected that was going on and could have expected Sandy would talk about it, but how do you talk about suspicion without making it into a big deal and getting into a big nasty fight? Or—worse — you get stuck in one of those big "Our Relationship" talks that are so uncomfortable. But as I said, their relationship was obviously changing, and it wasn't really the sort of thing Sandy could easily bring up. Under the circumstances.

That's one of the things about a close relationship. The more you get to know someone, the more you expect to confide in them, to check out stuff, see what they think of it, find out if you are really doing the right thing, get a respected opinion from someone who knows you well. When you have been hanging out as long as Chris and Sandy and have been through so much, then you get to know how someone really thinks and feels. You know what pushes their buttons, what makes them feel mad or nervous, what they hate, or how things make them feel. So they really are great as sounding boards for you, too, because they know you so well. You trust them, they trust you.

But in a way, that very closeness makes you vulnerable. You know how they work, so you know what hurts them, too. They know how you work, too, so they could tell someone else. I mean if they ever wanted to. When you're close you have a whole lot of things that you could tell other people about your close friend if you ever wanted to. But you don't do that. That's the point about a close relationship. You don't do that.

When the relationship gets into trouble, though, all those things—those secret, vulnerable, private things—are up for grabs and, if the person really starts to hate you or become an enemy or get really ticked off at something you did, then there's a lot of secret stuff or personal stuff that becomes a kind of currency they can use against you like a set of sharp weapons. You can use the information to hurt the very person you cared so much about, just by telling what was said when you were getting close to the person.

Of course, Chris was always good to me like that. Some of the things we shared were really, really deep and I learned things about Chris that I could never share with anyone else. The truth about the party after the game for example. But more than that, I learned some of Chris's deeper thoughts and secrets—in particular a few things about Chris' father that I really wish I didn't know. You don't expect most fathers to do thing like that to their little kids, and it obviously left psychological scars on Chris. It also explains a few things about the way Chris would act sometimes, though!! But that sort of stuff is kind of personal, and obviously this was very deep and affected the way Chris saw other people and relationships and the whole trust thing.

Well, when Chris first got concerned about Sandy, a lot of what happened was just the typical worrying, just "inside-the-head stuff," mulling it all over, wondering if it could be true—looking for evidence, replaying things that Sandy had said and done. Or not said and not done. Chris was obviously looking for changes or signs that could clear up the suspicions, but without having to bring it up to Sandy directly.

Chris was really just mulling it over, getting angry alone, not really talking to anyone about it very much but obviously stewing a lot, and getting really bugged by it. You could tell because Chris was normally so outgoing, but during that semester Chris just seemed to close down a lot more and go quiet and sort of brooding. I read something for one of my Psych classes about it: the guy called it the "intra-psychic phase of relationship breakdown" where people just brood, basically, not really knowing if anything is really wrong but thinking it over, trying to get a handle on it.

I heard a bit later from one of my old friends who is still at Bistarsky High on the other side of town that Chris had talked with her about it, not really wanting it to get back here to Sandy, but needing someone to bounce things off to see if the concerns were real or if it was all just imaginary. My friend didn't really have much to say except general stuff, since she didn't really know Sandy or have a network of friends that talked about Sandy or the people here at college much. At least she wasn't sure she did.

But it couldn't go on for long like that, just staying inside Chris' head. After a while Chris became totally freaked out and convinced that something was really, really wrong. Apparently some dork had told Chris that Sandy had been down at the lakeside—at that familiar hook-up spot there. It was a really dumb place for Sandy to go when you think about it, I suppose, unless there was some sort of unconscious desire that the whole thing would come out into the open. Maybe by that time it didn't matter. Anyway, the story got back to Chris via some poor dumb innocent guy who didn't even know that Chris and Sandy were lovers. He just mentioned the lakeside sighting all very casually, like he had heard a rumor, not having a clue about what it would do to Chris. It must have totally shocked Chris to hear that. A Bolt From The Blue, I'd say.

Well, Chris was mad, of course, and very hurt too. I was just about the only one who knew about the real relationship between Chris and Sandy—how the friendship thing had really become an act just to cover up the real relationship. So Chris was very upset when the rumor got started and naturally wanted to find out what was behind it.

Chris really got talking to a lot of people and started asking around and trying to reduce uncertainty about Sandy by checking out what people knew or suspected. Finally, of course, the two of them had it out right then and there with some really deep discussion about The Future and The Nature of The Relationship. It was tough for both of them, and of course I got caught right in the middle. Chris still wasn't sure if it was any more than a rumor, and Sandy didn't want to let on at first, obviously didn't want to be open about it. They both told me all about the whole thing and what it was doing to them. Sandy obviously felt a lot of guilt; Chris a lot of anger and suspicion. But it really was all over between them by then, and I knew it but didn't really have the heart to tell Chris what I thought. In any case, I didn't think it was my place. I thought that should come from Sandy. And of course it eventually did, but not very directly. People started talking about Chris, after hearing things about the party incident that could really only have come from Sandy. Or from me I suppose, but, . . . hey! Why would *I* say anything?

And the way things are, before long there was a big set of stories going around, and Chris looked like a bad person. Chris did this; Sandy did that. You've seen it before, a thousand times. The different groups of friends from school started taking sides, some with Chris, some with Sandy, obviously—but not really knowing the whole truth, which I guess we never really know, human nature being what it is. But there was a lot of talk: some people finally admitted that they'd never really liked Chris, or that they'd suspected the real nature of the relationship with Sandy, or that they were glad it was all out in the open now because it made them uncomfortable to play along with the act about the relationship. And Sandy and Chris had assumed nobody knew about them! That was a bit of an eye-opener for both of them, I think—finding out that more or less everyone knew. And people can be really mean when they talk about stuff like that, even if they don't intend to hurt people's feelings.

Mostly, though, what happened after the break-up seemed to be a big PR exercise anyway. I mean almost anything anyone does can be seen in a good or a bad way, can't it? To know all is to forgive all—as they say in France (in French obviously!).

Those who favored Chris soon talked about Sandy as the Beast from Hell. I mean, like they had never done anything remotely like that themselves. Come ON! Never two-timed or stepped outside the bounds. GET OVER IT!! Where have they been living? Anyway, the different people told different stories and took different sides, spreading their versions of what Sandy did, or what Chris did, and how it all fit into the breakup scenario. There were some quite interesting things that came out in the open that way. It was almost like a war zone sometimes, with big time gossip against one or the other of them, depending on whether you were for Chris or for Sandy. It didn't do the relationships among the whole group of us much good either, with everyone taking sides or feeling awkward around either one of them. Eventually, Chris tended to lose out and become a kind of outcast. There were just more people taking Sandy's side.

Well Chris and Sandy split up after that, not only as lovers but also as friends, and they seemed to spend most of their time telling their side of the break-up to anyone who would listen. Sandy was pretty smart about it. Chris wasn't quite so smart, but anger and bitterness can do that to a person. Chris was a bit unstable, if the party story was true anyway, and had all that baggage about trust issues after the way the father had acted. Sandy was clear that Chris was basically a good person, but despite the unusual nature of their relationship and the special closeness that it brought, it couldn't ever work till they really decided where their heads were. Sandy could understand Chris's feelings or motives for saying some of the things that got said and was really pretty saintly about the whole thing. But realistically, it was the kind of ending that Sandy had always seen coming to their relationship. Anyway, Sandy needed space and time to settle into the new relationship without all these other hassles.

Chris was angrier and felt very betrayed and didn't care who knew. Chris called Sandy all sorts of names, talked about back-stabbing, and called Sandy a

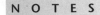

"traitor" and actually pissed off a lot of people by being so nasty about Sandy—even though, when you think about it, there was some justification. Anyway, Chris seemed determined to make sure that no one would ever consider going out with Sandy ever again or even risk being friends and it kind of back-fired, but you can understand why someone would try to do it. To paint that kind of picture, I mean. No one would ever want to go out with or trust someone who was basically untrustworthy, and might tell other people all the secrets you shared when you were close. So I guess Chris was trying out a trick that a lot of us would use if we were in that position.

Not that it really matters, though, since most people remembered how Sandy stood up for Chris over smoking pot at the game, and all the stories about "disloyalty" and "betrayal" and "treachery" were really easy to argue with because that story about the Vice Principal was so widely known and people had obviously come to trust Sandy for themselves. And once the truth about the party incident came out, it was actually Chris who looked bad. Anyway, perhaps I'm biased. I liked them both, but I have to admit that Sandy is just about the best lover anyone could wish for.

FOR FURTHER THOUGHT AND REFLECTION

1. What are the main elements that lead someone to feel a sense of betrayal?

2. Does a sense of betrayal come out of particular individual acts, or does it depend on your whole experience with the person who you believe betrays someone?

3. What do you think is the role of a network of other friends or family in confirming or denying, supporting or resisting a betrayal? Does the network play a role in defining whether betrayal has occurred? How does the network serve to reinforce or undermine the sense that a betrayal has occurred?

4. In this case, who betrayed whom? You should be able to find at least three answers to this question.

5. How should individuals who are friends with couples that are breaking up support each/both of the partners? Is it possible to be loyal to both people when a couple breaks up?

6. What sex did you attribute to Sandy and to Chris? Does the sex or sexual orientation affect your interpretation of this case?

NOTES

REFERENCES

Anderson, J. (1998) *Gendered Constructions of Sexuality in Adolescent Girls' Talk*. Ph.D. dissertation, University of Iowa.

Berger, C. R., & Kellermann, K. A. (1989). Personal opacity and social information gathering: Explorations in Strategic Communication. *Communication Research, 16*, 314–351.

Bergmann, J. R. (1993). *Discreet indiscretions: The social organization of gossip*. New York: Aldine de Gruyter.

Boon, S. D. (1992). *Love hurts: An exploration of the psychology of risk in dating relationships*. Waterloo, Canada: University of Waterloo.

Boon, S. D. (1994). *Dispelling doubt and uncertainty: Trust in romantic relationships*, In S. W. Duck (Ed.), *Dynamics of relationships [Understanding relationships 4]*, (pp. 86–111). Thousand Oaks, CA: Sage.

Duck, S. W. (1982). A topography of relationship disengagement and dissolution. In S. W. Duck (Ed.), *Personal relationships 4: Dissolving personal relationships*. (pp. 1–30). London: Academic Press.

Wood, J. T., & Duck, S. W. (1995). Off the beaten track: New shores for relationship research. *Under-studied relationships: Off the beaten track*, 1–21.

IF THE WORST HAD COME FIRST

Violence and Abuse Between Intimates

Katherine R. Allen

KEY WORDS

■

abuse
distressed marriages
family violence
inequality

Marty and Susan had been living together for about a month, a very exciting experience following a summer of only seeing each other on weekends. Susan graduated with honors from college the previous June, and Marty was finishing his senior year. He had to support himself while going to school, as he came from a large single-parent family. By contrast, Susan had more privileges growing up than did Marty. Her parents lived in a wealthy suburb, whereas Marty's family lived in a working-class neighborhood.

After Susan graduated, her parents wanted her to move home, but Susan was very much in love with Marty and decided to be with him. It was not easy breaking the news to her parents that she and Marty were going to live together. Susan's father was having his own problems. He'd been arrested a few times for drunk driving, but he had a good lawyer and always managed to get off. Her parents were not dealing well with her father's alcoholism; they hushed it up and focused on what their children were doing wrong. Susan's mother was embarrassed that her daughter was living with a man without getting married. She would not tell her friends or family, and she told Susan to lie if asked where she was living. Despite her parents' disapproval, Susan's desire to be with Marty kept her from moving home. She and Marty found a landlord who would rent an apartment to an unmarried couple.

Marty and Susan had a lot of fun setting up their apartment. They slept on a mattress on the floor. Marty made a couch out of old lumber, and Susan sewed the cushions. The furnishings were spare, but they didn't mind because they were surrounded by other young people with limited means. Although they loved being together, there were occasional tensions. Several times Marty shouted at Susan and called her names, but Susan thought that was only because he was worried about school. She didn't like his temper, but she thought it was no big deal.

After three months of looking for a job, Susan found an entry-level position, making little money but being offered the opportunity to receive excellent training and supervision. Marty returned to school for his senior year. Unlike Susan's parents, Marty's mom accepted their cohabiting relationship. She thought Susan was a nice girl, but she did wonder how high strung she was.

One Friday night while cooking dinner, Susan was acting very agitated. The next morning, she was going to take her graduate school entrance exam. She wanted to get her Master's degree the following year. Susan was very ambitious, and she felt it was imperative to do well on the exam. Yet, she'd heard horror stories about this standardized test. She thought, *What if I don't do well? What if I'm not as good as I think I am?*

Marty stood at the stove cooking an omelet, and Susan stood to his right side, hammering away about her current agitation. *God, she talks so much,* Marty thought. *I wish she'd just shut the hell up. What's the big deal anyway? Why is she so upset? She's got everything going for her, and she knows she'll do well on the damned test, just like she always does. At least she's got a career path mapped out, which is more than I do*, he fumed to himself. As Susan kept on talking, she seemed to be getting louder and faster. Marty thought, *She sounds like a horn honking*. Suddenly, she started telling Marty that she was upset when he came home late last night. *Oh God*, he thought, *there she goes again, getting on me about how I'm not pulling my weight around here. I can't stand it when she starts in on me. Who the hell cares if I'm late? What business is it of hers? God, she is so uptight!*

Susan was desperately trying to get Marty's attention, but instead, he just stood there, stirring the eggs around in the pan, slower and slower. She felt frantic, and thought, *He looks like a robot! Why won't he talk to me?* She said excitedly, "Marty, Marty, talk to me, please!" Marty heard Susan's words coming out of her mouth, but it just sounded like, *Yammer, yammer, yammer. Yap, yap, yap.* "What the hell are you saying?" he yelled back. "Bitch, just shut up the hell up!" And then, he flipped the omelet out of the pan, over his right shoulder, and onto her face. She stood there with hot yellow egg all over her, stunned, silenced, humiliated. His heart was racing, but all he was aware of was that she had finally shut up.

Susan realized what happened and felt as if the walls had caved in on her. She sobbed and thought, *Oh my God, this will ruin my chance to do well on the test!* She yelled at Marty for hurting her, "I can't believe you just did that!" Deep inside, however, she felt responsible—as if she provoked his attack. She felt guilty and silently agonized, *What did I do to make this happen?* The whirl of feelings, along with a sickening slosh in her stomach, fueled her anxiety and she cried out loud, "Marty, how could you do this to me?" He grabbed his jacket and keys, slammed the door shut, and grumbled through clenched teeth, "I'm out of here."

"God, now what do I do?" Susan cried. She was alone in the tiny apartment. She went into the bathroom and saw the red spots all over her face from where the omelet had hit her. She returned to the kitchen and wiped up the egg mess from the floor and walls. She felt sick and vomited on the floor. Then she took a shower to get the greasy feeling off her face and body and out of her hair. She cried inconsolably. She felt as if she has ruined her own life. She yelled at herself, "It's all my fault, I started it."

She didn't know what to do. She called her friend, Ellie, and asked if she could come over. She drove wildly to Ellie's house and told her the story—sobbing uncontrollably, feeling alternately angry and betrayed. She wished she could rewind the night and start over again. If only Marty had not thrown the omelet. She wondered aloud, "How am I going to get up at 7 A.M. to take that damn test anyway?" Ellie offered to let her stay the night, but all Susan could think of was getting back to her apartment because maybe Marty had come home. Maybe he'd apologize. Maybe they could make love and erase all this hurt and mess. Maybe, maybe, maybe.

Susan raced home, hoping and praying Marty had returned. It was late, about midnight, and his car wasn't in the driveway. The apartment was dark. Susan hated to admit it, but she was afraid of the dark. She thought, *How the hell am I going to enter that basement apartment without Marty in there to protect me? Where is he anyway? Where did he go?* She sat up crying most of the night. She drank wine to ease the pain and smoked cigarettes for comfort, mostly because she didn't know what else to do. She pushed aside thoughts that a hangover from drinking and smoking wouldn't be much help when taking a test. She felt like she was in a trance: *Inhale, exhale, take a sip, sit on the sofa Marty made and wait for him to walk in the front door. Keep all the lights on so I can't be surprised by a monster or a stranger hiding in the closet. Hug my knees close to my chest, just try to calm down.* She spoke to Marty, as if he was in the room, "Why don't you come home? What did I do to deserve this? How the hell am I going to take my exam tomorrow? Oh, Marty, please come home right now!"

She wandered into the bedroom and bundled up in the bed covers to protect herself from the scary things that could happen in the night. She dozed off and on, and set the alarm for 7 A.M. The alarm failed her, too, and didn't go off. She awakened, startled and frantic, at 7:35. She jumped out of bed, washed her face, threw on some clothes, grabbed a piece of bread to eat, and tore out of the apartment and up the hill to campus.

She stood in line next to a nice young man, who looked like a bit of a nerd. After the test, he asked if she wanted to have lunch and she awkwardly agreed. She didn't want to lead him on because she was, after all, living with her boyfriend. But she felt so lonely and confused, she thought, *What's the harm?* She needed to get her mind off the horrible omelet incident. While they were eating sandwiches at a local pub, she wondered, *Why can't I be attracted to some nice guy like this who seems gentle and sweet?* He asked her out again, but she declined, saying she had a boyfriend. She felt reassured that she wanted to be with Marty. She felt connected to Marty, even if he did that horrible thing to her.

At home, Susan felt more secure, so she decided to take matters into her own hands by calling Marty's family and friends. She started with his mom, who didn't know where he was. She went down his list of friends and learned that Marty was staying with their friend Bill. She called Bill and asked if she could speak to Marty. When Marty came to the phone, she said, "When are you coming home?" As usual, Marty was noncommittal and said he didn't know. She could tell that he had no intention of apologizing for throwing the omelet at her. She realized, too, that she desperately wanted him to come home. She felt wild inside, like she'd burst if she couldn't get him to come home. They started to argue, but she was so scared of losing him that she just begged him to come home. He said he didn't know when he was coming home and hung up on her.

Susan jumped into her car and drove back over to Ellie's house. Ellie calmed her down, let her talk and smoke, cry and shake. Susan felt better after this because she got attention and released some of her anxiety. She went home and spent another fitful night alone, but this time managed it a little better. Two days later, Marty casually walked in as if nothing had happened. Susan knew that she wasn't going to get an apology out of him. She knew that if she wanted him to stay, she had to keep her thoughts to herself. She knew her need for connection with him was stronger than her need to settle the score. They warily approached each other. That night, they crawled into bed and wound up making love. He was unusually responsive and tender. She thought she could sense his regret for hurting her. She was relieved that they were close once again and that he came home. She was so scared when he was gone.

Marty and Susan eventually got married. Susan talked him into it. At first he put up a fight, but eventually he gave in. Susan finished graduate school and accepted a teaching position in another state. They moved across country, and Marty got a decent job in his field. About once a year, a physically violent incident occurred in which Marty pushed Susan against a wall, or socked her in the stomach, or hit her in the mouth. These violent acts always occurred in the midst of a screaming fight, and they were always followed by lovemaking and attentiveness from Marty. Susan and Marty didn't quite understand the pattern that characterized their marriage, but they also didn't talk about it.

After Marty hit her for the tenth time, Susan went to a counselor. Marty refused to attend marital counseling, but Susan's therapist agreed to help her deal with her growing dissatisfaction about the marriage. Then, the unexpected happened. Susan got pregnant. Shortly after the baby was born, Marty had an affair. When Susan confronted Marty about the affair, he yelled at her and hit her so hard she fell against a table corner, cutting the side of her head and leaving a huge bruise.

Despite having a personal life that was out of control, Susan was a successful professional. She was asked to teach a women's studies course at her university and diligently went about selecting feminist texts. One of the books she chose offered a feminist perspective on wife abuse. In preparation to teach the course, she read statistics, causes, consequences, and personal narratives of women who had experienced intimate violence. For the first time, Susan felt on a gut level that she, too, had experienced such abuse. She had a career, a husband, a child, social success, and financial security. She was a role model to other women. She was attractive, loving, and kind. She was also a woman with an abuse history. Susan realized that one of the ways she and her husband maintained their marriage (and her greater success and ambition) was to use violence as a way to shore up his power in the relationship. Marty's pursuit of other women was just another way for him to try to control her and boost his self-esteem. Although she weighed 110 pounds, Marty was constantly telling her she was too fat. Now, Susan had a real baby, an infant, and began to name her own misery in this relationship. She could no longer deny that she did not feel respected, loved, or cherished. She could no longer tolerate the sacrifices she had accepted as a way to fit into a relationship she had outgrown. She confronted herself and the fact that she had to make a drastic and unpopular change in her life.

Marty wanted out, too, but he didn't want to take the first step. Marty realized Susan had always been the leader in their relationship. Sure, she was bossy and pushed him to the point of losing his temper, but she was a really good person. He knew they couldn't make it on just what he earned. Deep inside, he believed she was smarter than him, and he knew she was more ambitious. He felt scared: *What will I do without her? I'll be alone again.* Susan and Marty knew how hurt he was when his father abandoned his mother and family years ago. He never really got over it. Still, he knew he hated being married to Susan. He never could live up to her expectations. Nothing he did seemed to please her, and he felt worn out from trying. He thought, *Nothing scares her, she's so tough, let her get the divorce!*

For the first time as a couple, Marty and Susan found a marriage therapist. Susan cried a lot in their sessions, especially about how Marty abused her. Marty had little to say, but was always thinking: *What's the use trying to explain myself? She talks so much anyway. It's hard for me to get a word in with her blabbing all the time. She just makes me mad.* His one bold act was to ask the therapist for a date. He wanted to prove he wasn't as bad as Susan said he was.

One day, the therapist said to them, "Marty is physically abusive, but Susan is verbally abusive." This was a cathartic moment for both Susan and Marty. Here was a person to whom they were paying a lot of money and who was blaming Marty's abuse of Susan on her! Susan snapped out of her self-pitying denial, realizing that no matter how verbally aggressive she had been, he had no right to hit her. It had taken her all these years to come to terms with the fact that she deserved some basic human respect, especially from the person who was supposed to love her the most. She seethed with anger at the therapist. Even if the therapist was using some paradoxical technique to get them to recognize their self-defeating patterns, the therapist was blaming the violence on the one who was violated!

In the car on the way home, Marty said he was surprised about what the therapist said. "I can't believe the therapist took my side and blamed you for my behavior. Susan, I'm sorry for hurting you. I know it is over now, and I just want us to get on with our lives. I do love you, but you are just too much for me. I don't want to live with you any more." Marty cried as he told Susan all of this. He asked her not to abandon him, to help him get on his feet while they went through the divorce. He asked for her forgiveness. She cried, too, and said she would try.

That night, Marty called his mother and told her that he and Susan planned to separate. Susan was in another room with the baby, and as she walked past him on her way to the kitchen, he was saying, "Mom, I've hurt Susan. I used to hit her, and I don't think she can ever get over that." Susan was shocked to hear that he was taking responsibility for his actions.

But Susan was worried about breaking the news to her parents. When she finally told her mother the truth about the violence in the marriage, there was silence on the phone and her mother responded, "Well, he's not hitting you now!" Susan's mother reminded her how hard life would be as a single parent. She said, "A boy needs a male role model at home." Needless to say, Susan felt very little support from her family for her decision.

Years later, after Susan and Marty had divorced and formed happier second partnerships, they worked together to plan the celebration for their son's high school graduation. Marty and his family visited Susan and her family to make the arrangements for the party. Susan's car was at the repair shop, and Marty offered to drive her to retrieve it. As they got in Marty's car, Susan thought, *Wow, this seems like old times! There he is, clearing his throat, just like he always did, and here I am, adjusting the seat to fit more comfortably.* They looked at each other and smiled. Susan said, "You are a lot more mellow than when I married you." Marty replied, "You sure have done a great job raising our son." Susan responded, "Thanks for saying that, and thanks for helping me." They drove to the garage, going over old territory. But this time, they were taking a new route. He had matured and was good to his second wife. She had matured, too, and had become an outspoken critic of family violence, personally and professionally. Although the future didn't look anything like they'd imagined it when they separated years ago, they now knew what it took to end a violent and harmful relationship. They could look each other in the eyes and be grateful for their willingness to face reality and make the necessary changes.

FOR FURTHER THOUGHT AND REFLECTION

1. In Marty and Susan's relationship, how did traditional gender scripts for men to be dominant and women to be passive play out?

2. What were the transitions in Marty and Susan's relationship? How did major life events affect their relationship and career experiences?

3. What societal attitudes did Marty and Susan rebel against, from the beginning to the present time, in their relationship?

4. Where did Susan find support for her desire to change the nature of her relationship with Marty? What obstacles did she face?

5. What were some of the early warning signs that Susan and Marty's relationship could become violent?

REFERENCES

Emery, B. C., & Lloyd, S. A. (1994). Women who use aggression in close relationships. In D. L. Sollie & L. A. Leslie (Eds.), *Gender, families, and close relationships: Feminist research journeys* (pp. 237–262). Thousand Oaks, CA: Sage.

Greven, P. (1992). *Spare the child: The religious roots of punishment and the psychological impact of physical abuse.* New York: Vintage.

Johnson, M. J. (1995). Patriarchal terrorism and common couple violence: Two forms of violence against women. *Journal of Marriage and the Family, 57,* 283–294.

Milardo, R. C. (1998). Gender asymmetry in common couple violence. *Personal Relationships, 5,* 423–438.

Thompson, L., & Walker, A. J. (1989). Gender in families: Women and men in marriage, work, and parenthood. *Journal of Marriage and the Family, 51,* 845–871.

West, J. T. (1995). Understanding how the dynamics of ideology influence violence between intimates. In S. Duck & J. T. Wood (Eds.), *Confronting relationship challenges* (pp. 129–149). Thousand Oaks, CA: Sage.

Yllo, K., & Bograd, M. (Eds.). (1988). *Feminist perspectives on wife abuse.* Newbury Park, CA: Sage.

WHEN A RELATIONSHIP WON'T END

Stalking after Relational Termination

William R. Cupach, Brian H. Spitzberg

KEY WORDS

■

stalking
threat
obsessive pursuit
privacy invasion
unrequited love
jealousy

Alex and Anna, now 27 and 26 years old respectively, worked together in the information systems division of a large insurance company. After knowing each other at a distance for about a year, they were both assigned to work on a large development project. Alex and Anna enjoyed working together and, about six months into the development project, they started dating. That was almost two years ago. Now they don't speak to one another, and each is extremely uncomfortable on seeing the other. Alex and Anna each provide a perspective on what happened between them, and why.

ALEX'S STORY

From a distance, I always thought that Anna was cute. She seemed bright and friendly, precisely the type of woman I would want to spend time with; in fact, the type of woman I might eventually want to marry. I wanted to try to get a date with her, but it never seemed to work out. Our encounters at work were cordial, but infrequent and brief. I was dating other women off and on, and I figured someone as attractive as Anna must have lots of boyfriends. I almost got up the nerve to ask her out when I struck up a conversation with her at a division picnic, but suddenly other people were part of the conversation and the opportunity slipped away. Then one day I suddenly found myself assigned to work on the same project as Anna. I secretly felt really excited, figuring I would now be able to get to know her better and lay the groundwork for dating her.

As soon as we began working together, things really seemed to click between us, professionally and personally. We made great strides on the project, and our skills seemed to complement one another. We often had to work late together, but neither of us seemed to mind. In our conversations, I tried to find out as much as I could about her, though I was never satisfied that I knew enough. I asked some colleagues about Anna's social life, trying to figure out if she was "available" for more than just a working relationship.

Anna was very friendly toward me. She always smiled at me, listened to me intently when I talked, and offered sincere words of encouragement and support whenever I talked about personal problems. We teased and joked quite a bit, and I could tell that she really liked me. I started to feel as if we were destined to be together, so I felt I had to make my move. Confident that she found me attractive (she gave me numerous compliments), I decided to ask her out on a "real" date. We started seeing each other every weekend and, within a month, we went out a couple of times during the week as well.

For the most part, I enjoyed our dates. We laughed, talked, and enjoyed each other's company. The first few months were the best of my life. But I started getting suspicious that Anna didn't feel the same way about me as I did about her. Anna wanted to cut back a bit, saying she needed time for other things in her life. Whatever those other things were, I couldn't understand why I couldn't be a part of them—unless of course she was seeing someone else. I did what I could to confirm my suspicions on my own, but ultimately I simply raised the issue with her. This led to our first big fight, where I accused her of dating other men and hiding the fact from me. She denied it, but her anger made me wonder why she was being so defensive if there really was nothing to hide.

Although I was upset that Anna might be seeing another guy, I wanted to smooth things over with her. I apologized for not trusting her (though I had lingering suspicions). If anything, I felt I had to work even harder to win her loyalty and affection. I redoubled my efforts to show her how much I cared for her. I frequently would leave messages on her desk and bought her flowers and greeting cards. I called her almost every night but, about half the time she wasn't home or wasn't answering. When I would ask her later what she did, she sometimes told me but often seemed evasive. If I couldn't get a hold of her until late at night, she seemed annoyed that I called.

The more I pursued Anna, the more she seemed to play hard to get. This simply fueled my desire for her. I told her I loved her on several occasions, but she never said it back to me. When I asked her whether or not she loved me too, she said she wasn't sure. I was convinced that, even if she had been seeing other guys, she loved me and was simply afraid to admit it.

Anna seemed to be at home less and less, and she starting making excuses for not being able to go out on nights when we normally would see each other. I became very frustrated as we were now seeing each other maybe once every week or two outside of work. The strain in our personal relationship began to take its toll at work.

Then one Friday afternoon, without warning, Anna broke up with me. We met for a drink at one of our favorite places, and she calmly told me that she thought our relationship had "run its course." She said she thought I was a "nice" person, but that we were incompatible. She claimed we were both unhappy and that it was adversely affecting work. She said something about remaining friends.

I was devastated. I begged her for another try, but she was steadfast. I went home that night, feeling numb and humiliated. What would everyone at work think? What would my family think? What would Anna tell people behind my back? How could she do this to me! I got drunk that night and called Anna, hoping to reconcile. She was pleasant as always, and I got a glimmer of hope when at least she said we should put things on hold.

I knew Anna just needed some time. But I also knew that persistence was the key. You don't obtain things in life for nothing; sometimes you have to struggle and push to get what you want. If I did nothing, Anna and I would never be partners. If I pursued her vigorously, I had a good chance of winning her over. After all, Anna left the door open for a relationship between us, and I've seen persistence pay off so many times before.

All I could think about was getting back with Anna. I believed I couldn't be happy unless I restored our relationship, so I spent lots of time plotting my strategy to win her over. I sent her cards, letters, poems, . . . even flowers, just to let her know I was thinking about her. I continued to call Anna several times a week. When she wasn't home (or wouldn't answer the phone), I left her messages. When she did answer, our conversation was cordial. I felt like she was trying to be "nice" to me—but nice is not what I wanted. I was happy to talk to her, but I missed the intimacy and closeness in our talk, as well as our dates and times together.

Anna posted for and got a job in a different division, and she seemed pleased to be transferring to a different building. I couldn't understand why she would want to change jobs when she was so good at the one she already had. Since she still wouldn't go out with me, and since we no longer saw each other at work, I devised what I considered to be safe ways to see or communicate with her. I sent her humorous e-mail messages, interoffice notes, and cartoons that I thought she would enjoy. I knew some of the bars and restaurants Anna and her friends liked to visit. I would sometimes casually show up, hoping to make brief contact with her. Often I went alone, other times with my friend, Randy. I increasingly wondered what she was doing and where she was going. Once or twice at the end of a work day, I even waited in my car and followed her when she drove away, to see where she was going.

I also would occasionally drive by Anna's house—thinking I might see her coming or going. Finally I noticed a car I hadn't seen before parked in front of her place. My *God*! She *was* seeing someone else and she hid the fact from me. When I called to confront her, she first said it was none of my business. Then she admitted she was dating someone else and told me that I needed to get on with my life. She said not to call her anymore.

I was outraged. How could she betray me like that?!? I felt angry and hurt. Apparently I wasn't good enough for her.

Anna was now screening all of her calls, so I had to settle for leaving messages on her answering machine. Sometimes a man would answer—presumably her new boyfriend—and I would just hang up. I no longer wanted to get back with Anna. I wanted to get back *at* her. I wanted her to know the grief she had caused me, and I wanted to punish her for hurting me. I wanted to scare her a little, so I made some empty threats. One day I left a letter opener in her mailbox. The next thing I knew, the police visited me and served me with a tempo-

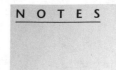

rary restraining order. I was told that they could send me to jail if I tried to contact Anna in any way.

Now Anna and I are bitter enemies. I feel ashamed and embarrassed for behaving foolishly, but I am deeply resentful toward Anna because I feel she led me on, humiliated and betrayed me.

ANNA'S STORY

Alex seemed like a good guy—until I got to know him. Although I apparently met him a few times before, I never really noticed him until we were assigned to work together on the development project. At first I found him to be charming and attractive. I could tell he was infatuated with me, and I enjoyed the attention he showered on me. Our personalities seemed to mesh and this fostered a good working relationship between us. I respected his contributions to the project, and I felt that he admired what I had to offer as well. When Alex asked me out on a date, I wasn't surprised. In fact, some of my friends told me he had been asking all kinds of questions about me for several weeks. I was concerned that dating someone at work could pose problems if it didn't work out, but I decided to take the risk.

The first few weeks were a whirlwind. We both got caught up in the excitement of new courtship. But before long, I knew Alex and I were not going to be long-term partners. I just wanted to enjoy his company and date for awhile. Although we worked well together on the project, it didn't take long for me to realize that Alex was not the sort of guy I wanted to spend my life with. Early on, it was apparent that Alex was very controlling. He insisted on making decisions about where we went, when, and with whom. He seemed constantly to test my loyalty to him. The attention he paid to me quickly became smothering and needy. I liked Alex as a person and I enjoyed our dates, but I didn't like the fact that he was so jealous and suspicious of my private life. I thought to myself, *My God, how can he be so possessive when we've only been dating six weeks?!* One time at my place, when I returned from the bathroom I found him looking through my mail lying on the kitchen counter. This angered me and sent up a red flag that I would have a difficult time trusting him.

I thought of breaking it off with Alex after a few months, but I kept putting it off. I didn't want to hurt him, and I didn't want the ordeal of defending my desire to break up. So I decided to simply scale back the relationship. I made excuses so that our dates were less frequent. He compensated by calling me more and more frequently, despite the fact that I saw him every day at work. If

I was out or didn't answer the phone, he apparently kept calling until he could reach me. One night I just refused to answer the phone and it rang every fifteen minutes. I finally couldn't stand it any more and around one o'clock in the morning picked up the phone. I asked him to please not call me so late, but he continued to do so. I finally started turning off my phone ringer some evenings so I could get some sleep. Whenever I did this, it angered him and he would make sarcastic and snide remarks to me at work the next day.

Alex began to be more of a pest than a dating partner. The more I got to know him, the more apparent it became that he had a very fragile ego. I wanted out of the relationship completely, but I feared he would go into a rage. The more I withdrew from him, the harder he pressed. It became increasingly difficult to work with him, but it was essential to the project that we collaborate. The relationship was costing me time, sleep, productivity at work, and more; I was getting nothing but aggravation out of it.

Because I had cooled off the relationship, Alex assumed that I was dating someone else behind his back. I wasn't, and I told him so. Nevertheless, Alex undertook a campaign of spying on me to find out for himself. He would drive by my house frequently and sometimes come to the door, especially if I told him earlier over the phone that I was busy. He really just wanted to see if I was entertaining another man. He also annoyed my friends by asking them my whereabouts all the time. He seemed to follow me everywhere. He started showing up at social gatherings and public places he normally wouldn't have gone to, just to "run into" me. I swear, sometimes I had this creepy feeling he might be following me or waiting for me around the next corner.

I jokingly mentioned to my friend Karla that I sometimes felt as if Alex were stalking me, and that I must paranoid. But Karla wasn't so sure I was paranoid. She told me about a recent article she read in the newspaper about stalking and obsession with relationships. The researchers in the article reported that stalking is not all that uncommon, and that it can be dangerous. I was surprised to learn that nearly two million people in the United States are the victims of stalking each year. I always thought that stalkers were "sociopaths" who harassed celebrities. But Karla told me that the most common type of stalker is a former intimate partner, and that the vast majority of victims are female. My annoyance regarding Alex was turning into serious concern.

I decided enough was enough. I tried to break it to Alex gently because I knew he would be hurt. I wished him no ill will; I just wanted my life and my freedom back. I told him that we could still be friends but that I didn't want to date him any more.

After I broke up with Alex, he seemed to push even harder than before. He called me constantly—sometimes six or eight times in an evening. I avoided him as much as I could. Work became intolerable so I asked for a transfer and got it, even though I hated to leave the work I was doing. Moving to another building made it difficult for Alex to badger me at work—although he managed to clog my computer in-box with unwanted e-mail.

One day I answered the phone when Alex called, and I firmly told him never to call me again. After that, I got caller ID and would not answer the phone when he called. He eventually figured this out and started calling from other locations—his friend's house, phone booths. So I just stopped answering all calls and told my friends to leave a message when they called because I was screening.

I started dating another man that I met through my cousin. About this time, Alex was driving by my house frequently, and he started leaving threatening messages on my answering machine. He would call me nasty names, like "frigid bitch," and tell me that I would pay for making him miserable. He also made derogatory remarks about my new boyfriend, though Alex really knew nothing about him. One of the things that angered me the most was that Alex tried to spread rumors about me to co-workers and friends. He told people that I was a slut and that I gave him a sexually transmitted disease—an embarrassing outright lie! I couldn't believe I ever saw something attractive about this guy. How could I have been so wrong?

One day I came home to find a dagger in my mailbox. It really scared me. Alex's messages had become increasingly threatening, and I always had the feeling I was being watched. He would show up unexpectedly almost anywhere I went—including dates with my new boyfriend. So I finally called the police. Because I kept track of Alex's recent threatening behaviors, and because I had some of his threats recorded on my answering machine, I was able to get a restraining order against him. But it didn't keep me from being afraid. I've read too many stories where a restraining order can send the restrained person "over the edge" with anger. I really feared Alex would do harm to me. I changed my phone number and my locks. I don't walk my dog alone at night anymore. I frequently change my routine so that my schedule is not predictable.

Alex said he'll "get" me. But I haven't seen him since I took out the restraining order, except once at work, where he flashed me a sick smile and glared at me. I am anxious. I am resentful. I am angry. My life has been completely disrupted. I am less trusting of people, and men in particular. I wonder why I waited as long as I did to break up with Alex. I wonder why I couldn't see sooner that he had an obsessive personality. I wonder what I could have done differently after the break up to prevent his anger from escalating. Now I wonder how I can protect myself. How can I get back to leading a normal life? Will he pop up again unexpectedly and do harm to me?

FOR FURTHER THOUGHT AND REFLECTION

1. Our culture seems to promote a script that says persistence in pursuing relationships and potential partners pays off. Where does this "script" or societal message come from? What factors perpetuate and reinforce the belief that persistence ultimately leads to success, particularly where relationships are concerned?

2. At what point does pursuit of a relationship become obsessive? How do you know when you should abandon the goal to have a relationship with someone?

3. Many people enjoy seeing their partner be a little jealous. When is jealousy productive, and when is it unproductive, in relationships? How can you manage your own jealousy so that it doesn't become destructive?

4. Anna struggled with deciding when "enough was enough" and when Alex's behavior had become excessive. At that time, she broke off the relationship, avoided contact, and eventually called the police and took out a restraining order. In her place, what, if anything, would you have done differently? Why? What advice would you have given Anna at various points in her relationship with Alex? Why is hindsight, or the view of a friend, so much clearer than what we see when we are directly involved in the relationship?

REFERENCES

Bratslavsky, E., Baumeister, R. F., & Sommer, K. L. (1998). To love or be loved in vain: The trials and tribulations of unrequited love. In B. H. Spitzberg & W. R. Cupach (Eds.), *The dark side of close relationships* (pp. 307–326). Mahwah, NJ: Lawrence Erlbaum.

Cupach, W. R., & Spitzberg, B. H. (1998). Obsessive relational intrusion and stalking. In B. H. Spitzberg & W. R. Cupach (Eds.), *The dark side of close relationships* (pp. 233–263). Mahwah, NJ: Lawrence Erlbaum.

de Becker, G. (1997). *The gift of fear*. Boston: Little, Brown and Company.

Fremouw, W. J., Westrup, D., & Pennypacker, J. (1996). Stalking on campus: The prevalence and strategies for coping with stalking. *Journal of Forensic Science, 42*, 664–667.

Jason, L. A., Reichler, A., Easton, J., Neal, A., & Wilson, M. (1984). Female harassment after ending a relationship: A preliminary study. *Alternative Lifestyles, 6*, 259–269.

Meloy, J. R. (Ed.). (1998). *The psychology of stalking: Clinical and forensic perspectives*. San Diego, CA: Academic Press.

Tjaden, P., & Thoennes, N. (1997). *Stalking in America: Findings from the national violence against women survey*. Unpublished report, Centers for Disease Control and Prevention and NIJ Grant # 93-IJ-CX-0012. Denver, CO: Center for Policy Research.

FAMILIES AND ADDICTION:

Narratives of Pain and Healing

Karen Rasmussen

KEY WORDS

■

addiction
alcoholism
denial
rules
conflict
separation
connection

N O T E S

Lit in lavender we met.
Wry glance and grin, droll
Words—at once soft, silly, sharp, serene.
Women people, casting a circle to
Shout, cry, laugh, and then pray.

Now we embrace a time for all things.
A time for struggle, silence, pain, and peace.
Shared time to treasure,
A legacy textured richly
To comfort and sustain.

from "Passage" (in memory of Anne Stein)
Karen Rasmussen, 1 August 1998

For nearly a year, a group of us went weekly to the home of a friend who was in the process of triumphing over addiction as she battled cancer. As we participated in the process of living and dying, our practice was to share with our friend and she with us. And, as so many others have, we affirmed the power of human stories. We felt anew their capacity to show us how people are, how many ways we can be, how rich but sometimes cruel the world was and is. Our words were her medicine and ours, for they instilled deep within us a sense of continuity, a centeredness, a ground from which we could cope with our lives and the passage of one of us.

This special, almost sacred, time was uniquely liberating for its intensity permeated barriers, allowing us to share secrets we ordinarily would have hoarded. In essence, we've learned that in speaking and hearing we collectively cleanse and heal. For me, four of my friends' stories are especially striking. Each is the tale of coming to terms with being raised by parents in the throes of alcoholism or some other kind of addiction. In the pages that follow, I'll do my best to re-present the narratives of four of them to you as I portray lives that move from the **confusion** of early memories to the **chaos** and destruction that accompany addictive behavior to the kinds of **conciliation** each has reached. I've altered names and details to honor their privacy, included a collage of voices to highlight the similarity which exists across the diversity of these people. Some of you may encounter the familiar; others may gain insight into the lives of friends. And many may see, as have they and I, the compelling complexity of lives altogether human.

CONFUSION

(Eleanor) I'm from Guam, a forty-something with a life very different from the way it started out. My first memory is from when I was very young. It was on the island, and I was playing with an Anglo friend. I had to leave in a hurry when her dad came home because she wasn't supposed to have anything to do with me. See, my olive skin and almond-shaped eyes looked too Japanese, a bad thing on Guam during the early '50s. Whenever my mom repeated that story, she used it as an example of why we couldn't take anything from anybody. She meant what she said. After losing a fight at school, I remember her sending me back, saying not to come home 'til I won. She had this rage deep inside that never ever went away. You see, when the Japanese invaded our island the women in her family got beaten or raped or both. I don't know just what happened to her. But I grew up knowing that I always had to defend myself and that I shouldn't trust anybody, especially men. She forbade us to learn our native language, too. She said it was hard enough looking different without making things worse by *sounding* different.

(Michael) Okay, I know this isn't very *macho*, but when I was a little kid one of the best things was coming downstairs in the morning, finding my mom in the kitchen. I'd sit with her and she'd massage my neck, talk some, take care of bills, whatever. . . . Yeah, she drank then. But for a long time she managed to hold everything together. She ran the house, went to work, kept all of us on track. She'd do stuff like cook dinner at three in the afternoon, in case she passed out too early in the evening. She was caring and reliable. Not like she is today, which is so sad because she's gone from a world-beater to a shell of a woman who's afraid to leave her house. Hardly the person I clung to as a kid. And I needed her. My dad was scary—he's one of those big men who radiates energy and can stop you with a look. When my mom had to go off on trips— she's a design consultant—I would just freak out at the thought of being left with him because, even as a kid, I knew I'd never be the "man" he wanted me to be. Hell, when I got bigger than he was and didn't take his pounding any more, I still didn't measure up.

Mom picked me up after school, went to conferences with teachers, did Cub Scouts and Boy Scouts—all that mother stuff. Dad's "flair-ups," as we'd call them, and their fighting with each other was another whole thing. He'd just go off and beat on whatever was handy, which was nearly always me after about age eight. Then his solution was to disappear, eventually come back, and keep his distance 'til the next time. He could go weeks or months, but he'd always explode eventually. He'd also be absent, with a good excuse, of course. But she knew. See, he's the kind of man who's a magnet for women—you know, the looks, the charm, the stories. Sometimes my parents wouldn't talk to each other—for weeks, even. That was another of my dad's tricks. He'd decide you just didn't exist. He defined me out of existence, made me into nothing until he got tired of it, I guess. Good thing *he* didn't drink!

(**Erin**) After I got help for my own addiction—several of us kids followed in my parents' footsteps—I had this memory of my mother telling me about my birth. She was twenty years old, painfully thin as well as rundown and anemic, and she had two little kids already so she wasn't overjoyed to be pregnant. The doctor told her that if she wanted to keep her baby she should take care of herself, but if she wanted to lose the child she should go home and clean her house—the floors, the walls, everything. Do hard work. So she went home. And she cleaned. I guess she had to slow down or something, because she started to think that, being Catholic, she couldn't kill her baby. So I got to live, but she decided I was going to be a boy. When I was born, she didn't want to hold me, didn't care what my name was, stayed depressed for months. I grew up knowing that I owed her my life, that she was special because she had sacrificed to do the "right" thing by having me. So I always worked to please her, to earn her love. I tried to be smart, to be pretty, to help around the house. To be the perfect child. It never was enough, though. As an adult I came to think that I'd made the whole story up. I mean, I can understand being young and desperate, but who would tell a young *child* such a story? She did, though. A few years ago, she started to tell the same tale, just as I'd remembered it. After that, I looked at my birth certificate. It has "baby girl" on the front, no name, except that "Erin Margarette," the name my grandmother gave me, is on the back.

(**Elizabeth**) I was supposed to get married, raise a good Christian family. I didn't, except that I think my boys are wonderful kids. My earliest memories are about Mom holding me. She'd sit in a rocker, and I remember lying with my head on her shoulder, staring at shadows as the chair went up and down, up and down. I was very shy, very timid. Because there were six years between my sister and me, I probably have better memories from being at a friend's house. It was fun because there were kids my age and we'd climb trees and mess around in the barn and run in and out of the house, and I didn't have to worry about making trouble for my mom or being tormented by my brother or irritating my prissy sister.

Our house was messy and cluttered, except when Pops was home. Then we had to clean our rooms and keep everything neat. He did stuff with us, but he was so stern—"Get your room cleaned before I boot you in the butt. . . . Don't give me any lip. . . . Do that again, and I'll smack you." He didn't hit us, but he didn't have to. He had little patience with children, especially with my oldest brother and me. Sean was my mom's first kid who took lots of her attention, and I was the afterthought who was totally attached to her. For as long as I can remember, Pops and I have been at war. See, everybody else would toe the line and back down, but I couldn't be quiet. And he got pretty abusive, which increased when his drinking picked up. By the time I was a teenager, my sister and brothers were busy messing up their lives, and he'd tell me that I'd never amount to anything, that I'd be just like them. When I'd say I wanted to go to college, he'd tell me I wasn't college material, that I'd better find some poor slob to support me. So we'd have screaming matches, which of course would upset my mom. But I just couldn't seem to keep my yap shut—which is pretty much the way it is today. Pops and I do better with each other now, but we're not buddies, like he and my sister are.

CHAOS

(Elizabeth) When my brother died (I was twelve), everybody's world turned upside down. It happened in July, right after we came to Southern California. My mother became withdrawn, depressed, listless—as if *she* was dead. That's when Pops started drinking heavily and they seemed so angry at each other. She at him for moving the family—as if it wouldn't have happened if we'd stayed put. He at her for blaming him. He at himself. Everyone at everyone. Yet during the funeral I remember thinking that they all were so *composed!!* I mean, I wanted to throw myself on the floor and scream, "What is your problem??!!! Don't you *feel* anything? Don't you *care?* He's *dead*. He's *not* coming back, *ever!!!*" I didn't, of course. I'd stare up at them and look for the pain in their faces, but I'd just see the mask, the perfect control. And I just couldn't understand.

Nobody told me what really happened. *I* had to be "protected." But I knew that it was awful. I remember going out into my brother's garage and seeing this bottle of Jim Beam on the floor—see, they left everything the way it was when they found him. I didn't know exactly what went on, but I connected "it" with the alcohol. And I was right—except it was alcohol and drugs. My brother was so loaded he couldn't save himself. See, he was on his knees on the ground, using this cord on his neck. And all he had to do was stand up. But he couldn't. He *couldn't . . . even . . . stand up*. So he suffocated.

(Michael) I knew alcohol was a problem for my mom right after the first time she and Dad separated. She'd had some sort of crisis at work and, when my dad wasn't where he was supposed to be, she called his boss and told him to dig up my father so that his children could be safe. He went on a rampage and moved out, but he found his favorite punching bag first. And then she just started drinking, as if she never could get enough of the stuff. One day I found her passed out on the bed, except I didn't know about "passed out" then. I thought she was dead. But she wasn't, so I got mad—after all, at age nine I was the "man" of the house—and my sister and I ran away. We made it as far as the bushes in the park across the street and sat waiting for her to come rushing after us. But she didn't come, didn't even know we were gone. So we went home. I remember being scared because she was sleeping in her clothes with the light on—as if she was ready to make an escape. Then we'd have to live with Dad, and I couldn't face that without her.

But she wasn't always there. On the day of the football game that kicked off my high school career, my parents walked in, announced that they were going out to dinner to talk about getting divorced, and then left. *They . . . just . . . left!* Okay, so I knew they had problems, but they weren't supposed to get *divorced!!!* Not when I was starting high school, for God's sake. At halftime we raided my parents' bar. And of course I got wasted, *really* wasted. I ended up sprawled in the ivy in front of everybody, puking my guts out. My mom was cool; she tried to talk to me and help me. My father slapped me around and then just wrote me out of his life for about three months with his patented silent treatment. I'd just started high school, and I didn't exist in my own home.

(Erin) I couldn't be friends with people because I had all kinds of fears nobody could know about. When I was eight, my dad started sexual abuse toward me. I'd wake up and he'd be there, smelling of alcohol, doing disgusting things that made me freeze, made me wish I'd die. When I got older I remember being afraid that he'd want to have intercourse and that I'd get pregnant, and that I'd just go insane. So I came up with a plan. I bought the tightest pair of jeans I could find, the kind you have to lie on the floor to zip. I knew he wouldn't be able to get them off me, so I'd be safe. For the first time, I was hopeful because I was protected. When I woke up to the jeans being undone and him there one more time, I freaked out!! I jumped up and threw on every light in the house. And started yelling and shrieking. "You're never *touching* me again. I'll kill you! I'm going to call the *police!* You're *evil!!* I'm going to *stop* you!!" I just snapped because I couldn't keep myself safe. And so I went downstairs and told my mother, "Your husband's abusing me!! I'm never going to let him touch me again!" I expected her to react, to protect me because she's my mother, and mothers protect their kids! But . . . she . . . started to *whisper* to me, "Okay, . . . Okay, . . . Sshhh. . . . You'll wake the other children up. Go back to sleep. Just *go*

. . . back . . . to . . . sleep!" And I remember just shutting down right then. Because she knew. She *knew!* She *knew* and she did *nothing!*

(Eleanor) When I went to live with dad, I thought it was going to be just us and I'd be the center of everything. But he had a life, he had a girlfriend, he still liked to party. His speech to me when we were coming home from the airport was that I should get on the pill and that I could smoke weed and I could drink. But "just don't do any downers, and no acid." When I had a baby at fifteen he was no help. So I went to his older sister who probably gave me the first good piece of advice anyone had. She said, "Get yourself a piece of paper, and write down the reasons you should keep the baby and the reasons you shouldn't." The only good reason I could think of to keep him was that I would have something of my own. So I gave my son up for adoption. Somehow I knew I couldn't keep a child and not be there for him. See, my dad was a runner. Not too much later he gave me a hundred dollars, and told me to go buy some clothes or have fun or whatever and come back the next day. When I returned, he was gone. I learned all about running and all about the hurt it causes.

CONCILIATION

(Eleanor) Today I'm moving toward being at peace with both my parents. Dad and I have a wonderful relationship. He came back into my life after about fifteen years and after getting a lot of therapy. Plus he's been sober a while, as have I. Mom died of cancer when I was twenty five. And I took care of her, because of guilt, mostly. I sold everything I had, bought a one-way ticket, and landed on Guam with ninety dollars in my pocket. At the time I wasn't anywhere close to being ready to quit my own drinking, so of course no real healing could take place. What I'm trying to do today is to remember the good things about her. I know that she gave me gifts—a fierce determination, a creativity, an abiding curiosity. I know that she was a deeply damaged person whose battering created a rage that spawned cruelty. Having compassion for her doesn't excuse the behavior. It was destructive, awful. But the more compassion I feel, the less resentful I become. And the more I can built a trusting relationship with my husband and a stable home for my children.

(Michael) I always had to protect my sister and my mom. My dad had giant mood swings, so if he came home in one of his moods there was incredible pressure because we could do nothing right. The yard wasn't picked up, our rooms were a mess, the kitchen wasn't spotless, the dogs weren't washed, the trash was piled up, the house wasn't vacuumed. And so I would jump in and say, "It's my fault. I didn't do that," just to avoid his anger being directed at anyone but me. I mean, I was going to get it anyway. I guess I just thought it was my job to be a protector. Later on, when my mother wasn't holding it together so well, I'd take care of her. I'd call in for her at work, I'd get her to bed, I'd clean her up, I'd do all that stuff. Especially when they were split up. Maybe I just needed her to have someone to trust. She sure didn't trust him.

Today, she's afraid to go out of the house, and that drives me crazy because she's not *really* that way. But she won't stop drinking. He doesn't drink any more—hasn't for years. And he hasn't hit me since I backed him down when I was 16 or 17. My sister lives in the same town. She and her husband seem to have a good life and seem to be able to deal with the parents. I just can't go there very often. If I do, I get caught up in the frustration and the anger—especially the anger. So I keep my distance. I see them for short periods of time. I do some of the things a "good" son should do. But my life has to be separate from theirs. Because when I try to help them, I hurt myself. And I won't do that any longer.

(Elizabeth) I do triangles—with my parents, my kids, my siblings, my relationships. It started with my parents. Pops drove a truck and probably—we discovered later—was out having affairs. I guess Mom knew, but she just decided to stay. My bother and sister were gone, so it was just us three. Mom was my security, and Pops was my tormenter, and he was her tormenter, and therefore I had to be their buffer because I could get in his face. What happened is that we all had relationships through the third person. I didn't understand this until a lot later when I was in therapy and saw that I was doing it with my son and his stepfather. It's as if I have this split personality: there's the little mediator who helps cover up all the problems, and then there's the confronter who gets everyone together and makes them face up to stuff. I remember doing that with my parents. We all knew he'd been putting the make on my girlfriends but nobody would talk about it. So I made everyone face up to what was happening, which they didn't like much. But I'd rather do that than create more lies.

I've heard horror stories of other families whose alcoholic was lots worse than Pops. He always worked, he kept the family together financially, he at least kept up outward appearances of being a "good family man." He's still not the most nurturing person. You should see the circus when my boys can't quite keep it together, which is frequently. But he and my mom finally are happy. Thank God she did Alanon when he was at his worst, or she wouldn't have survived. Today they have a great life—friends, trips, hobbies, everything. He fell apart when she was so sick with cancer. He says he can't imagine life without her. So maybe she was right to stick with him. I do know that because of things I've done, I understand what it's like to be judged by others. And maybe that has helped me to come to terms with him. Perhaps we'll always have part of a wall between us. The bottom line is that he's my dad, flawed like I am. I'm not the type who forgives easily, but I can keep memories from ruining my life. My boys and I see my parents pretty often, and they even stay with their grandparents—until they or Pops can't stand it any more. He does love them, and he does love me. Which is good, because I love him like I always did. Today, I even *like* him a fair amount of the time.

(Erin) After I got sober I couldn't figure out why I didn't feel better, like lots of other people did. I mean, my life was no longer total chaos, but I was sure I would fly apart at any moment. So I went to therapy and eventually began dealing with childhood issues, especially the abandonment and the abuse. I went to support groups. I worked with therapists. I participated in groups. I worked. I stayed home. I did everything I could. And eventually, so that I could heal and so that my own family could have a chance at being healthy, I had to cut myself off from my birth family. It was the only way I could have enough peace to heal. That went on for several years. As time passed, my kids grew older, and they were happy kids. And my husband and I came to terms with each other, mainly because I wasn't ripping him apart any more. Then my brother was killed in a freak car accident that left his wife with two young children to raise.

So I had to deal with the family again. It was bizarre, having these people I'd cut out of my life like a cancer sharing "grief" with me. Now, to all outward appearances, my family looks good. It always has. And both my parents can be charming. Naturally my kids wanted a relationship with their grandparents, even though when they became old enough I told them about my childhood in a general way. So, now I see my parents on holidays and other important occasions. I always make sure that it's for a limited period of time, that I can leave if things get too crazy for me. Some people seem to be able to transcend traumatic pasts. From my point of view they act as if nothing happened, which doesn't seem right. But that's an outside view. Right now I have a workable relationship with my parents. I don't know what will happen in the future, but I do know that I will do everything possible to keep myself and my family safe. Today I can do that because I've made choices that are lots more effective than buying a tight pair of jeans.

NOTES

FOR FURTHER THOUGHT AND REFLECTION

1. A *mantra* among people coping with alcoholism/addiction is that it is a disease of denial, or the refusal/inability to recognize the power and destructiveness of addiction. What kinds of denial do you see in the stories? What communicative strategies support the denial? What strategies do the narrators use to overcome denial?

2. Each of the narrators goes through the process of separating from her or his family and then re-establishing familial connections. In doing so, what behaviors do they abandon, what new ones do they adopt, and what old ones do they retain?

3. Over time, the communicative rules in each family change. Compare the rules implicit in each person's experience across the three stages (confusion, chaos, conciliation) by examining in each case: (1) who can speak, (2) about what, (3) with whom.

4. Each person's story is rife with conflict. Using the typology below, analyze the kinds of conflict strategies used by each of them:

a. *Avoidance:* ignoring or "side-stepping" a conflict/problem

b. *Accommodation:* meeting the needs of another rather than ones own

c. *Competition:* working to meet ones own needs rather than those of others

d. *Compromise:* giving up something to get something; "horse-trading"

e. *Collaboration:* working to find an optimal solution which best meets the needs of all involved, to the extent that's possible

REFERENCES

Affilia: Journal of Women and Social Work

This journal publishes essays that focus on women's issues. The following two essays are examples of work related to women and alcoholism:

Rhodes, R., & Johnson, A. D. (1994). Women and alcoholism: A psychosocial approach. *Affilia: Journal of Women and Social Work*, 9(2), 145–156.

Turner, S. (1992). Alcoholism and depression in women. *Affilia: Journal of Women and Social Work*, 7(3), 8–22.

Al-Anon Family Groups, Incorporated.

Al-Anon is a support group that grew out of Alcoholics Anonymous. Its purpose is to provide assistance to persons with significant others who suffer from alcoholism and other addictions. The group publishes a variety of literature, including the following two items:

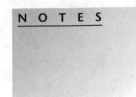

Al-Anon Family Group Headquarters, Inc. Staff. (1998). Having had a spiritual awakening . . . Virginia Beach: Al-Anon Family Group Headquarters, Incorporated.

Al-Anon Family Group Headquarters, Inc. Staff. (1977). What's "drunk," mama? New York: Al-Anon Family Group Headquarters.

Biggers, J. (1998). *Transgenerational addiction*. New York: Rosen.

McGovern, G. (1997). *Terry: My daughter's life and death struggle with alcoholism*. New York: Dutton.

Peele, S. (1983, April). Through a glass darkly. (M. L. Pendery's criticism of M. B. Sobell's and L. C. Sobell's study of controlled drinking). *Psychology Today*, 38–42.

Rivers, P.C. (1996). *Alcohol and human behavior: Theory, research, and practice*. Englewood Cliffs, NJ: Prentice Hall.

Schuckit, M. (1993, Sept/Oct.). The natural history of alcoholism. *Psychology Today*, 24–25.

SHARING THE SECRET

Social Support among Adult Incest Survivors

Eileen Berlin Ray, Beth Hartman Ellis, Leigh Arden Ford

KEY WORDS

■

dialectical tensions
disclosure
reframing
support group
sexual abuse survivor

The local Rape Crisis Center (RCC) offers support groups for women who are adult survivors of incest. Diane and Michele are counselors at the RCC who specialize in working with survivors of sexual abuse. Both have received additional training in facilitating support groups and have run numerous groups for the Center. Groups meet once a week, for two hours, over 16 weeks.

The members of this group look like those in other groups Diane and Michele have run. There is nothing to distinguish them from any women you would see anywhere.[1] Different races, religions, socioeconomic statuses, and occupations are represented. Despite their diversity, the women share at least two things: each of them is a survivor of incest, and each hopes that this support group will help her deal with issues, heal, and move on with her life.

"Well, it's time to get started, so let's begin, as always, with check-in," Diane said. For the next 10 minutes, each group member highlighted her past week and brought up concerns she wanted to talk about at tonight's meeting.

"Jenny," Michele observed, "you said you wanted to talk about some of your anxiety about telling your boyfriend about your abuse. Why don't you start?"

"Well, okay," Jenny replied. "I've been thinking a lot since last week, especially about why I can't seem to tell my boyfriend about the abuse. But I've really been having a hard time, flying off the handle, crying at the drop of the hat. My boyfriend wants to know what's wrong, but I'm afraid to tell him. I feel as if it's my fault and nobody would believe me because, the few times I did tell people, nothing was done. But I can't keep acting this way and not tell him why. He thinks it's about him, that I want to break up with him. But it's really about what happened to me. How do you tell the guy you think you love that your brother and your cousin raped you from the time you were seven until you were twelve?" Tears welled up in her eyes and Claire, sitting next to her, passed her the box of tissues. "What's he going to think of me? I'm damaged goods."

Carol immediately responded. "I know exactly what you mean. I always believed it was my fault, that I could have stopped it if I had wanted to. That's what my stepfather always said to me. 'You know you want this, you know you like this. Who's going to want a girl like you?'"

Marsha added, "My father said that if I told my mom, they would get divorced. I believed him. I didn't want them to get divorced, so I didn't tell."

"I wasn't even sure what was going on," observed Lashanda. "I remember my Gramps was supposed to be somebody who loved me, and for a long time I thought that was a part of the way people show you love. I was always confused about why my father didn't do it to me, too. Why doesn't my dad do this? When my grandfather did it, it was supposed to be some kind of affection."

Marsha echoed this. "Yeah, I remember feeling really confused too. On the one hand, it felt good so I didn't mind up to a point. But on the other hand, I felt so dirty and yucky. And somehow I knew it wasn't right."

"I didn't put it all together until one day at school," said Carol. "We were talking about sex in class and they said something about molestation. I read the definition of it and freaked. It was like, 'Oh my gosh, that's me.' I think it made it easier because I had a word for it. Once I could define and place it, it was like a wave of relief."

"I wasn't sure what it was called, but I knew it had to be wrong because my dad kept saying that, if I told, people would hate me and that my mother would leave and I would be there alone with him," said Francine. "He said if I did what he said God would forgive me."

"With my father," Rita noted, "he just kept telling me it was my fault and I liked it and, if I told, everyone would hate me and think I was a liar."

"Well, it's hard not to believe that stuff," noted Ellen, "especially when you do tell people and that's the kind of thing they say. A similar thing happened to me. From the time I was six until my first year of high school, I didn't tell anybody. One day after church on Sunday, I told some friends that my uncle was sexually abusing me and I asked them for help. They called me a liar and told me never to come back to church. They just didn't want to deal with it."

"I remember one night," Claire reminisced, "my grandfather abused me really bad and I just couldn't handle it anymore. I was terrified and shaking. I told my grandma that I needed to tell her something. I remember telling her but I don't know the words I used. She got really angry and she called me a liar. She said I was a whore and a slut and I had brought it on myself, I deserved it. After I went back home, I got a letter from her saying that I was never welcome to come back. I was just devastated."

"Wow," sighed Gail. "I can't believe people can be so cruel and screwed up, especially your grandmother, Claire."

"Yeah, well, for what it's worth, I found out later that she had been abused by her father when she was a girl and that my grandfather had done the same thing to my mother when she was growing up. I guess that's pretty common."

"Are you kidding? That makes it even worse, as far as I'm concerned," cried Gail. "How could your grandma even put you near him? How could she not protect you? And then not believe you? And where was your mother in all this? How could she let you go visit them? These people are crazy!"

Through the muffled crying, group members laughed. "You're right, they are crazy. And it's taken me quite a few years to really believe that it's them who are crazy and not me," said Claire.

"Oh, Claire, your story really makes me feel sad," Fran said. "I would feel horrible if my mother had reacted like that. I guess I was luckier. My mom said she knew something was wrong when I was a teenager but she couldn't figure out what. We fought a lot. I used to curse her out. I hated her and I used to tell her that all the time. We had a really bad relationship until about six years ago, when I finally told her what my dad had done to me. She actually kicked him out. We've been in therapy together ever since and now we're like best friends."

"Yeah, you *were* lucky," Marsha said. "I know I could never tell my mother. But I did have a great experience with a neighbor of mine. We like to visit when I walk my dog. One day we were talking and I told her. And she said, 'You're not going to believe this. My mother, not too long ago, told me she was sexually abused by her father.' So she could understand what I've been through and what her mother's been through."

"I had a good experience, too," offered Carol. "I told Michael, my boyfriend at the time, and he disclosed that a family friend had fooled around with him when he was a teenager. When he told me that, I knew he believed me."

"I told my sister before I told anyone else," added Lashanda. "I had been away at college and my sister and I wrote letters and became very, very close, putting aside sibling rivalry. She would have been, at that point in my life, the first person that I told about really anything."

"I never told anyone about what my father did to me," said Rita, "until just before Steve and I got married. I can't even tell you why I told him. We were in the living room watching TV and I just turned around and said, 'I have something to tell you.' He didn't say much of anything, and we never talked about it after that. But then when my daughter turned three, it was bothering me, just seeing Steve and Emmy together. I used to want to spy on them to see if he was doing something to her. When I told him, he got really upset. He couldn't believe I would think that of him. And I had to try to tell him that it wasn't him; it would be anybody. Now Emmy's eight and I've been in therapy for about four years. But as time goes on, I keep having trouble with sex. I expected that it would get better. But it's gotten worse. Sometimes I have flashbacks and sometimes I just can't feel anything. That puts a strain on us. I don't like to talk about the abuse, not with him. It's so personal, and it may get into something that I don't want to deal with, or I think *I don't want to open this up again.*"

"That's kind of how I feel, too. I'm having enough trouble dealing with it by myself. I don't want to have to deal with my parents, too," observed Kathy. "Right now I don't feel ready to tell them what my brother did to me. I really don't know how they would take it. I don't see the positives that would come out of it. I might at some point tell them, but right now I'm just not ready."

"You'll know when the time is right," responded Diane. "And there may never be a right time. You should only tell them if you need to for yourself, not because you want them to do or say anything. Because they may not do or say the 'right' thing."

"That's really true," said Claire. "I knew the time wasn't right to tell my mother, but I couldn't help myself. She was bitching at me about my weight. She's done that for 20 years; even before I put on the weight, she bitched at me about it. I finally turned around and looked at her and told her, 'drop it or I will tell you why, and I know you don't want to know.' She kept on, and I turned around and looked at her and told her, 'I am this heavy because your father raped me.' It just exploded from there."

"Well, you just can't count on people's responses, and that's really scary," said Ellen. "When I finally told my family, I thought they'd be concerned and ask me things like 'Do you want to see a counselor? Do you need help with this?' But nobody asked me anything. I think I told them because I wanted them to make me feel better, but all they did was make it worse."

"Yeah, that's the mess. You know what you want them to do and you feel that, if they really love you, they'll do it. And you really need to feel that someone loves you that much," Carol observed. "When I told my mom about my stepdad, she said something like 'oh, shit!' But she didn't fly off the handle. She didn't say 'I don't believe you' but I felt bad for bringing it up. She cried, but it seemed like she cried more for herself than for me. And she made it clear he wasn't going anywhere. I thought she should have told him, 'Get your toothbrush. Get the hell out of here.' But she didn't. I felt really hurt and let down by that."

"I sure know that feeling," agreed Marsha. "I read this article about 20 years ago that really helped me understand the abuse. So I brought the article and had dad read it. And I said, 'That's how I felt.' He apologized that he hurt me because he loves me, but he never said he was wrong to have done it. I haven't brought it up to him since then because I know he won't give me what I want; he won't say, 'I was wrong. I shouldn't have done that.' I am not going to get that, and I don't want to set myself up to get hurt again."

"Yeah, it's really risky because the rest of the family has a lot at stake, too. A big part of the problem is that everybody wants to keep it secret, keep up the facade," added Jenny. "In my family, there was so much trying to protect the family, trying to give the illusion that we were a normal family. Mom said that it would destroy so many people. I told her that it practically destroyed me."

"I fell into that trap too," Marsha stated. "I didn't tell my husband about my dad for the longest time. It was this weird thing with protecting my family image, and he had gotten along well with my dad before. I was trying so hard to protect the family."

"In my family," said Teresa, "there was always this undercurrent—we're a model family, we're well known in the community, dad was a banker, mom was a teacher, they were active in the church. It would be horrible enough if anyone ever found out that I was being sexually abused, but it would be even worse if they knew it was my mother! I mean, usually when you hear about it, it's the father or stepfather or grandfather or brother, some male. Never a woman, especially your own mother. I'm sure my mother would have denied it and no one would have believed me. She's been dead for about four years, but I can still see how screwed up it made me. I did so much drugs and drank so much and slept with tons of guys. I've been in AA now for about 15 years. I've been sober for 14 of those years, and I've been in therapy for most of that time. I'm just now finally beginning to feel that I have some control over my life, that I'm not such an emotional cripple, that maybe someday I'll find a decent guy who will love me."

"I'm sorry for you, but I'm really glad that I'm not the only one who was abused by a woman," Sharla spoke quietly. "My aunt, my mother's sister, is the one who abused me. It was horrible because it was real seductive so it actually felt good. I was sure that meant I was a lesbian. I didn't have any relationships until I got to college, and then I had a few lesbian affairs but they weren't really satisfying. I slept with some men, too, to check that out, and that wasn't too thrilling either. So now I just don't hang out with anyone, at least in terms of sex—partly because it's too painful. She stuck lots of things up my vagina, and I never totally healed from that."

"You know, speaking of physical things, I've always had a lot of stomach aches and headaches. And as a child, I had really awful eczema," offered Rita. "I missed a lot of school, I spent a lot of time in the hospital having tests run. My parents always said I was faking but I wasn't. The doctor could never find anything wrong but it was real. And now, as an adult, I get lots of migraines."

Jenny nodded in agreement. "I've spent almost my whole life being depressed, really depressed. I can't tell you how many times I've seriously thought about killing myself. I finally got on medication and that's helped some, but it's still a daily battle. Through my therapy, though, I can trace it back directly to the incest. I'm finally getting mad about it, mad that my brother and cousin raped me, sodomized me, made me perform oral sex on them. And I'm finally believing that I couldn't have stopped it and that I wasn't to blame. So I guess turning that depression into anger towards them is good."

"Absolutely," agreed Michele. "Getting to that anger is a very important turning point. And there's something really important to keep in mind here. It's very easy to be labeled, or to label ourselves, as physically sick or crazy or depressed or emotionally ill, or whatever. Psychiatrists do it all the time. But you do not have an illness, your reactions are not pathological. They are the coping mechanisms you used to survive a horrific trauma. Think about it. Rita, when you were in the hospital, your father couldn't touch you. So that worked! Fran, when you got depressed and shut down emotionally, you didn't have to feel anything. So that worked, too! The only unsuccessful coping strategy is suicide. But you're all alive, you're all working on your issues. It's just that now you don't need those same coping mechanisms. I guess I just want all of you to be careful that you don't look at successful coping as a negative, as a weakness in you."

"That's an excellent point," agreed Lashanda. The other women nodded. "I think it's been really important to me to focus on the positives—not that there's anything really positive about incest—but, while I wish it hadn't happened, it has made me a better person. It has made me stronger and more compassionate. I wouldn't wish it on my worst enemy, but I don't think I would change my life in any way because I like me. And it has taken me a long time to say that."

"I think, for me," Rita said, "talking about the incest has been the key to releasing the shame. Letting someone into that horrible, ugly place and having them respect you and love you. It makes you feel affirmed, that it's not your fault. That's the only way that I get it away from me. I felt that I was bad, a slut, until people confronted me and said, 'Wait, he was a bastard.' Seeing them get angry helped me get angry. Seeing them grieve for me helped me grieve for me; so for me it was extremely difficult, but it was also what saved me."

Several of the women nodded in agreement. "That's what we hope this group will help with," said Diane. "To give all of you a safe place to talk about your incest, to be angry, to be sad, to be happy, to be whatever you need to be, and to see how old patterns show up and mess up our adult relationships. It's time to break for tonight."

The women made their way to the snack table. Some were hugging, some were crying, some were speaking, some were silent. Gradually they left and headed back to their families, jobs, and everyday lives. They were all struggling to juggle life's demands while dealing with the impact of their incest on their adult lives. But at least they knew that one night a week they had others who shared their pain and a place where they could let their guard down and focus on their healing.[2]

END NOTES

This case is drawn from in-depth interviews with adult incest survivors. We thank these women for their willingness to share their stories with us. All names used are pseudonyms.

1. The support group in this case study is comprised only of women. Our choice was in no way meant to negate or minimize the experiences of men who were incestuously abused as children. Rather, group composition reflects our data; all stories included here were told by female interviewees.

2. You may have noticed that these women, while sharing much of their pain, did not share much explicit detail of their abuse. This is quite typical in the early stages of support groups of this type. As their trust with each other develops, details may emerge. However, each woman will progress at her own pace. The support group is not a panacea and is not a blanket recommendation for survivors of sexual abuse. However, for many, support groups provide a safe place where incest survivors can have their experiences validated, where they can learn to trust others, and where they can candidly talk about their abuse.

FOR FURTHER THOUGHT AND REFLECTION

1. What are some of the benefits of support groups such as this one? Give examples of these benefits from the case study. What are some potential drawbacks? Are any of these drawbacks apparent in the case study?

2. Communication in support groups can function to reframe or alter the meanings participants attribute to their experiences. What are some of the ways this support group accomplishes this reframing?

3. The theoretical perspective of dialectics suggests that many human communicative experiences are characterized by opposing tensions or pulls in opposite directions, and that we use communication to manage these tensions. What tensions or dialectics do the survivors in this support group seem to experience (such as secrecy vs. disclosure, denial vs. acknowledgment, or reality vs. fantasy)?

4. The theoretical perspective of Communication Boundary Management argues that individuals develop rules for determining their self-disclosure choices. Can you identify disclosure norms that seem to be in operation in this support group?

REFERENCES

Bass, E., & Davis, L. (1994). *The courage to heal: A guide for women survivors of child sexual abuse* (3rd ed.). New York: Harper Perennial.

Baxter, L. A., & Montgomery, B. M. (1996). *Relating: Dialogues and Dialectics.* New York: Guilford.

N O T E S

Ford, L. A., Ray, E. B., & Ellis, B. H. (in press). Translating scholarship on intrafamilial sexual abuse: The utility of a dialectical perspective for adult survivors. *Journal of Applied Communication Research.*

Petronio, S., Reeder, H. M., Hecht, M. L., & Ros-Mendoza, T. M. (1996). Disclosure of sexual abuse by children and adolescents. *Journal of Applied Communication Research, 24,* 181–199.

Poston, C., & Lison, C. (1990). *Reclaiming our lives: Hope for adult survivors of incest.* New York: Bantam Books.

Ray, E. B. (1996). Challenging the stigmatizing messages: The emerging voices of adult survivors of incest. In E. B. Ray (ed.), *Communication and disenfranchisement: Social health issues and implications* (pp. 273–291). Mahwah, NJ: Lawrence Erlbaum.

PART V

CHANGE AND CONTINUITY IN LONG-TERM RELATIONSHIPS

BIG CHANGES COME WITH SMALL PACKAGES

Communication Processes in the Transition to Parenthood

Gail G. Whitchurch, Sarah E. W. Dargatz

KEY WORDS

■

relationship redefinition
self-identity
family development theory
role negotiation
boundaries

Sometimes they call me their shrink; one couple even called me their shrink-lady when we first started our work together. I can tell that people who have come to me for couples therapy are expressing affection for me when they call me that, but actually I don't help people *shrink* anything. What I do is help people *expand* the ways in which they think about their world, and the ways they interact with each other. When I start working with new clients, I always tell them that there's no big secret to therapy: We'll try to find out what doesn't and does work and do *less* of what doesn't work and *more* of what does.

People who come through my door usually have put sincere effort into doing what they think is needed to "fix" their problems. If only they could hold onto the emotional "high" that developed between them when they went on that marriage renewal retreat; if only they could remember to behave in the ways they saw on the TV talk show; if only they had been able to follow all the steps in the self-help books and articles they read. Especially the steps to better communication—you know, the "six steps to better communication about sex/money/the kids" articles advertised on magazine covers at the grocery store checkout area.

Sometimes a couple who asks for my help has tried to solve relationship problems by having a baby. That's not an unusual way for couples to try to establish intimacy when they feel it is lacking in their relationship. People have babies for all sorts of other reasons, of course, and sometimes the reason is that the pregnancy is unplanned. But what all new parents have in common is that, until they actually become parents—whether through adoption or through giving birth—no individual or couple fully realizes the extent of the changes a baby will bring to their individual lives and to their relationships with one another and with others.

I'll demonstrate my point with the following composite case study, which is drawn from a variety of sources, including published research and theory on the transition to parenthood. Although my research with single mothers' transition to parenthood and my experiences conducting couple and family therapy also informed my writing of this case study, the confidentiality of my research interviewees or my clients has not been compromised.

When I began working with them four years ago, Marcy and Roland had not realized the changes that would come with the birth of their first child. They are both Caucasian, from the United States, and in their early 30s at the time I first began seeing them. Marcy is a high-school chemistry teacher, and Roland is a certified public accountant. Their daughter, Anna, was three months old at the time we began working together, and they have since had twin boys. On that day four years ago, it was Marcy who called to make their first therapy appointment. On the telephone she said that the reason she and her husband wanted counseling was for "communication problems."

Couples often truly believe that "communication problems" are at the root of their unhappiness—that if they could just learn to communicate more and/or better with one another, they would be happy. To make matters more complicated, each partner in a couple usually sees the "communication problems" as stemming from the *other* partner's behavior: "If she would just communicate more, then our problems would be solved." "If only he would not nag me all the time, everything would be fine." Sometimes I hear what can be the most damaging statement of all, because it suggests that the inevitable conflicts of a relationship are being played out in indirect ways rather than being addressed directly: "My spouse wasn't complaining, so I didn't know there was a problem."

During my first session with a couple, I always point to the mobile made up of cardboard birds that hangs from my office ceiling, and I ask them to tell me what is hanging up there. The partners invariably look at me incredulously, and then they often look at each other as if to say, "And we're paying *money* for this?!" Finally, one will say tentatively, as if expecting a trick question, "a mobile?" "Right!" I exclaim. "I ask every couple who comes in here that same question, and not one person has ever said, 'It's eight birds.' Everyone has always seen one mobile." After I asked that question of Marcy and Roland, I continued, "In the same way that nobody ever says, 'That's eight birds up there,' during our work together I view my 'client' to be the entire family system represented by that mobile: you two, Anna, and your extended families. We won't blame anybody for anything, because we're not concentrating our attention on any one of you as an individual. We'll focus on the interaction *between* you and help you change your interaction in ways that will help you meet your goals for coming to counseling."

Next I looked at both Roland and Marcy and asked what brought them in to counseling. They looked at each other, as if deciding who would answer for the couple. Roland nodded to Marcy and she said, "For about the past year, we've just not been happy, and we fight a lot. I try to talk to Roland about things, but after a few minutes he finds a reason to go into the den and work at the computer—that's when the fights begin. His disappearing act is not going to help us be happier, so I follow him in there and say something like, 'Roland, you can't just hide behind that computer! We have to talk about why we're so unhappy.' "

Roland had been nodding while Marcy was talking and then said, "That's about how it goes. When Marcy starts one of these fights with her griping about being unhappy, I try to help by talking for a little while, but pretty soon we're just going in circles. When I can't stand it anymore, I just have to escape; so I go into the den and turn on the computer to try to get away from things for awhile. But no! She can't just leave it alone! She has to follow me in there, and she starts in again that we have to talk! When I try to ignore her badgering me by concentrating on the computer screen, she comes over by the computer and keeps insisting that we have to talk about things. After that's gone on a while I shout at her, 'Damn it, Marcy—leave me alone!' or something like that. The fight finally ends when one of us gets so mad we go out to the store to get a carton of milk or something. Sometimes the baby is crying by this time, and if a fight gets really bad, one of us goes off to bed and tries to fall asleep before the other one gets there."

I asked Marcy and Roland a few routine questions about whether alcohol or drugs were ever involved with their "fights," and whether there ever had been any physical violence between them. If there had been even "just" a slap or shove, I needed to know about that to work with Marcy and Roland on their "communication problems." When I was satisfied that there was no drug or alcohol abuse and no physical violence and I had detected nothing that suggested underlying psychiatric problems with either Roland or Marcy, I moved on to the main thing I try to get accomplished in my first session with a couple: the story of their relationship and family history.

Marcy and Roland had been married for five years when they first came to see me. They had met about a year before they married, when Roland was giving a speech about his work as an accountant on Career Day at the high school where Marcy teaches. They began dating casually at first. Roland had been married briefly before he met Marcy, and although there had been no children in that marriage and he and his ex-wife had parted amicably two years before, he wasn't in any hurry to be in a serious relationship again. (I then asked several questions of both Roland and Marcy and ascertained that no leftover "baggage" from Roland's first marriage was contributing significantly to Marcy and Roland's current relationship problems.) During a few months of dating casually, Marcy and Roland's relationship had gradually become more emotionally intimate; eventually it also became a sexual relationship. Both Roland and Marcy described the sexual aspects of their relationship as mutually satisfying early in their relationship, but less so in the year before they began couples therapy.

Marcy and Roland said that, after they had been married about four years, they wanted to "start a family." Marcy was delighted when she conceived within a few months, but throughout her pregnancy she felt that Roland was more "into" the pregnancy than she was. She said that early on, while she was nauseous and fretting over her disappearing waistline, Roland was already reading books on childbirth and parenting. Roland researched strollers and car seats thoroughly in *Consumer Reports* before purchasing the best ones. During the second trimester of pregnancy Marcy was less nauseated and even had a little more energy than before, so she and Roland worked together in clearing out all the boxes stored in their second bedroom and making it into a nursery. They planned on equal parenting responsibilities, so they wanted to share the preparations for the baby, too. Together, they decided that Marcy would take a semester off from teaching after the baby was born. It was advantageous timing that the baby was due in March, because they would have the extra money Roland earned during tax season.

During her third trimester, Marcy tired easily and often, so by the end of a school day she was content to leaf through the book of babies' names Roland had bought for them. They knew by then that their baby was a daughter, so together they decided on the name Anna Elizabeth, for two of their grandmothers. Marcy's and Roland's grandparents all had died by the time Marcy was pregnant with Anna, but all four of their parents were still alive. Roland's parents, Bob and Linda, already had a grandson who was the son of Roland's sister Kate, but Anna would be the first grandchild for Marcy's parents, Peggy and Chuck, who had no other children besides Marcy.

Anna was born a couple of days before her March due date. As they had planned, Roland was in the birthing room with Marcy during her labor, and he got to cut the umbilical cord after delivery. Roland and Marcy had taken prepared childbirth classes so, although Marcy had to work hard during the labor and delivery to maintain her focus and breathing, with Roland's coaching she was able to give birth without medication. Marcy and Roland had planned that she would breastfeed the baby; both said they had wanted to give their baby the best start they could, so within moments after her birth Anna was placed at Marcy's breast. Marcy's and Anna's postnatal examinations showed that both the pregnancy and Anna's prenatal development had been without complications.

I explained to Roland and Marcy that the period of time between one family life-cycle stage and the next, which is very stressful for both families and individual family members, is called a *transition*. They had recently passed through the most complex transition of all in a family's life cycle, the transition to parenthood, and they were now in the stage of their family life cycle when they were a family with an infant.

I further explained that during individual and family life-cycle stages, stage-specific *developmental tasks* (that is, milestones that must be achieved) have to be accomplished. If the developmental tasks of a particular stage are not successfully completed, there will be difficulty with the developmental tasks of subsequent stages. For example, as she progresses through her individual life-cycle stages, a baby like Anna must learn to crawl before she will be able to walk. Similarly, a couple must accomplish the tasks of their life-cycle stage when they were a couple without children and progress successfully through the transition to parenthood, before they can negotiate the developmental tasks of the life-cycle stage of the family with an infant.

I told Marcy and Roland it was significant that their "fights" had begun about a year before and not earlier in their relationship. That timing led me to speculate that they had successfully accomplished the developmental tasks of their "couple without children" stage but now were having difficulty with the profound changes of the transition to parenthood and the developmental tasks of their "new parents" stage. Based on that speculation, I spent considerable time on their relationship history—ascertaining that, indeed, they seemed to have accomplished the main tasks of the prior stage. Those tasks included developing a shared definition of their relationship, intimacy without extreme costs to each individual spouse's sense of autonomy, and satisfactory patterns of managing relationship conflict.

Sure enough, as I probed their relationship history, Roland and Marcy's "fights" and unhappiness were the tip of an iceberg of deeply underlying relational issues that had developed during the pregnancy. They had not recognized these issues, so they had not talked about them directly. No wonder they labeled the relationship issues that had brought them to counseling as "communication problems"!

Although Anna was a healthy baby, things had not gone as smoothly during her weeks as a newborn as Marcy and Roland had planned. When they had planned their pregnancy, mid-winter had seemed like a good time to have a baby because they would have the needed extra money Roland earned during tax season. However, that year Roland worked far more hours than they had anticipated. Business was especially brisk for Roland, and—feeling so much financial responsibility with new fatherhood—he didn't want to turn down any new clients. Anna and Marcy adjusted quickly to the breastfeeding and Marcy enjoyed it, but she didn't want to give Anna even an occasional bottle. As a result, she had to be available for Anna at all times. Also, Marcy and Anna spent so much time together that Roland sometimes felt a little jealous of the closeness that developed around breastfeeding.

Marcy and Roland had thought that, once the baby was born, their couple relationship would go back to the way it had been before the pregnancy—after all, babies sleep a lot, right? But Anna's preferred sleep times were during the day and for short periods during the night. At first, Roland got up with Marcy during the night when she nursed the baby, but soon he slept right through Anna's crying because he had worked long days preparing tax returns. Within a couple of weeks, Marcy and Roland's conflict patterns from earlier in their relationship had gone by the wayside, and they snapped at each other from fatigue.

Marcy's main complaint was, "Just because I'm nursing, you expect me to do the entire night shift!" Roland would retort, "You can catch up on your sleep during the day. I have to work then because I'm the one bringing in the income around here!" Before long, they didn't talk much about caring for Anna's needs. They didn't want to argue, so both assumed Marcy would take care of Anna's needs because she was on leave from teaching and Roland was gone so much.

Their old ways of feeling close as a couple didn't work very well either. Marcy had some mild postpartum depression and lingering soreness from an episiotomy she had had while giving birth. So, when they came to therapy three months later, they had not yet resumed having intercourse. Roland secretly worried that Marcy's reluctance to have intercourse meant that she was rebuffing him. Maybe she didn't appreciate all his extra work to earn money for the family. But he didn't want to sound like all he cared about was sex, so he hadn't said anything about it to Marcy.

Earlier in their marriage, they used to spend time in bed just talking and laughing together. After Anna was born, Roland complained that he felt no sense of privacy in their own bed because Marcy often nursed Anna there. Marcy knew he was right about needing some privacy just for the two of them, but because she was so tired from childbirth and she knew her night's sleep would be sporadic anyway, it was easier to bring Anna to their bed so Marcy could doze while nursing.

Even with all the changes in their lives, Roland and Marcy often talked between themselves about how glad they were they had had Anna. Both were thrilled with the closeness they felt with Anna, and they felt proud when Anna's pediatrician praised them for giving her so many health benefits from breastfeeding. Other stories in Marcy and Roland's relationship history from Anna's newborn period also indicated that parent-child attachment had proceeded well. For example, both Marcy and Roland said that on the rare occasions when they left Anna with Marcy's parents, they often returned early from their outing because they missed their baby.

Chuck and Peggy loved caring for Anna, and although they thought Marcy should be a little more "laid back" in caring for her newborn, they never said anything about it. They wanted their daughter to know they respected the fact that she and Roland, not they, were Anna's parents. Privately, Roland thought it was a little weird that Peggy and Chuck took so little interest in the baby; his own parents often gave advice to him and to Marcy about child care. Marcy said she resented Bob and Linda's "interference," so Roland discussed things with his sister Kate. Kate said that during her pregnancy and after the birth of her son, Justin, she had depended a lot on their parents, especially their mother. Kate said, "I didn't have a husband the way Marcy has you. If Mom hadn't been there for me to talk to while I was pregnant and after Justin was born, I don't know what I would have done."

By the time Roland finished relating this part of his and Marcy's relationship history, we were nearing the end of the time allotted for our first session. Therefore, I moved on to an initial discussion of their goals for therapy. Their goal was that their "fights" would stop; they said they wanted me to teach them the communication skills they would need to reach that goal. I told them that stopping the fights was a realistic goal but that new communication skills alone would not stop the fights. I told them that I was optimistic we could change the way they experienced relationship conflicts because, once we had begun to deal with their underlying relationship issues, they would be able to draw on their previous, more productive, conflict management patterns.

As spouses who were invested in each other, Marcy and Roland would always have conflicts, of course. I told them that is normal and healthy for a committed couple. They had a lot going for them, which boded well for their success in therapy and for the longevity of their marriage: Each was functioning well as an individual; Anna was a healthy baby; there were sufficient time and financial resources to support them all; they had a relationship history of trust and respect for each other. Although we needed to work on establishing mutually-satisfactory boundaries with their parents/Anna's grandparents, the support from their extended families was a plus for this family. I knew that Roland and Marcy would need to learn to identify and interact effectively about their underlying relationship issues. Most of all, though, they would need to learn to negotiate the complexities of their redefined relationship, which included *both* their roles—as Anna's parents and as each other's spouse.

FOR FURTHER THOUGHT AND REFLECTION

1. What are some misconceptions couples have about their relationship communication?

2. Dialectical tensions (simultaneous "pulls" in opposite directions) are normal occurrences in couple relationships. The autonomy/connection dynamic becomes particularly prominent for many couples after the birth of their first child. Identify some examples of Marcy and Roland renegotiating this couple dynamic after Anna's birth.

3. What are some of the changes for Marcy and Roland as a couple that occurred during their transition to parenthood? Changes for the each of them as an individual?

4. One developmental task that must be accomplished during the transition to parenthood is the appropriation of the parental role. This comes about through three overlapping processes: *role expectations* (trying to predict what parenthood will entail); *role enactment* (each partner both facilitating and inhibiting the appropriation of the other's parental role); and *role negotiation* (interacting about care of the child) (Stamp, 1994). When and how did each of these occur with Roland and Marcy?

5. Find examples of social developmental tasks involving boundaries in the nuclear family system of Marcy, Roland, and Anna. Then, find examples of their social developmental tasks that involve boundaries in their wider relational systems (that is, their *suprasystems*).

REFERENCES

Aldous, J. (1996). *Family careers: Rethinking the developmental perspective.* Thousand Oaks, CA: Sage.

Bradt, J. O. (1989). Becoming parents: Families with young children. In B. Carter & M. McGoldrick (Eds.), *The changing family life cycle* (2nd ed., pp. 235–254). Boston: Allyn and Bacon.

Berger, P., & Kellner, H. (1964). Marriage and the construction of reality. *Diogenes, 46,* 1–24.

Hess, R., & Handel, G. (1959). *Family worlds.* Chicago: University of Chicago Press.

Rodgers, R. H., & White, J. M. (1993). Family development theory. In P. G. Boss, W. J. Doherty, R. LaRossa, W. R. Schumm, & S. K. Steinmetz (Eds.), *Sourcebook of family theories and methods* (pp. 225–254). New York: Plenum.

Rogers, L. E. (1989). Relational communication processes and patterns. In B. Dervin, L. Grossberg, B. O'Keefe, & E. Wartella (Eds.), *Rethinking communication, Vol. 2* (pp. 280–290). Newbury Park, CA: Sage.

Socha, T. J., & Stamp, G. H. (Eds.) (1995), *Parents, children, and communication: Frontiers of theory and research.* Mahwah, NJ: Lawrence Erlbaum.

Stamp, G. H. (1994). The appropriation of the parental role through communication during the transition to parenthood. *Communication Monographs, 61,* 89–112.

Whitchurch, G. G., & Constantine, L. L. (1993). Systems theory. In P. G. Boss, W. J. Doherty, R. LaRossa, W. R. Schumm, & S. K. Steinmetz (Eds.), *Sourcebook of family theories and methods* (pp. 325–352). New York: Plenum.

Whitchurch, G. G., & Dickson, F. C. (1999). Family communication. In M. B. Sussman, S. K. Steinmetz, & G. W. Peterson (Eds.), *Handbook of marriage and the family* (2nd ed., pp. 687–704). New York: Plenum.

PARENTS, CHILDREN, PEOPLE

Stages in Parent-Child Relationships

Kathleen M. Galvin

Annie's roommate knows the drill. When Annie's mother calls, Stephanie is to say she is really busy and will call back soon, even if Annie is flopped on the bed in their dorm room. When Annie does talk to her mother, her roommate is primed to create appropriate noises to suggest Annie is wanted elsewhere. Sometimes Stephanie gets the signal to "go into her act;" at other times she senses she can leave Annie chatting away. Yet if Annie's father calls, Stephanie will make an effort to find Annie if she is in the hall. Freshman year of college has been an important transition time for Annie and her mother as they try to redefine their relationship. Annie will be returning home for a long winter break in two weeks and hopes it will prove to be a good experience for both of them. She sees the break as a time for reconnecting with her father, for different reasons.

As Annie prepared to leave for college, her mother, Jan, told the neighbors, "I thought it would be tough to send my first child off to school, but Annie's adolescence has made that moment easy for me. I'm actually counting the days!" Annie had the days and hours numbered also, ceremoniously crossing them off on the kitchen calendar with dramatic flair. But in August Jan shopped for trinkets to send to Annie during the first semester, and Annie indicated she expected Jan to attend the Fall Parents Weekend.

Annie's departure for college left Jan feeling sad, regretful, and relieved. After two stressful days of arguing and packing, the four-hour ride to campus was quiet and tense. As the residence-hall staff enveloped an excited Annie, Jan found herself watching as other parents unloaded their children, wondering if they felt as conflicted as she did. After unpacking, Annie barely managed a quick good-bye before racing off to catch up to her new suitemates who were heading to a dorm barbecue. Jan drove home, wistfully reminiscing on eighteen years of motherhood that had proved quite different from her expectations.

On Parents Weekend, both women tried hard to survive with limited friction, although there were a few tough moments when Jan saw the state of the dorm room and heard about some of Annie's midterm grades. There was little talk of dating, since Annie deflected most of the relevant questions; Jan made suggestions for selecting a sorority, to which Annie responded in a noncommittal manner. Annie and her roommate planned a number of events together, so time alone for each mother-daughter pair was limited. Annie's dad, a musician, was playing a concert that weekend and could not attend. Again Jan drove home, wishing she could have some years to live over again and aiming at a different outcome for this mother-daughter relationship. She imagined the upcoming holidays as a time for greater closeness and less tension, but she foresaw some continuation of the stressful interactions that characterized the last years with her daughter.

Jan had always held very clear ideas about the importance of strict parenting and appropriate behavior for children and adolescents—ideas she did not hesitate to share in an unrelenting manner with her three children, Annie (18), Tim (14), and Paul (12). As a primary parent since Annie was ten, Jan felt personally compelled to raise highly responsible children who would be resourceful and appropriate in all situations. The divorce, which Jan resisted, was particularly painful because it challenged her personal and religious sense of commitment, shattered her image of what a family should look like, and forced her to give up her expectation for an active male partner who would support her positions on parenting. At 20 she had fallen in love with Josh, a carefree, spontaneous young musician who challenged her rather rigid upbringing. Against her family's advice, she proceeded to marry Josh within the year. Eleven months after the wedding, Jan found herself with a new passion, motherhood, a role she took very seriously while Josh tried to maintain his fluid lifestyle.

Jan, the only divorced sibling in her family of origin, saw her situation as a personal failure although she had experienced Josh's growing distance for years. The divorce left her determined to make this family work well and look good to extended family and neighbors. Jan remained concerned about the family image and her role as a responsible parent, frequently preaching, "Only your best is good enough" and "You have to work for what you get." According to Jan, such values prepared her children to succeed in a tough world. According to her children, their mother was overbearing and only was concerned with what others thought.

The children's father, who lives in the same city, provides a counterbalance to Jan's attitudes. "Don't sweat the small stuff" and "Mistakes build character" were closer to his approach to life and parenting. Although Josh has had a number of long term relationships since the divorce, his musical career dominates his life. The boys tease that Dad's saxophone is really his "first-born child." All three children are attracted to his easygoing and spontaneous style, and they compete for his limited attention. They have learned to tell him the good stuff and to avoid problems, since Josh does not deal well with the latter. Josh enjoys his children, but he stays in touch with them on an irregular basis because he travels extensively for concerts and recording sessions. When he is available, the boys tend to hang out at his house since both of them are into music and sports. Annie tries to engage her father in her life, but sometimes she feels that she's on the fringe. Josh's current female partner is also a musician, something Annie resents.

Both Jan and Josh provide support for the successes of their children by trying to attend basketball games or drama performances, although Josh is frequently out of town. Family celebrations, such as birthdays or graduations, are shared by both parents, although an uneasy truce prevails during the informal parties in one or the other's home. Jan and Josh continue to argue predictably about approaches to parenting, but generally Josh defers to Jan because she is the consistently available custodial parent. True to form, he does not confront Jan's strong positions, if only to avoid the stress of disagreement.

Relations between Annie and Jan have not always been as strained as they are now. In elementary school, Annie was the dream child whom Jan relied on for female companionship and support while the two younger boys and Dad teamed as a counterbalance. Mother and daughter often shopped, went to the movies, or held video nights while the "boys" were otherwise occupied, often at music or sports events with Dad. Although Jan worked as a free-lance writer, she made time to assist with the Scout troop and field trips. Through these activities, she developed a network of other mothers who shared parenting tips and stories. Much time was spent with Jan's extended family, and Annie was an active member of the cousins' group.

By seventh grade, relations started shifting and the easy and consistent closeness between mother and daughter disappeared. Annie became secretive and isolated, complaining that her mother was overprotective. She balked at having to participate in countless extended family celebrations and clung to her girlfriends, some of whom Jan saw as manipulative and rebellious. Annie was part of a group of girls that shifted frequently over 18 months as members were "in" or "out." This was a painful period for Annie, who wanted desperately to be part of the "in" group by dressing and acting like the other girls. Jan resisted the group's impact, and most mornings began with a battle over clothes, hair, makeup, and attitude.

Over the years, Jan closely monitored each child's activities, but the teenage years brought conflicts over this behavior. For example, before Annie could attend a teenage party, Jan was likely to call the home to be sure a parent was going to be in the house. If Jan doubted that Annie gave her a true picture of plans for a Friday night, or if Annie was more than 20 minutes late, Jan would call around to locate her. Annie's friends soon learned to cover for her if Jan called. The following conversation occurred with countless variations:

JAN: Where are you going Friday night?

ANNIE: To hang out at Angie's

JAN: Will her parents be home?

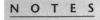

ANNIE: Sure.

JAN: What's her number? I want to talk to her mother.

ANNIE: You are the only parent who acts like a junior in high school is a five-year old. Other parents trust their kids.

JAN: Some parents are not responsible. . . .

ANNIE: And some think they're the police. . . .

After the divorce, Jan relied heavily on adult friends or teachers for advice on child-rearing, frequently asking how they might handle a particular situation or how she should deal with Annie's latest escapade. In such conversations, Jan's high expectations for her children were evident, although she was more tolerant of the foibles of other people's children. Jan rejected Josh's suggestions because she found him too permissive.

Teachers quickly learned that Annie's mother called to check on homework expectations or special project guidelines to ensure Annie's work would be absolutely correct. Sometimes Jan would use parent-teacher conferences as an opportunity to gain feedback on how she handled certain parenting situations. Such behavior was an extension of Jan's active involvement with all three children's teachers throughout their school years.

Much to her children's dismay, Jan felt called upon to monitor her children's behavior in public settings and directly requested they alter it if she believed they were not being polite or appropriate. When guests entered their home, she was likely to say, "Annie, didn't you see Mr. Goodman? Please say hello," or "Tim, you didn't tell Daryl you liked his birthday present." She displayed clear expectations for how children should talk to adults, particularly family members ("Don't answer back"), as well as standards for public appearance ("You can't go to school dressed like that"). Annie provided the greatest resistance, although Tim began to "Do an Annie" as he entered adolescence. Paul remained a compliant child.

Jan's "need to know" frequently clashed with her children's need for her "not to know." Occasionally, Jan lifted up the phone receiver and listened in on the children's conversations, explaining if someone caught her in the process that she thought the line was clear. Throughout adolescence, Annie took the position "the less Mom knows the better," and resisted sharing much about her life with her mother except the good stuff and the troubles some of her less-well-liked peers encountered. Therefore, Annie did not lie regularly, but she omitted many important topics from conversations with her mother, in the hope that no one else would bring them to Jan's attention. Topics Annie avoided included low grades on tests, detentions after school, missed athletic practices, money from her father, drinking, and some drug experimentation. Although

Annie mastered the parent deception routine, at times she envied her friends who talked about really important things with their parents.

It was quite common for Annie to "yes" her mother and then do whatever she chose. In certain situations, flat-out lying was the strategy of choice, which resulted in outrage if Jan discovered the situation. Knowing her mother was not likely to call her father's house casually, Annie reported spending the evening with Dad when, in reality, she was at a friend's party. On occasion, Josh was surprised to hear her coming in at 5 A.M. (four hours later than her mother's curfew time). If asked directly, he tended to cover for Annie by telling Jan he knew she was coming. After he figured out Annie had been experimenting with drinking and pot, he talked with her about the risks, but didn't tell Jan because he didn't want to deal with the predictable arguments.

Dad's home provided Annie with leverage in heated conversations, when she occasionally threatened, "I'm going to live with Dad," a painful message for Jan. This served to bring Jan in line and reduce her overt anger. Josh's history of broken promises in his marriage and the post-divorce parenting relationship made Jan worry that Annie would turn out deceitful "just like her father."

The following conversation typifies the mother-daughter interaction in Annie's later high-school years:

MOM: Annie, I received a phone call from your drama teacher, and he said you were sent home from rehearsal because you arrived over an hour late for the second time.

ANNIE: Mmmm. . . .

MOM: I was supposed to have signed a form before you could return, but he said Dad signed it. Why didn't I see it? I'm the custodial parent. When did you see your father to do this?

ANNIE: It's not a big deal! Mr. Murray needs me in that show. There's no decent understudy for my part. Don't worry about it.

MOM: Don't worry! I had no clue what the man was talking about, and he seems to think it's important. Why didn't I see this form?

ANNIE: I forgot.

MOM: Forgot?! How convenient. So you just signed Dad's name? That's wonderful. I guess he has to be good for something in your life.

ANNIE: Mom, it's no big deal. Lay off!

MOM: Anne Marie. Don't talk to your mother that way. I expect an explanation about what was going on.

ANNIE: Nothing was going on. I got into a conversation with Terrie and lost track of time. I told you—forget it. Get off my back!

MOM: Until we can talk in a civil manner about this and you can explain the whole situation, you can sit in your room and think about it.

ANNIE: (*stomping off*) Well, at least I'll get away from your jabbering!

MOM: And no talking on the phone. . . .

Although their time was characterized by repeated disagreements, there were occasions when Jan and Annie found ways to interact in a positive manner. Annie relied on Jan's help and support in large school projects, such as her poster display for the city history fair or numerous science projects. Jan was a solicitous parent when the children were sick, she chauffeured them to countless activities, and she prepared favorite meals on request.

One special experience occurred when Jan had a business trip to Mexico City and she carved out five days for herself and Annie to travel. Jan gave Annie travel guides and maps and told her to plan the trip. Annie spent hours poring over the information and came up with a reasonably well-organized itinerary, which Jan agreed to follow. This was a unique experience, and they negotiated each day effectively, meeting both of their needs. Jan was able to talk about missing out on such experiences as a young person and wanting Annie to explore many parts of life before getting tied down to marriage and family.

On occasion, Jan used Annie as a confidante or sounding board, particularly with respect to concerns about Paul. She asked Annie's advice about how to help Paul make his own friends or how to help him find a clearer identity apart from Tim. In the last year, Jan even talked briefly with Annie about a man she was dating.

Annie had many boyfriends during high school, but no one very special. Jan had strict rules about any friend of the opposite sex entering the house without a parent present. Jan suspected Annie violated the rules, but she was never able to prove it and Annie claimed that Jan was overreacting as usual.

Although Annie and her brothers argue regularly, they don't tell on each other. Annie will cover for the boys, and they pretend not to know Annie's business if Jan asks. At times, Annie appears to resent all the attention that Tim, a superb athlete, receives. She recently ended a phone conversation about Tim's invitation to a regional gymnastics meet, shouting, "I'm sick of talking about Tim's flips."

At this point, mother and daughter are viewing winter break with mixed feelings. Jan imagines some cozy conversations, during which Annie will really share stories about her life at college, her friends, dates, classes and thoughts about independence. Annie envisions moments when she and Mom will talk the way she hears her roommate discuss life with her mother. Each hopes there will be less tension between them, but each fears the same old patterns will prevail.

FOR FURTHER THOUGHT AND REFLECTION

1. Identify examples of the following dialectical tensions found in the relationship between Annie and Jan—openness/closedness and autonomy/connection. (*Openness/closedness* refers to the struggle two people encounter as they negotiate how much information in their lives to share with each other and how much to keep private. *Autonomy/connection* refers to the struggle two persons confront as they try to manage each one's need for independence and interdependence.)

2. To what extent has self-disclosure been used to build a relationship between members of this family?

3. What has been the effect of deception strategies on the relationship between Annie and Jan?

4. Identify some family themes and expectations that Jan and Josh each bring to their parenting roles.

5. What are two predictions you would make about Annie and Jan's relationship over the next five years?

REFERENCES

Blieszner, R. (1994). Close relationships over time. In A. L. Weber & J. H. Harvey (Eds.), *Perspectives on close relationships* (pp. 1–17). Needham Heights, MA: Allyn & Bacon.

Galvin, K. M., & Brommel, B. (1996*). Family communication: Cohesion and change* (4th ed.). New York: Addison Wesley Longman.

Petronio, S. (1994). Privacy binds in family interaction. In W. R. Cupach & B. H. Spitzberg (Eds.), *The dark side of interpersonal communication* (pp. 241–258). Mahwah, NJ: Lawrence Erlbaum.

Rawlins, W. K. (1992). *Friendship matters: Communication, dialectics and the life course.* New York: Aldine de Gruyter.

Rawlins, W. K. (1989). Rehearsing the margins of adulthood: The communicative management of adolescent friendships. In J. F. Nussbaum (Ed.), *Life span communication: Normative processes* (pp. 137–154). Mahwah, NJ: Lawrence Erlbaum.

Stafford, L., & Dainton, M. (1995). Parent-child communication within the family system. In T. J. Socha & G. H. Stamp (Eds.), *Parents, children, and communication,* (pp. 3–21). Mahwah, N.J.: Lawrence Erlbaum.

WHO'S THE PARENT NOW?

When Adult Children Become Care Givers for Parents

Julia T. Wood

KEY WORDS

■

parent-child relationships
gender roles
emotional conflicts
venting
honesty
sandwich generation

N O T E S

When I was nine years old, I was very sick with an serious case of mumps. I was miserable—achy, uncomfortable, and feverish. I couldn't speak without strain, and even swallowing was painful. I remember my mother sitting with me for hours on end. She rubbed my forehead with a cool washcloth to ease the fever, and she stroked my swollen neck gently. Although I didn't realize it then, mother was neglecting other things she'd planned to do in order to care for me. Perhaps she resented me (or my illness) for intruding on her plans; perhaps she felt frustrated at having to care for me; perhaps she was bored during the days she spent by my bedside. If so, she didn't show those feelings. I never sensed any reservations or resentments as she sat patiently with me.

The scene I've just described was replayed 32 years later; only the second time I was the one sitting patiently with mother, trying to ease her pain from the terminal disease that would too soon take her from me. As I cared for her, I felt sadness and deep love for this woman who had given birth to me and nurtured me all of my life. Yet I also felt resentment, frustration, and anger. I resented her needs because they interfered with my family plans and my professional responsibilities. I was frustrated by the unpredictability that her illness injected into my world. And I was angry at her for not acting like my mother—not being there for me, putting her needs aside for mine—and for provoking a reversal in our roles so that I was now acting like a mother to her and she was acting like a needy child.

Most of all, I felt guilty—horribly, wrenchingly guilty—for feeling resentment, frustration, and anger toward my mother. I despised myself for not willingly and lovingly giving her unbounded time and comfort. Why couldn't I be as selfless for her as she had been for me?

During the process of taking my mother through her final passage and recovering from her death, I learned many things about what was happening to me and between us. I learned that the mixture of feelings I had—love, sadness, resentment, frustration, anger, guilt—were typical of many children who become care givers for sick or dying parents. I learned that what I felt didn't make me a horrible person, because all of my feelings were normal. The case that follows illuminates what I learned about relationships in which children assume the role of parent with their own parents. The case, however, is about far more than my personal experience. It reflects insights from counselors and research on general patterns in relationships in which adult children care for parents.

"It's not that I don't want to take care of her; it's that I don't have the time," Kate says in an effort to tell her therapist what she is feeling about her mother who moved into her home two months ago. "I mean, I still have my job and my marriage and the two children—those responsibilities haven't gone away just because mother is living with us and needs constant care."

"Are you saying that if you had more time, you'd be happy to take care of your mother?" Sylvia asks.

Kate nods. "Yes, of course. I'm not a selfish person."

"Is that how it feels to you—that it would be selfish not to want to care for your mother?" Sylvia asks. Even before Kate answers, Sylvia anticipates that Kate will equate not wanting to do everything for her mother with being selfish. The role of women in Western culture is so firmly tied to caring for others that it's hard for any woman not to feel it's selfish to do otherwise.

"Of course. Any decent person would do that if she had the time." Kate feels compelled to answer this way, but part of her is relieved that her job and family limit how much she can do for her mother. She doesn't mind fixing meals and doing laundry or spending time talking with her mother. Other parts of care giving, however, do bother her. She dreads helping her mother in the bathroom and despises cleaning up when her mother loses control in her bed. That disgusts her, but she doesn't want to tell Sylvia she feels this way. It seems so heartless.

"Do you think your mother never resented taking care of you?"

"Of course not. She was always there for me."

"So maybe she did what you needed even if she resented it," Sylvia suggests. "Does that mean she was somehow less caring or less loving?"

Kate ponders the question. She's a mother now too, and there are times when she is frustrated by her children's needs—even times when she resents their demands on her time and energy. She tries to hide those feelings from her son and daughter, and she thinks she does so successfully. But sometimes she does resent her children, just as she sometimes resents her mother.

"If love means doing only what we want to do, it's not very admirable," Sylvia says. "Perhaps a more mature, authentic kind of love is doing what others need even when we don't enjoy it."

"Maybe," Kate allows. "But it seems dishonest to act as if you don't mind doing something when really you do."

"Okay, let's play that out. What would be the point of telling your mother you don't like doing some things, such as changing her bed when she's dirtied it? Would that do *you* any good? Would it do *her* any good?"

"No," Kate admits, "but sometimes I just feel the need to express my anger or frustration about all of her needs and how they fall on me."

"Nothing wrong with that," Sylvia replies. "And this is a safe place for it. You need somewhere where you can vent your anger and frustration without hurting your mother. You can do that with me; you can do it with your friends; you can do it with Mark. And you should."

"It just seems so selfish to feel anything but a desire to help her when she's so sick," Kate says. "I feel like a terrible person if I get angry when I have to rearrange my schedule for her or when I get disgusted about cleaning up after her. Those aren't nice feelings."

"So who says all of our feelings are nice?" Sylvia asks. "Does it mean you don't do what she needs? Of course not. You do it, in spite of anger or disgust. That's real love, not the storybook kind. Give yourself permission to have those feelings and express them in safe places where they won't hurt your mother."

"What I'd really like to do is express that anger to Sandy," Kate mutters. Her brother, Sandy, lives in the same town, but he never invited their mom to move in with him. Actually, it would have been easier for him because his and Alice's children are older—both in high school—and their home is larger. But when she and Sandy talked about the fact that their mom couldn't take care of herself anymore, both of them had just assumed Kate and Mark would make room in their home. When Kate had suggested tentatively that maybe their mom could live six months of the year with each of them, Sandy had dismissed the suggestion, saying, "That really wouldn't work because both Alice and I work." *So?* thought Kate. Both she and Mark worked too!

Since their mom moved in with Kate's family, Sandy has stopped by once a week for short visits, and he sometimes calls between visits. What infuriates Kate most is how much her mother appreciates the little that Sandy does for her. Just last week he stopped by for only 30 minutes. After he left, Kate remembers her mother said, "It's so good of Sandy to take time out from his busy life to visit me. I know how pressed he is." Kate had thought *He gets praised for giving her 30 lousy minutes, and I spend hours taking care of her every day!*

Sylvia nods. From her counseling, she realizes that Kate's situation is like that of many adult women who are caring for parents. Often there are brothers, but they don't volunteer to take over any of the care giving. Sometimes they help with expenses, but they seldom take much responsibility for the day-to-day nursing and personal care. Almost always, that responsibility falls on daughters or daughters-in-law whose husbands don't provide hands-on caring for their own parents.

Sylvia reflects on the lack of change in gender roles regarding caring for others. Although the feminist movement has enlarged women's political, economic, and professional opportunities, it hasn't transformed the traditional expectation that women are the primary care givers of young children and anyone else who needs care. Both women and men continue to expect women to fulfill that role. This sometimes creates extraordinary pressures on women of the "sandwich generation"—people who are caring for children at the same time they are caring for parents and parents-in-law. When those people are also engaged in full-time work outside of the home, the strains can be overwhelming. When more women were full-time homemakers and mothers, it was less of a strain for them to take care of relatives. Then, too, Sylvia realizes, life-spans have expanded significantly, so more people are living to ages when they require some assistance.

The problem is not just men who don't willingly assume equal responsibility for caring for parents and in-laws. It's just as much the problem of women who expect so much of themselves. Kate is like many of her clients—stretched to the breaking point to meet their responsibilities to jobs, children, husbands, and elderly parents. And they often feel guilty for feeling strained, angry, or resentful. Sylvia wishes she could do more to help her women clients challenge the internalized feeling that they should not only care for others but should always feel happy to do so.

"We can't control what Sandy does or doesn't do, so let's focus on what we can control," Sylvia redirects the conversation. "Tell me more about what your resentment and frustration and anger are like."

"Well, I just feel that I can't do it all and that I shouldn't have to," Kate begins. "It's like I have to fix all of her special meals and keep track of her records and make sure she gets to her doctors' appointments, and everything, and nobody is taking care of me."

That's what Sylvia had been waiting to hear. She's read a lot of research on adult children who become care givers for parents. What she's read leads Sylvia to suspect that Kate probably feels some sense of betrayal because her mother is no longer mothering her.

"So, not only do you have the responsibility of taking care of someone who is needy, but that person is the very one who is supposed to take care of you," Sylvia says.

"I miss my mother so much. She always took care of me, even after I was grown up and married. She was the one who would always support me and make time for me and help me."

"And now she can't do that for you, and you have to do it for her? Is that what it feels like?"

Kate nods, dabbing her eyes with a tissue. "I feel as if I don't have a mother anymore. It's as if she's my child, and that feels so strange."

Sylvia nods. One of the most difficult issues when children become care givers for parents is role reversal. Suddenly, they have to watch and protect the parents and oversee daily schedules in the home.

"Sometimes I feel as if I've *become* my mother," Kate continues. "I take her dinner to her room and start talking to her, but it's her voice —not mine—that comes out. I sound like she did when she was mothering me—her words, her tones, even her gestures and facial expressions."

"That makes sense. She's your primary role model for caring. When you step into that role, it's natural for you to act like she did," Sylvia says. "Do you also hear your mother in yourself when you're mothering your children?"

"Yes, but I am *their* mother. I'm not my mother's mother; I just act like it, and she acts like my child." Kate thinks about what happened this morning before she left for her session with Sylvia. After helping her mother bathe, Kate explained that she would be gone until about 5 or 6 o'clock that evening. Her mother had asked if she could have tomato soup and a grilled cheese sandwich for lunch. Kate cringed, thinking about that interaction. Her mother is 72 years old; why is a 72 year-old woman asking permission to have what she wants for lunch. Yet, the incident wasn't unusual. Her mother often asked permission for the most ordinary things, as if Kate were the parent who granted or withheld permission.

"That's the hard part. Being with her but not having her be the person she's always been for you," Sylvia empathizes. She knows that Kate is experiencing two losses: the loss of her mother as a mother, and the loss of her own role as the child. It's a double whammy. "And it's really hard to become that person for her, to be her mother when you so much still want her to be yours."

"It really is," Kate agrees. "After more than 30 years with our roles one way, it's so hard to deal with turning them upside down. I don't want to lose our mother-daughter relationship just because she needs a lot of help now."

"Okay, that's a good thought. Let's build on it by talking about ways you might let go of the mothering role with her," Sylvia says. "Can you define the parts of your relationship with your mother in which you feel most pushed into the mother role?"

Working together over the next several weeks, Kate and Sylvia figured out that helping her mother with personal care (baths, shampoos, changing clothes) made Kate feel like her mother's mother. Fixing meals didn't make her uncomfortable because Kate or she and Mark fixed meals for the family anyhow. In conversation with Sylvia, Kate also realized there were benefits to having her mother live with them. She liked talking with her mom about daily life, and she enjoyed seeing her mother interact with the children.

Following her discussions with Sylvia, Kate talked to Mark and then the two of them talked with her mom and Sandy and Alice. Together, they decided that they could afford to hire a nurse's aide who would come to the house for three hours each day to provide personal assistance to her mother. This relieved Kate of some of the responsibilities she disliked and allowed her to spend more time with her mother in ways that both of them enjoyed. Mark was willing to take over feeding Kate's mother, but when they proposed this, her mother said, "That's not a man's job." When Kate checked back with Sylvia as they had agreed, Sylvia explained that most people—women and men—feel more comfortable being nurtured by women than men. It was the persistence of gender roles.

There are still days when Kate feels some resentment or anger. Sometimes the aide has to cancel, and Kate is forced to juggle her schedule and provide personal care to her mother. Sometimes she still resents Sandy for not assuming a fair share of the responsibility for caring for their mother. And there are moments when she deeply misses having a mother who puts aside everything for her. Even so, letting go of the bulk of mothering tasks has reduced the strain on Kate and revived parts of their mother-daughter relationship.

FOR FURTHER THOUGHT AND REFLECTION

1. Is it fair or acceptable that women continue to assume primary responsibility for care giving? What aspects of socialization and education might be used to foster more balance in care giving in our society?

2. This case raises questions about whether honesty is always advisable in personal relationships. Do you think Kate should tell her mother she sometimes feels resentful, frustrated, or angry? Does not telling her mother about these feelings foster a dishonest relationship?

3. In Kate's situation, it was possible to hire professional help to reduce the burdens on Kate and to diminish Kate's need to be a mother to her mother. How might Kate have coped if hiring help had not been feasible?

4. Sylvia suggests that an admirable, mature love is based on more than doing what one feels like for another person. To what extent do you think "real" love includes meeting obligations and acting beyond personal desires?

REFERENCES

Aronson, J. (1992). Women's sense of responsibility for the care of old people: "But who else is going to do it?" *Gender and Society, 6*, 8–29.

Brody, E. M. (1985). Parent care as a normative stress. *The Gerontologist, 25*, 19–29.

Rubin, D. (1982). *Caring: A daughter's story.* New York: Holt, Rinehart and Winston.

Silverstone, B., & Hyman, H. (1989). *You and your aging parent: The modern family's guide to emotional, physical, and financial problems*, 3rd ed. New York: Pantheon.

Wood, J. T. (1994). *Who cares?: Women, care and culture.* Carbondale, IL: Southern Illinois University Press.

FRIENDS OF THE HEART

Communication Between Long-Term Friends

Mary E. Rohlfing

KEY WORDS

■

friendship
familial bonds
sex differences in friendship
cross-sex friendship

ophie had stood alone in her father's now-empty house for close to fifteen minutes. Knowing she'd never return to this place again, she wanted to allow herself time to experience the feelings of relief and sadness pulsing through her heart and gut. She visualized her father as she had often seen him during her annual visits "back home"—seated at the kitchen table, bathed in a low light, smoking cigarette after cigarette. She remembered the ever-present stacks of now discarded magazines and newspaper clippings he piled neatly on the floor near his feet. As she blinked back the tears filling her eyes, she turned one last time to look out the window overlooking the creek and meadow, where just this morning she had seen three deer grazing in the knee-high grass. She had tried futilely to remember the names her father had given each one, re-membering how nearly every time he had called her, he'd talk endlessly about them, and how she almost invariably would tune him out. Now, she wished she'd paid closer attention and knew which was which. Realizing that this thought, too, was hopeless, she dropped her face into her hands and sobbed.

This was the moment of finality she had both longed for and feared. The house sparkled. The furniture, clothing, cookware, books, and memorabilia had all been packed up, tossed away, or carted off by the auctioneer. There was nothing left but the memories. The smells her father had filled his home with were already fading, and soon they too would also be replaced by those of the new owners. Nothing would ever be as it had been, and she simultaneously ached to bring her father back and struggled to let him go. Dabbing at the tears that had begun to flow less freely, Sophie knew there was nothing now to do but go on. She sighed and said aloud, "That's it." Quickly and definitively she strode to the back door, opening and shutting it tightly behind her.

Stepping outside, Sophie squinted and blinked as her moist eyes adjusted to the bright sun. She saw Jay leaning comfortably against the driver's door of the rented moving truck parked in the driveway. She noticed that at his feet were three stubbed cigarette butts. "Now's a good time to quit that nasty habit," she called out as cheerfully as she could. "We have 2,000 miles of high-way ahead of us, and you are NOT going to smoke in that truck!"

"Screw you," Jay muttered sarcastically. "You ex-smoking, holier than thou, Miss Thing. I can't believe, after all I'm doing for you, you won't let me smoke in the truck. I'm warning you, it's going to take us three weeks to get back to Oregon, because we're going to have to stop every thirty miles so I can have a fix." Sophie laughed and, as she did, she made a noise like a horse. "There you go, snorting already." Jay shook his head in mock disgust. He reached toward her to take her suitcase. "You think I'm kidding? This provokes a lot of anxiety for me, Sophie. Driving and smoking go together like Brandy and Monica. One is no good without the other."

Sophie had walked around to the passenger door of the truck and Jay noticed that she was tugging at the locked handle to let herself in. He pulled the keys from his pocket and tossed them in a high arc over the cab of the truck to her. Sophie snatched the keys from the air, unlocked the door, and started to get in. "Nice catch, Willie Mays," Jay said appreciatively.

"Let's go, Thelma," she mockingly demanded. "Time to get this show on the road."

Jay tossed his cigarette on the driveway and climbed up into the driver's seat. As he did, he said, "Shut up, Louise," referring to Beverly's parting comments as she saw them off at the airport just four days before. As they hugged, Beverly had warned Jay, "Now don't go pulling any Thelma and Louise crap out there. Don't stop at bars, don't blow up any oil trucks, and for God's sake, don't go near any cliffs." The comment had humored them for the last three days. As they cleaned out Sophie's father's house, they had frequently referred to one another as Thelma and Louise.

While Jay adjusted the mirrors and got acquainted with the rental truck, Sophie poured herself a cup of coffee from the thermos. She ran her finger along the cassette tapes in a large wooden box between them on the seat until she located just the one she wanted. As she put the tape into the player, Jay started the engine. "Don't even think about playing Laura Nyro," he muttered. "I have not had enough coffee for that yet."

"You can't even see the tape; how do you know what I picked out?" she asked incredulously. As the engine began to purr, the first strains of a Laura Nyro song played loudly through the speakers. Sophie stared at Jay, waiting for his answer.

After a moment, he said, "Well, let's see. Maybe cause I've known you for, what? thirteen long, painful years? Maybe cause your girlfriend warned me that you have some weird ritual that requires you start road trips by playing Laura Nyro to 'bless the trip.' Maybe your musical taste is more predictable than a 'Lethal Weapon' movie? Gee, Sophie, I don't know; how could I have known?" He revved the motor and barked, "Now pour me a cup of coffee, woman, and let's blow this popsicle stand." Sophie laughed as she filled his request and then pretended to nearly spill the cup in his lap as she handed him the steaming mug. "So help me, I'll kill you," Jay sneered as he took the cup from her.

Jay took a sip then placed the cup on the dashboard. He leaned toward the stereo and lowered the volume. Gently placing his hand on her knee, he looked at Sophie and asked, "You ready?" Sophie smiled weakly and nodded her head. "You sure?" She looked away, knowing if she kept his gaze a second more she would burst into tears. "OK," Jay said, realizing this was the moment. "Thelma" he yelled, as he turned up the stereo to a near deafening-volume, "let's drive off this cliff!"

Maneuvering the long, overloaded truck out of the driveway and onto the street, Jay began to sing along, and Sophie couldn't suppress a smile. Just minutes before she had been ready to break down, but now she was light-hearted and excited. Besides Beverly—who couldn't come along since she was just two weeks into the new school year in a new position—Sophie could imagine no one she'd rather be with than Jay. "Hey, wait a minute," she said watching her father's house disappear behind them in the side mirror. "Did you call me 'Thelma,' Thelma?" Jay nodded affirmatively. "I thought I was Louise and you were Thelma. We need to get this straight."

Jay beamed at her. "Tell you the truth, Louise, I don't know which one's which. You be whoever you need to be. You be Cher, I'll be Sonny. Hell, you be Sonny, I'll be Cher."

Sophie grew amused thinking that they often delighted themselves arguing over some trivial pop culture tidbit and the great lengths each would go to to prove the other wrong. They had dubbed these disagreements their "culture vulture" wars. She recalled how they had gotten into it at parties over who had written this song or who had directed that movie. Invariably they cleared the room and found themselves alone. "Well," Jay would say at such moments, "we've once again run off the competition with our superior knowledge of all things popular and all things cultural."

For the first few hours of the trip, they rarely spoke, but Jay could tell that Sophie was restless. He noticed her open the glove box to retrieve the insurance and rental agreement, which she dropped to the floor. Cursing, she scooped them up and fished a rubber band from her pocket to bind the papers together before putting them back. Next, she placed the box of cassettes on her lap and began organizing each tape so their titles faced the same direction. Satisfied, she deliberately placed the box squarely between them before reaching under the seat to fetch the road atlas. This she set neatly on top of the tape box. Seeming to have run out of chores, she momentarily leaned back in her seat, then quickly jerked forward to adjust the balance of the speakers. With the sound just right, she settled in again, but not for long. Once more she opened the glove box, this time removing a crisp, new pocket notebook and pen. Shifting in the seat to face Jay, she asked, "How many miles have we gone?"

He squinted at the odometer and shrugged his shoulders. "Eighty miles? One hundred? I don't know."

Sophie admonished him. "Jay, look at the odometer. What's it say?"

Jay looked crossly at her. "It *reads*," he said elongating the word to indicate that she had misspoken, "1982 and six-tenths of a mile." Sophie sighed and rolled her eyes.

"Didn't you zero out the odometer?" Jay shrugged again. Perturbed, Sophie whined, "Jay, I need to keep track of this shit."

"What?" he asked. "What are you keeping track of?"

Sophie made no attempt to hide her irritation. "The miles, the gas, the hotel bills, how much we spend on food. That's what!"

Exasperated, Jay asked, "Why? Who cares how many miles we go, how much gas we use, or what the rooms cost? Don't go anal on me." He looked away from Sophie to avoid her glare.

Sophie responded, "I'm not anal. I have to keep track to be reimbursed. You know how my brothers are." Jay was unconvinced. The two times he'd met Ron, he seemed like an easy going guy, albeit tough to get to know. Her older brother, Mike, lived in California and had never ventured to Oregon to see his sister, nor had she ever gone to see him. He didn't think Mike or Ron would be counting pennies under the circumstances. After all, she had saved them both a lot of grief by taking on the task of dealing with their father's house and belongings.

Sophie yanked open the glove box and tossed the notebook inside. She remained silent as they drove west on the Pennsylvania Turnpike, passing one farm after another. Jay considered apologizing, but he wasn't sure why. He knew Sophie was trying to maintain her generally jovial demeanor, but the events of the last three weeks were beginning to wear on her. Although she'd sworn she could handle the aftermath of her father's death alone and claimed that she would relish "driving solo" in the rental truck across country, Jay had insisted on coming along. No way would he or Bev let Sophie face all the emotional and physical work that had to be done by herself. Since he was between jobs, he was the best choice to accompany her. Jay knew, though, that Sophie was too proud to admit she needed him, so instead, when they talked about the trip, he would say the main reason he was coming along was so that he could visit the east coast with someone who had grown up there.

In their thirteen years of friendship, Sophie and Jay had been through a great deal. They first met when Jay was 26, and Sophie was 25 years old. When Sophie missed a college class both were enrolled in, Jay offered Sophie his notes. He invited her to his house to get them, and they instantly became friends. Sophie liked to say that had they been heterosexual, theirs would have been a classic case of love at first sight.

As Jay got to know Sophie better, he revealed that his lover, Zach, had recently died of complications from AIDS. Ever since his death, Jay had remained single and celibate, telling anyone who asked that Zach had been his "one and only" and that he couldn't be "replaced." As the years passed, Sophie came to believe Jay's reluctance to become involved romantically with anyone new was a means of protecting himself from ever being hurt so deeply again. A few years back, she had begun to encourage him to date, and she worked up the courage, finally, to tell him what she thought was at the root of his long spell of solitude.

Doing so had been a mistake. Jay stormed out of Sophie and Bev's house half-way through the birthday dinner they had prepared in his honor. He accused them of meddling in his life and told them both to "fuck off!" For three weeks he refused to return their calls, and once, when Sophie stopped by his house to try to talk things out, he told her, through the closed door, to leave him alone. She stood outside his door, telling him how much he meant to her and how deeply she missed his friendship. Realizing he was not going to let her in, she finally walked away, unsure that she'd ever see him again. Then, a week later, he stopped by her work and asked her to lunch. As she tried again to apologize, he cut her short. "You did that already. Don't belabor the point." After that, Sophie never raised the issue with Jay again.

As he drove, Jay remembered how five years into their friendship, Sophie had faced her first real heartbreak when her lover left her for another woman. When she told Jay that what she missed most was having someone to say good-night to, he called every night for the next six months to "tuck" her in. He happily stopped doing so when, one night, Beverly answered the phone. He had known Bev for years and had long thought that she and Sophie would make a great couple. Now that the two of them had been going strong for seven years, he knew he'd been right.

Jay looked over at his friend. He noticed how tired Sophie looked, and he asked if she wanted to move the tapes and lie down on the seat to sleep. She shook her head and continued staring out the window.

Sophie had known for years that her father's health was fragile; still, she was shocked when he died. Three days before his death, she had phoned to tell him that she and Bev were off for a week-long hike in the wilderness. When she asked how he was, he said he was "a little under the weather" but it was "no big deal." As they bid each other good-bye, he told her to have a great time and to send his love to Bev. While Sophie and Bev were hiking in the Cascade mountains, Sophie's father had "slipped away," due to a massive infection in his lungs.

Sophie's big brother, Mike, was the first to hear of their father's death, and after two days of failing to reach his sister, Ron advised Mike to call Jay to find out where they were. Jay told Mike that Sophie and Bev weren't due home for four days and that they were 30 miles from a phone. He volunteered to hike in where he thought they would be to tell Sophie what had happened, but Mike refused Jay's offer, thinking it best that they enjoy their trip. Their father had been cremated and there would be no funeral. Mike was assured that their father's attorney could handle the other details. Since none of the children wished to return to Pennsylvania and live in the home their father had bought after their parents' divorce, all that remained to be done was for the house to be cleaned out and put up for sale.

Talking with Mike, Jay understood why Sophie found him so difficult to connect with. While Mike was friendly, he was terse and officious, offering no hint that he felt much sadness about his father's death. Mike, Sophie said, thought their father had "lacked ambition" and was to blame for their parents' divorce. In his eyes, their father was not a "real" man. Despite knowing all of this, Jay thought it odd that Mike could be so cool. Before their conversation, he'd always thought Sophie was too hard on her brother. After talking with Mike, he understood why she was.

Sophie loved her brothers, but she was not as close to either of them as she was to most of her good friends. Mike's values, it seemed to her, were exactly opposite of her own. He was a staunch and vocal conservative whose conversations were frequently laced with sexist and racist remarks. He'd been married three times, and each wife was younger than the last. On those rare occasions when they spoke, Mike used financial terms to answer her questions about how he was. Sophie, on the other hand, didn't much care about money. She didn't make much at the women's shelter, but Beverly had a well-paying job as a school administrator. They had plenty. Still, Sophie thought Mike believed she was less than successful in life. That she was a lesbian also didn't sit well with him, and it hurt that he never asked about Bev. Jay knew Sophie thought Mike was a bigot and, that although she tried to dismiss him, she was hurt by Mike's disapproval of her.

Ron, Sophie's younger brother was nearly ten years her junior. He respected and looked up to Sophie, but since he and his girlfriend lived three hours away, the siblings got together to visit only once or twice a year. Sophie felt closer to Ron, but he had been only eight years old when she left home for good. In her mind, it was as though they had grown up in two different families.

Hoping to break the silence that had engulfed them, Jay turned on the radio. He noticed that Sophie was tapping her foot to the beat of the song. He'd known her for over a decade, and felt more comfortable with her than anyone else, but he realized that it wasn't until he made this trip back to where she had been born and raised that he felt he had a handle on her life. He asked Sophie about her favorite places here in the east, what she had done as a teenager, and what it was like, at eighteen years of age, to drive cross-country alone to go to college in Oregon. Sophie warmed to the questions, providing details she had never before shared with Jay. She was animated as they made their first stop for food and gas, and she told him a funny story about traveling with her family when she was ten, and how at this very Howard Johnson's, her mother had absent-mindedly driven off without Mike before he returned from the men's room. It wasn't until they were three miles down the road that Sophie realized Mike wasn't in the car. When she did, she cried and screamed loudly for her parents to go back to get him.

After they ate and filled the truck with gas, Sophie took over driving and Jay curled into a fetal position, using his wadded up sweatshirt as a make-shift pillow. Sophie drove for close to four hours when she realized that she was too sleepy to go any further. She pulled off the Turnpike and drove to the nearest hotel. As she parked the truck, Jay awoke and asked her what was going on. She told him it was time to stop for the day. Jay rubbed his eyes and looked at the hotel sign. "Let me wake up, and I'll go in and register with you," he said quietly as he tried with little success to flatten his mussed hair. Stretching his mouth so as to regain feeling in his face, he asked what time it was. Sophie told him and he asked, "Have I really been asleep that long?"

"Yes. Thelma," Sophie answered. "And by the way, you're fabulous company on a road trip. Your insightful remarks, pointed questions, and generally interesting patter are really making the miles fly by, pal."

Jay blinked his eyes and rubbed them, "I'm sorry. I should have stayed awake to talk to you." He yawned and stretched his arms. "I just couldn't. These last few days have been rough on this old queen. Packing this truck and carrying all that heavy furniture is more labor than I'm used to. You would have done better bringing some big, butch dyke, my darling." Sophie laughed at him as he continued, "Now, when we get to Oregon and start trying to figure out how to mix your dad's furniture with that funky, Bohemian, college student decor of yours and Bev's, I'll be a real Martha Stewart. At the moment, though, I'm just a warm body."

Sophie stroked his hair, helping to smooth down a stray strand or two he'd missed. She then reached up to the dashboard and grabbed Jay's cigarettes. She shook one loose from the pack and put it between her lips. "Got a light?" she asked. Saying nothing, he reached into his pocket and pulled out his lighter. Sophie took it from him and lit the cigarette. He noticed that, although she had quit two years ago, she didn't cough as she inhaled. Before handing it to him, she took another drag. Exhaling, she said, "This will help you wake up."

Jay was genuinely confused and quickly turned to roll down the window so the smoke could escape. "I thought this was a nonsmoking truck."

"It was. I can't ask you to go all day without smoking. You stay here and enjoy it." Before he could thank her, she had opened the door and jumped out.

After showering, writing postcards, and clicking through the channels on the television, Jay popped up from his bed and announced, "I'm going to get a six pack and some burgers for us. Please take advantage of my absence to call your sweetie and do that kissy face thing. I don't want to be subjected to that crap."

Sophie smiled at him as he walked to the door. "Wait," she said. "I have to tell you something." Jay turned back to look at her. She continued, "I've been a jerk today. I just . . . I just . . . oh, Jay, how can I repay you? You're so good to me. You've been such a huge help these last few days. I could never have got all that done without you."

When it appeared that she might tear up, Jay cut her off. "Sophie, you know I despise this kind of verbalized sentimentality. Stop it before I vomit."

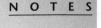

"No," she said seriously. "Most of time I honor your inability to link words to feelings. Just shut up, and hear me out." Jay rolled his eyes and sat down. As he did, she said simply, "I love you, friend."

Jay sat looking at her, expecting Sophie to continue. Realizing that she was through talking, he exclaimed, "That's it? That's all you have to say to me?" They began to chuckle. "You are so incompetent as a woman sometimes, Sophie." Standing to leave, he said, "So, that was the big heart to heart? I can't believe you. You're pathetic."

As he opened the door, he turned back to her. "Tell me again, which am I? Thelma or Louise?" She shrugged, unable to recall. "OK, well, whichever one slept with Brad Pitt is the one I'm going to be, got it?" As he walked out the door, he called over his shoulder, "I love you, too, Sophie. And when you call Bev, tell her I only thought about killing you twice today."

She knew he wouldn't hear her but called after him anyway. "You have to love me, I'm your best friend, Thelma!"

FOR FURTHER THOUGHT AND REFLECTION

1. What qualities define a friend?

2. How do friendships differ from relationships with family, neighbors, and co-workers?

3. Some researchers have claimed that men and women enact friendship in different ways. Can you see differences in how Sophie and Jay express their feelings of friendship for each other?

4. Many people believe that men and women cannot have successful friendships. What has been your experience with cross-sex friendships? How do those friendships differ from ones you have with same-sex friends?

5. Do long-term friends communicate differently than short-term friends do?

REFERENCES

Adams, R. G., & Blieszner, R. (1989). *Older adult friendship: Structure and process*. Newbury Park, CA: Sage.

Bell, R. R. (1981). *Worlds of friendship*. Newbury Park, CA: Sage.

Rohlfing, M. E. (1995). "Doesn't anybody stay in one place anymore?" An exploration of the under-studied phenomenon of long-distance relationships. In J. T. Wood

& S. Duck (Eds.), *Under-studied relationships: Off the beaten track* (pp. 173–196). Thousand Oaks, CA: Sage.

Rose, S. (1984). How friendships end: Patterns among young adults. *Journal of Social and Personal Relationships, 1,* 267–277.

Wood, J. T., & Inman, C. C. (1993). In a different mode: Masculine styles of communicating closeness. *Journal of Applied Communication Research, 21,* 279–295.

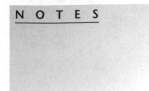

N O T E S

'TIL DEATH DO US PART

Retirement and Communication in Lasting Marriages

Fran C. Dickson

KEY WORDS

■

context
connection/autonomy
role reversal
life continuity theory
lasting marriages
different marital experience

MARTHA AND ROBERT:
FRIENDS AND LOVERS FOREVER

"We have been married for 58 years and never once did I think about leaving him. We weren't always this close and there have been hard times, but I never thought about divorce." Martha felt a strong need to stress how long she and Robert have been happily married.

Robert was quieter about it, but he too had a great deal of pride in their relationship's longevity and success. "It really hasn't always been a good as it is now," stressed Robert.

During the first few years of marriage, Martha and Robert really enjoyed life. The first year they were married, Robert was sent overseas, and he and Martha rarely saw each other. However, it was common for Martha and Robert to write each other daily. This way they could stay connected in their letters.

Martha replied, "We were apart during the time when love and romance should be at its peak and a time when couples are getting to know each other." Martha added that she had read a great deal about World War II brides and knew that it was common for young couples during the war to have only a few face-to-face meetings (or dates) before they decided to marry. Then, after the wedding, they were separated by the war. Many women had more contact with their husbands through letters than through actual physical contact. She finished by stating that this is very different from the way couples establish their relationships today.

Somehow near the end of Robert's tour, Martha was able to go overseas and saw Robert more than many other war brides. The two really enjoyed this time together. Even though the war was going on, they were happy and in love. After the war, they settled in Iowa City. Their first and second children came soon after they moved to Iowa City. That's when things changed. Martha said, "I had two babies, one right after the other. It was a nightmare. I never slept, visited with my friends, or saw my family. I missed my family."

Robert added, " Having those two babies, one after the other, was really hard. I tried to help, but I had to work. On weekends I would change diapers, which many of my male friends wouldn't do, and try to get Martha to go for walks with the kids and me, but she was just too tired. So I tried to take the kids somewhere and give her a break." Martha added that she couldn't wait for the weekend because she knew that Robert would be around to help her with the kids. She "lived" for those few hours alone. But she also missed going dancing or to the movies with Robert. Since they started having children, they rarely had time alone.

Once the children where older, Robert and Martha started spending more time together. They had to find activities that they both enjoyed. The kids were getting ready to go to college, and Martha and Robert were going to be alone again, just like at the beginning of their relationship. They were excited about the prospect of being alone, but both felt apprehensive about the children leaving home. It was particularly hard for Robert when their youngest left for college. He became withdrawn and sad. He and Martha talked about how he was feeling. Robert said he felt that he hadn't spent enough time with the children and now they were gone. He wondered if they really knew him, or if he knew them. He was concerned that he had missed the best part of their lives. Martha reassured him that he was a good father and spent more time with the children than most men of his generation. She reminded him of all the times that he helped her on the weekends, and she told him how much she appreciated that time.

Martha had different feelings about the children leaving for college. On one hand, she felt relieved. She would have time to relax, do what she wanted to do, read a book, visit with friends, spend more time with Robert, or even get a job. It would be nice to have her own money. On the other hand, she felt guilty that she was feeling relief about the children leaving. *Is this the way a mother should feel?* she often wondered.

Robert's retirement presented other challenges for both Robert and Martha. Martha was not used to having Robert around the house so much. She was used to running the house "her" way. Would Robert interfere with that? Robert was worried about how he would spend his time. Martha had a number of suggestions, but he just wasn't sure. When Robert's retirement finally came, there was a period of adjustment. Martha felt that Robert was interfering in her kitchen work. Robert believed he could help and show Martha more efficient ways of doing things. Since she had read a great deal on the retirement process before it actually occurred, Martha knew that researchers reported that this is a common problem when a husband retires. Robert laughed about the way the Martha "researched" a problem. He said he enjoyed watching her in the library; it was like she was a private investigator.

Finally they adjusted to Robert's retirement. Martha got a job in a local department store and loved it. She let go of a number of tasks that were previously hers. For example, Robert now did the grocery shopping. Martha said, "Robert does a far better job at the grocery shopping than I did; he pays attention to coupons and specials when I could never be bothered with that." Robert has also taken on some of the cooking. He gets up before Martha on mornings that she is working and makes breakfast for her. She loves it. However, Robert does remind her that she never did that for him when he was working. They laugh about that a lot.

Martha and Robert describe their marriage as being like a U shape. The beginning years were very happy, the middle years were more difficult, and now their senior years are very happy again. Martha said, "The best years are now." And Robert strongly agreed. Martha said, "It's funny, sometimes we think the same thing at the same time and can even finish each other's thoughts." There was evidence of this in their storytelling, it was common for them to finish each other's sentences and know what the other was going to say.

Robert says, "It's very strange that we can read each other's mind." Martha says they can read each other's mind because they are so close emotionally, but it wasn't always like that—only in the recent years. Neither can imagine life without the other.

TRUDY AND BILL: MARRIED STRANGERS

"We have been married 55 years," says Trudy. "That's a long time; it feels like a long time." Bill, her husband, sits in silence. They sit in their living room, in separate chairs. Neither makes a great deal of eye contact with the other. When they talk about their marriage, they are very deliberate, distant, and clear. They also take turns telling their relational story, never talking at the same time or reinforcing the other's story. It is as if it is her story, and then it is his story.

Trudy starts by talking about how they met. She states in a neutral tone that they met at a dance. At that point Bill adds that he loves to dance, and that they saw each other maybe three or four times before they decided to marry. They knew that right after they were married, that he would be sent on his overseas assignment for the Army, but they still married. "All our friends were doing it," Trudy adds. Bill says it was love at first sight and that he knew he wanted to marry her the moment he saw her. Trudy says nothing. She goes on with her story.

Trudy said the wedding was very simple and she didn't even have a wedding gown since they didn't have any money. They had two days together in New Orleans, and then he had to leave, so Trudy went to live with her mother and sister. She was pregnant. She had their first child, Jon, while Bill was in Germany. He came home when Jon was about two. They described this time as very stressful. Trudy was used to doing things her way, and now she and her son had to get used to a "stranger" being around. Bill agreed that his return home was difficult. He said he felt like a stranger to his wife and son. Trudy added that he *was* a stranger to them. It took a long time for Jon to accept his father's presence. Trudy admitted that at that time she would have preferred to stay with her mother and sister, rather than move into an apartment (they called it a flat) with her husband. Bill said that he found a flat that was suitable and moved his family out of her mother's house. He said he wanted things done his way, not the way the women ran things. He said they were spoiling Jon. Trudy said that she was lonely for her mother and cried every day.

As time went on, they got used to each other and had more children together: Janet and Susan. Bill worked in an accounting firm while Trudy stayed home with the children. Trudy said she resented staying home, even through women didn't work then as they do today. She felt trapped. Bill was working very hard and enjoyed going out with his co-workers after work. He also enjoyed dancing and had several dance partners during their marriage. Trudy appeared uncomfortable when Bill was talking about the dance partners. It was obvious that this was an issue in their marriage, but Trudy changed the conversation topic quickly.

It was also common for Trudy to take the children to visit her mother in Florida. Bill never joined them. Trudy said those trips reminded her of the old days when she and Jon lived with her mother. She said she was happy then.

It was very clear that in their family Trudy was responsible for the home and children and Bill was responsible for bringing in the money. Trudy mentioned that Bill once lost his job and said that was a very hard time. He was home more than usual, sometimes drinking, and even told of the time when he hit Susan so hard she fell down the steps. During the telling of that story, Bill was quiet and distant, but Trudy appeared to take pleasure in the telling of the story.

Trudy also appeared to have a desire to talk more about Bill's unemployment. She is proud of the fact that when Bill was not working the children never suspected that their family was in financial trouble. She stressed that she had survived the Great Depression and World War II and she knew how to "get by on less." She believes that surviving these two historic events taught her how to be satisfied with less. She finished by stating, "Couples today have such high expectations of life and their relationships; that's why the divorce rate is so high. They just can't meet their expectations, and everything is a disappointment. If you expect less, you will be happier."

Since Bill's retirement they have been involved in separate activities. Trudy enjoys her reading group and the women at the Senior Center. Bill goes dancing twice a week with his dance partner. Trudy did not want to talk about the dance partners. Bill also enjoys working in the garage, building things, and playing poker with a group of men. They rarely do things together, talk together, or seem affectionate. Bill has also taken an interest in cooking. He says it's a creative outlet for him and thinks maybe he should have been a chef instead of an accountant. Trudy says she hates to cook so its great that Bill is doing the cooking and now also the shopping since he knows what he is making for dinner.

Trudy and Bill are polite to each other and show respect toward each other, at least in most cases. Since Bill's by-pass surgery, they have had separate bedrooms. Trudy says it's been five years since they shared a bedroom. Bill thinks it has been less. It appears to be fine with both of them that they sleep separately. Bill talks a great deal about his surgery and how it was the worst time in his life. This surprises Trudy, and she said that when their son was young he had cancer, and that was the worst time for her. Bill says, "Oh, yeah, I forgot about that time."

Trudy stresses that they have very little in common and is not sure why they even got married. Trudy also wonders out loud if World War II put pressure on many young women to marry men they really didn't know very well. She remembers how after their wedding they were apart for many years. She quietly said, "Maybe since we didn't get to know each other well in the early years of our marriage, we were unable to become close in the middle and later years." She knows that the way they started their marriage (Bill being overseas; her giving birth alone, raising Jon alone, and living with her mother) may have had an impact on how they set up and experienced their marriage through the years.

She says she thought of divorce a number of times; but it wasn't being done back then, and she wouldn't have been able to find a job. She feels that women today are lucky that they have options, financial security, and independence. She finishes by stressing that she taught her daughters not to rely on anyone but to be independent. Bill adds that both their daughters are now divorced.

When Bill talks about their marriage, it has a different flavor than Trudy gives it. Many of his stories are about the "good" times, and Trudy seems confused and disinterested in his stories. Much of his stories revolve around his career, his dancing, and time spent with his friends. He says that you have to have good friends to be successful in life. He does not stress family.

When looking at this couple, one might wonder how they stayed together for so long. When they were asked that question, they gave two different answers. Trudy said that she respected her husband and did her job of taking care of the children and their home—that divorce was not an option. Bill stated that Trudy was just as pretty as she was the day he first saw her and that he loves his wife. He appears to have survived by ignoring Trudy's unhappiness.

NOTES

FOR FURTHER THOUGHT AND REFLECTION

1. What are the major differences between the two couples? What are the characteristics of the happily married couple and the unhappy married couple?

2. How do these couples compare to couples you know that have been married within the last twenty years? How might they differ from couples that were married during the Vietnam War or the Prussian War?

3. What can we learn about communication and marriage from these cases? What are the differences in the communication among the four people and between the two couples?

4. What kinds of relational themes exist for each of these couples? How might these themes influence their relational experience?

5. The life continuity theory helps us understanding marital quality over time, claiming that the level of marital happiness at the beginning stages of the marriage are predictive of the level of marital happiness at the later stages. How do you see this theory demonstrated in these two cases? Do you agree with this theory?

REFERENCES

Ade-Ridder, L. (1989). Quality of marriage: A comparison between golden wedding couples and couples married less than 50 years. In L. Ade-Ridder & C. B. Hennon (Eds.), *Lifestyles of the Elderly: Diversity in relationships, health, and caregiving* (pp. 37–48). New York: Human Science Press.

Cole, C. L. (1984). Marital quality in later life. In W. H. Quinn & G. H. Hughston (Eds.), *Independent aging: Family and social support perspectives* (pp. 72–90). Gaithersburg, Maryland: Aspen Systems Corporation.

Dickson, F. C. (1995). The best is yet to be: Research on long-lasting marriages. In J. T. Wood & S. Duck (Eds.), *Under-studied relationships: Off the beaten track* (pp. 22–50). Thousand Oaks, CA: Sage.

Duck, S. (1994). *Meaningful relationships: Talking, sense, and relating.* Newbury Park, CA: Sage.

Nussbaum, J. F., Thompson, T., & Robinson, J. D. (1989). *Communication and aging.* New York: Harper & Row.

Pearson, J. (1992). *Lasting love: What keeps couples together.* Dubuque, IA: William C. Brown.

DISTANCE MAKES THE HEART GROW ANXIOUS

Managing Long-Distance and Commuter Relationships

Marcia D. Dixson

KEY WORDS

■

long-distance relationships
relational rules
self-disclosure
social support
turning points

Lindsay had just finished unpacking the last of her CDs when she heard four taps followed by two quick taps on her dorm door. She smiled knowing the "tapper" to be her brother Lance, a junior at the same college where she would begin taking classes tomorrow. She opened the door and was amazed to still be struck at how "cool" she thought her older brother was. Of course, he enhanced this effect by standing languidly in the hall, leaning against her doorframe with one of his best "you'd be lucky to know me" poses. The pose gave way to a big smile and very uncool hug for his little sister as soon as the door opened.

"So, Sissy, how do you like life at ole' UI so far?" Lance asked as he sprawled across her bed.

"Fine, but you know I hate being called Sissy! I have since I was twelve. Don't you think that now I'm in college you could quit?"

"Sure, Sissy!" he responded with a grin. "Seriously, is there anything you need? Want to know where the best bars are? Need to know where to get cash after midnight? I might even be able to hunt up the library if you're interested."

"No, thanks. I went on the freshman tour. I can probably show you where the library is, as well as the writing center, the speaking lab, the foreign language lab! Geez, I hope I don't end up needing all the special help they have here!"

"So, what about that guy you've been seeing, Tom, John, Lon?"

Lindsay responded by sitting in her oversized chair and looking glum but determined. "It's Ron, oh feeble-minded one. We've decided to stay together even though we're at colleges 450 miles apart. We'll call and write; it'll be fine. Besides he's the greatest guy I've ever dated. He's kind, smart, thoughtful, gorgeous, funny and a gentleman. Hey, come to think of it, he's everything you're not! Maybe that's Freudian or something, looking for the perfect man who's everything your brother isn't?"

"Very funny, ha ha! And this from a woman with a vast repertoire of, what, *two* other dating experiences?" her brother responded sarcastically. He then continued in a more serious tone, "Are you sure this is what you want to do? How can you have a relationship when you don't see each other? Besides you'll miss out on half the fun of college if you can't go out and enjoy yourself."

"Why wouldn't I be able to go out and have fun? I may not be dating other guys but I don't have to sit home and vegetate! Yes, I'm sure. Ron is really special and he's too important to me to blow off just because of an inconvenience like a few hundred miles. Besides, haven't you heard? Love conquers all. Speaking of which, what about that girl Terrie, Carrie, or Mary you were dating last spring?"

"Oh, Jerrie, she went back home for the summer. I don't know if she came back to school or not. Maybe I'll run into her at our fraternity party next weekend.

That'd be ok. She's kind of cute and fun. You coming to the Phi Kappa party? I don't want you going to other parties, I won't be there to protect you, ya know."

"Right big brother. I think my black belt in TaeKwanDo will protect me just fine. Yeah, I'll be there. See ya then."

Two weeks later at the party, Lindsay finally spotted her brother across the room. "LANCE!" Lindsay tried to get her brother's attention over the music and voices.

"Hey, you made it! You remember Jerrie?"

"Hi, Lindsay, it's nice to see you again. Do you have a date, or would you like for Lance and me to introduce you around?" Jerrie inquired as they moved away from the music to a quieter corner.

"No thanks, Jerrie. I'm seeing someone," Lindsay responded.

"Oh, where is he? I'd like to meet him."

"He's not here. He's in Indiana—he goes to Purdue."

"Yuck, that's not much fun!" said Jerrie.

"Oh, it's not so bad."

"Don't you miss him? Don't you wish he were here?"

"Yeah, I do miss him. But what's odd is that while I miss going to parties like this and movies and stuff, I miss just being with him even more. You know, like on Sunday afternoons he'd watch football and I'd listen to music. Just having him around is what I miss the most."

"Really? I'd think you'd want someone here for the really important stuff. You know, to take you to fraternity parties or sneak into your dorm room, huh, Lance?" Jerrie looked at Lance suggestively.

As usual, Lance was paying little attention. "What, oh yeah, sure, I told her this long distance thing wouldn't work, but she's like our old dog, loyal to the end . . . unhh."

A quick elbow jab finished Lance's sentence for him.

"My roommate and I came together, do you see her?" Lindsay asked to change the topic. "Oh, there she is, leaving with some guy!"

"Uh, I know that guy, I wouldn't expect her back soon," Jerrie whispered conspiratorially. "Come on, let's see if Lance misses me while we go get something to drink."

The next day over a lunch of pizza, Lindsay noticed Lance's nauseated expression, "Judging by how you look, the party went pretty late last night."

"Yeah, I was there 'til three. Did you have a good time? You looked kind of like a lost puppy."

"You can stop with the dog metaphors any time. The party was fine. I just felt a little out of place. I have the same problem with my friends and roommate. I don't want to go guy hunting with the single girls, but I can't double date with the girls who have boyfriends. I don't fit. My roommate keeps telling me to lighten up 'cause it's not like I'm in a *real* relationship! I wish people would see that it is a real relationship, even if he isn't here."

"Well," Lance interjected while his sister took a breath, "you could date just for fun you know. That might get people to leave you alone."

"I don't think I should have to go to those lengths just to be left alone!" Lindsay objected. "And by the way, the Phi Kappas have the same problem. They kept hitting on me, saying that Ron was probably out partying with other girls anyway. Do I have to carry proof of relationship involvement or something to be taken seriously?"

"I told you this long distance thing wasn't going to work out. Why don't you give it up before you've wasted the entire rush season?" Lance reminded her.

"Because Ron happens to be more important to me than the entire rush season, thank you very much. I just wish we could see each other more often. But, we've worked out a plan. We make sure we are in on Friday nights for our phone call. We write every week. Hopefully, these slow computer people will get my email account set up soon, so we can stay in contact that way. But we don't expect each other not to have friends and go out. We've both agreed that while being apart is a pain, it does lessen the distractions from accomplishing what we're here to do, which is get an education so we can both get good jobs, get married and, some day start our family."

"Yeah, but isn't the distance a real problem?" Lance asked.

"Well it's changed our relationship in some ways I didn't expect. Not all bad, such as we don't argue about stupid stuff anymore because the time that we have on the phone is too important to waste that way.

"We both know that we need open, honest communication. That means telling each other about how hard it is to have a long distance relationship. But we won't give up! Hopefully I can visit him soon. Speaking of giving up, how is Jerrie?" Lindsay ended, determined to change the subject and be optimistic.

"Don't ask. I have no idea what her problem is. We have only been seeing each other for two weeks and you would think she owns me! She got all ticked off last night for no reason that I could figure out. Something about me missing or not missing something. I have no clue. She was great when we first started seeing each other, interested in lots of the things I am. Now she always wants me to take her to stupid sorority events, and if I don't call her every day she pouts. She has to share every detail of her life with me or she's not happy. Frankly, her life isn't that interesting! She's way too much trouble."

"Wow, short relationship! I'm glad Ron isn't like you. He still listens to me when we get the chance to talk. Maybe good relationships are good whether or not they are long distance relationships."

Lance responded with his best looking out for little sister tone. "So, you're really happy? Even though you never see Ron?"

Lindsay seemed pensive as she considered her answer. "It's hard. Last night seemed weird because everyone was pairing off. I wondered how Ron would act at a party. I missed him so much I went back to my room and called him, even though it wasn't our night to talk. Big surprise, he wasn't there. He was probably out with his roommates or something. Right?"

"Are you trying to convince me or you?"

"Both, I guess. I have no reason to think that Ron would ever cheat on me. He talks about this girl, Pat, who is just a friend. They have a lot of classes together since they're both engineering majors. I don't know or particularly care about the structure of bridges and skyscrapers, but Ron gets all excited talking about what he is learning. I guess I'm a little worried. I feel like I'm missing out on so much. When we were together, I knew what was happening with him everyday. Now I get an update once a week. It's too expensive to call more often. I don't really have any reason to worry. I have male friends here. That doesn't mean I'm looking or anything. I'll get better once I get used to this, won't I?"

"Maybe, but, you have to do what is right for you. If the relationship is going to cause you this much worry, is it really worth it?"

Lindsay considered for awhile before answering. "Yeah, it is worth it. We just have to figure out how to do the long-distance thing."

"Is there anything I can do to help?"

"No, but thanks for listening to me whine."

"Aw, what are big brothers for? Hey, how about seeing a movie this afternoon?"

"What, with you and Jerrie so I can feel like a third wheel again?" Lindsay answered dubiously.

"Naw, just you and me, a family thing."

Three weeks passed before Lance and Lindsay saw each other again. When they did, it was a Monday morning and Lance spotted his sister on the way to class. "Lindsay, hey wait up!" he called to her.

"Hey, Lance, how was your weekend?"

"Fine, I think I'm in love!"

"With Jerrie?" Lindsay asked, surprised.

"Nah, she's history. I had a date with Toni, one of the football cheerleaders. She's hot, I mean attractive. Oh, she's also smart and nice, so you and Mom would approve. How'd your weekend go? Wasn't this the BIG VISIT?"

"Yeah, I went to see Ron at Purdue. It was great, but it was also weird. I had dreams of how romantic it would be after being apart for over a month and how he would meet me with flowers and a dinner reservation at a nice restaurant. Instead, when he first picked me up at the bus station (no flowers, no dinner reservation) it was like we barely knew each other. I mean it's only been a couple of months so we haven't changed that much, but it was still strange. It took us a while to get comfortable again. Then it was better.

"I met his roommates, so now I have faces to go with the names when he talks about them. I also saw the campus and the town. It makes it easier to picture him when I have a setting to put him in. After we got over being shy again, we had a great time. It was romantic and new and wonderful. He really missed me!"

"Was there any doubt about that? Who wouldn't miss my little sister! He's lucky to have you."

"Yeah, well it was nice to hear it from him and be able to see him when he said it. Talking on the phone is great, but I get a better feel for how he feels when I can see him. And we talked a lot! I had so many questions."

"You didn't make the poor guy talk about the relationship all weekend did you? Guys hate that."

"Well, guys may hate it but when you are apart as much as we are, I need to talk about the relationship."

"What's there to talk about? Are you still worried about that girl Pat?"

"No, I'm not worried about 'that girl' Pat. I met her this weekend. Ron thought I'd feel better if I knew her. He was right. She's pretty and very nice. I liked her."

"If she's all that, why do you feel better about it?"

"Well, I trust Ron and I trust her, and I also met her girlfriend."

"You mean she's a lesbian?" inquired Lance.

"Yep. I don't know why I always assume that everyone is heterosexual. I mean, I'm not stupid; I know better. But I have to admit I do feel better knowing that Ron really isn't her type."

"That's dumb, Sissy."

"Calling me 'Sissy' is dumb!" Lindsay punctuated this with a smile and a jab to his right arm. Lance noticed that his sister seemed less nervous and happier than she had been since she started the semester, but she still didn't seem entirely secure in this relationship. He only hoped she didn't let this long-distance relationship get her down.

A week passed before Lindsay and Lance reconnected and then it was by phone.

"Hello," Lindsay said.

"Hey, Sissy!"

N O T E S

"Would you please stop that, Lance! How are you? How's the latest love of your life?"

"I'm great, Toni's great, life is great. How about you and Ron?"

"We're better. I finally got my email account activated here and got Ron's email address. Now we email each other everyday. I feel as if we get to keep up now, you know. I can complain about my loads of homework or my roommate without feeling that I'm wasting our few minutes on the phone each week. We still call on Friday nights, but now I can ask about the little things going on in his life because I know what they are! I feel much more connected. And guess what?"

"What?" Lance answered.

"My communication instructor told me about this program that the local Y and the university put together for college students and other people in long-distance relationships."

"You mean a support group or something?" Lance inquired incredulously.

"Mm-hmm. And I went to my first meeting yesterday afternoon."

"Was it weird, being around all those lonely lover types?"

"Kind of. But I got lots of information. Like the worries I've had are natural for people in LDRs—that's what they call long-distance relationships."

"So, is there a twelve-step program to cure you of this LDR disease?" Lance asked mockingly.

"Funny, and no," she replied. "But there are ways to cope. One is to find other people in LDRs, so I know I'm not alone in this situation. There are tons of us right here on campus! We're thinking about having t-shirts printed. What do you think of 'I'm surviving an LDR!'?"

"Not much. Did you really get anything useful out of this group?"

"Yeah, I learned about disadvantages, advantages, and coping strategies for LDRs. I feel that I am being proactive now rather than just waiting for a problem to happen and hoping we can work it out."

"What do you mean, being proactive?" Lance queried curiously. "It sounds like you have a battle plan for your relationship. Isn't that a lot of work? Is it *really* a good relationship if you have to work so hard?"

"No, yes, and yes, big brother. It is not a lot of work. It's mostly little things like buying a card or sending Ron a video of me. By the way, one of the coping strategies is not to talk about the relationship too much when we do see each other, but to just try to enjoy the time together."

"Well, I told you that!"

"And, yes, it is a good relationship even if we have to work at it. As a matter of fact, there are some advantages to LDRs. We don't argue about little things because our time together is too important. We don't take each other for granted, and we have better communication even though we don't have as much communication."

Lance shook his head. "Still sounds like an awful lot of work to me."

"All good relationships involve some work. You know, Lance, that may explain your relational score card. I'm emailing Ron a copy of the information. I'll send you a copy as well. Maybe you can use it to try to make ONE relationship IN YOUR LIFE last longer than a month."

"Ha!" Lance replied undefeated. "Not if I have to go to that much trouble! Hey, that reminds me, do you want to meet Toni? We are having another party at the house this weekend, and I thought you might want to come—that is, if Ron doesn't mind."

"Ron won't mind. He knows he has no competition. I'm looking forward to meeting this latest goddess."

"Great, see you at the house Saturday night. Bye, Sissy!"

"La-a-a-ance!"

```
From: lindsdi@uiowa.edu
To: roneng@purdue.edu
CC: lancedi@uiowa.edu
Subject: LDR information


Ron:


Here is some of the information I mentioned in my last
email. I will write a longer note later.


LDRs


1. Recognize the disadvantages to LDRs
        Concerns about partner cheating
        Less frequent interaction
        High expectations of time spent together
        May feel left out due to new hobbies/interests de-
           veloped by partner
        Trouble with in-town relationships not acknowledg-
           ing or affirming the LDR
        Missing everyday talk about little things


2. Use coping strategies
```

Find creative ways to communicate (videos,
    gifts, cassettes)
Discuss relationship ground rules
Use face to face time wisely: some relational
    talk, some just enjoying being together
Look for positive aspects

3. Enjoy the advantages of LDRs
        Allows partners to focus more on school
        Less likely to break up
        Have higher quality communication
        Relationship satisfaction, intimacy, trust & in
            timacy is identical to other personal rela
            tionships
        Can explore new hobbies/interests not appealing
            to partner

Let me know what you think.

Miss you,

Lindsay

FOR FURTHER THOUGHT AND REFLECTION

1. Of the advantages and disadvantages listed in the information Lindsay received, which seem to be present in the relationship between Lindsay and Ron? What can she and Ron do to minimize the disadvantages?

2. Lindsay talks about relational rules that she and Ron have agreed to. What are they? Why are they important in LDRs? Do other kinds of relationships (romantic, friendships) have these kinds of rules? Are they usually explicitly discussed? What kinds of relational rules are likely to be explicitly discussed?

3. Turning points in relationships are events which qualitatively change a relationship (i.e., first kiss, getting engaged, breaking up). What turning point(s) is(are) there in Lindsay and Ron's relationship?

4. Lindsay experiences at least two forms of social support which help her cope with being in a long-distance relationship. Identify each form of support and discuss the differences each makes to Lindsay.

5. What is the role of self-disclosure in Lindsay and Lance's relationship? How important is it? Is there any self-disclosure in the relationship between Ron and Lindsay? If so, what kind seems to have occurred?

6. What differences, if any, do you notice between Lindsay's relationship with Ron and Lance's relationships with Jerrie and Toni?

REFERENCES

Gerstel, N., & Gross, H. E. (1982). Commuter marriages: A review. *Marriage and Family Review, 5,* 71–93.

Gross, H. E. (1980). Couples who live apart: Time/place disjunctions and their consequences. *Symbolic Interaction, 3,* 69–82.

Govaerts, K., & Dixon, D. N. (1988). . . . until careers do us part: Vocational and marital satisfaction in the dual-career commuter marriage. *International Journal for the Advancement of Counseling, 11,* 265–281.

Guldner, G. T., & Swenson, C. H. (1995). Time spent together and relationship quality: Long-distance relationships as a test case. *Journal of Social and Personal Relationships, 12*(2), 313–320.

Rohlfing, M. E. (1995) Doesn't anybody stay in one place anymore? An exploration of the under-studied phenomenon of long-distance relationships. In J. T. Wood & S. Duck (Eds.), *Under-studied relationships* (pp. 173–196). Thousand Oaks, CA: Sage.

Stafford, L., & Reske, J. R. (1990). Idealization and communication in long-distance premarital relationships. *Family Relations, 39*(3), 274–280.

Westefeld, J. S., & Liddell, D. (1982). Coping with long-distance relationships. *Journal of College Student Personnel, 23,* 550–551.